Solid Ideas for a Fluid World.

ves and millennials like me. It is one of those books that make you laugh, cry, reflect, and apply the knowledge not only to your personal life but also to your professional life. These words stay with me: **"You mustn't worry, but rather deal with your problems." There is so much wisdom in that single quote.** - Jorge Branger, Digital Entrepreneur and Strategist, Flyt! & Fluence Co-Founder, Madrid, Spain.

I'm sure that once in your life, you had an **"enlightening" conversation** with a friend—those conversations that left a mark in you because they are both profound and simple. That is what I felt while reading these pages... I felt challenged by enlightening dialogues, reasoned answers to essential questions, and encounters with the crucial aspects of life and the person that often come to my mind: truth, the self, happiness, our aspirations, God, among so many other topics.

A perfect book **for all the young people looking for solid answers,** written in a clear, attractive and appealing way. It will stay on my nightstand! - Ernesto Kaltwasser, Santiago de Chile.

From the first moment I spoke with Fr. Jorge Obregon I thought it would be incredible to read a book written by him. A few months later, I had the surprise of having his book in my hand, and it certainly **exceeded all my expectations.**

"How to achieve happiness?" "What is man's ultimate goal?" "Who am I?" These are some of the many questions this book has answered for me. I identified with the stories told in its pages as if they were my own. This book **helped me understand the root of vices that I have experienced and which have not allowed me to advance on a path of peace and fulfillment.** It touches on themes related to our wounds, God, the actual concept of the word sexuality, and life's questions, among many others. I highly recommend this book, not only for young people but also for adults who want to grow personally. - Ricardo Motiver, Speaker and Entrepreneur, Mexico City.

I found reflections that I had already had but had not shared, and that made me read it in almost one sitting. **This book is a must-read.** It touches readers through timeless stories, capturing the attention of any generation. It's undoubtedly, an entertaining and light narrative from the first page. Each situation presented has been experienced at some time, so it achieves a feeling of closeness and proximity. My favorite quote and lesson of life from the book is: **"every human aspiration must be based on something solid."** - Daniela Obregón Solórzano, TV Azteca Host, Mexico City

A solid book that explains naturally and straightforwardly the deepest questions that we carry inside: Is there a truth? Who am I?

Where am I headed? The dialogue between Luis and Alejandro brings up questions for personal reflection, for meaningful conversation among friends, and ways to discover—while turning the pages—our ultimate meaning in this life. - Fr. Miguel Guerra, L.C., México.

\

PUBLISHING

Solid Ideas for a Fluid World
What is wrong with this generation?

Jorge Obregon, L.C.

First edition 2020

ISBN: 9798559408798
Independently Published

Illustration and graphic design: Fiorella Esquivel T.

SOLID
IDEAS
FOR A

WHAT IS WRONG WITH THIS GENERATION?

JORGE OBREGÓN, L.C

CONTENTS

FOREWORD

It was a sunny Friday afternoon. After the work week, we were meeting a group of friends in the backyard of a house in the eastern hills of Bogota. We listened to a presentation about Regnum Christi summer programs offered to children and young people in the United States and various European countries. When I gave a quick look at the group of people, I calculated that I knew two-thirds of the guests, but there were new ones. There were several priests I hadn't met before as well as a group of consecrated women who were in charge of making the presentation. I vividly remember a large fire that burned in an immense bronze basin, situated in the center of the garden and, in a corner of the yard, surrounded by perfectly pruned vines and flowering roses, a beautiful image of the Our Lady of the Miraculous Medal.

I met friends I hadn't seen in a while, and we had a good time catching up with each other about our work as well as our faith journey. There was good music, delicious Spanish tapas, and an exquisite Rioja wine. Add to this the sound of wood burning and the light of the sunset, and it made for a pleasant and welcoming atmosphere. When the flames had burned down, someone took out a large Paella pan and put it on the fire. It was a real delight to see how they prepared a delicious Valencian-style paella in less than an hour. I have always liked the cuisine and all the guests got to enjoy some. My wife and I had dinner with two other couples, and the topic we discussed was our doubts about educating our children in a non-denominational school and our concerns about moving them to a Catholic school. A young, outgoing priest joined the group and, upon hearing our conversation, introduced himself. To be precise, he was not a priest yet; he was Brother Jorge Obregón. His opinions were accurate and to the point. His words were full of wisdom, and his way of speaking projected humility and simplicity. He shared solid and well-articulated ideas about the importance of alignment between school and the home, coupled with the principles upon which spiritual education is based. His words were enlightening for our own thinking process and decision making.

When I met him, I was sure that Brother Jorge would be a great priest, but it did not cross my mind that he would be such an important person in my own and my family's life. I never imagined that he would be the one that supported us with his prayers, advice, and acts of love in different moments of our lives, in moments of glory and as well as those of trial. I also had no idea that he would help me discover and enjoy reading great Catholic thinkers and authors such as Henri Nouwen or Bishop Robert Barron. Nor did I have the slightest inkling that it he would be the one who would give First Holy Communion to three of our four children (we hope that he will be the one to give First Holy Communion to our youngest daughter Guadalupe in a few years). In that moment there in Bogotá, I couldn't imagine that I had before my eyes a true and great entrepreneur: an entrepreneur of faith.

Entrepreneurship has been the defining theme of my professional life. I have created several companies, some successful and some not. I have worked in large companies, always trying to promote a culture of entrepreneurship. Since 2014 I have dedicated myself exclusively to promoting entrepreneurial thinking and the development of virtues in life and work through conferences and digital content. I invest a lot of time and effort in studying entrepreneurs, their stories, and attributes.

Once, while watching an episode of Bishop Robert Barron's "Catholicism" series, which focused on St. Peter and St. Paul, the idea came to my mind that these two great saints have been perhaps the greatest entrepreneurs in history. Wearing their robes and espadrilles, without any material resources, but armed with their faith and illuminated by the Holy Spirit, they built the pillars of our beloved Catholic Church. It was undoubtedly a titanic undertaking.

I can imagine them saying: "We have to build this together, you go to Greece and I'll go to Rome and start to share the good news. We'll convince everyone that Jesus Christ has risen and that we should all live in His image and likeness. Let's build a great Christian community based on the teachings of the Lord." That is what I call thinking big.

Almost two thousand years later, we are witnesses to many men and women who, giving continuity to what Peter and Paul began, have contributed to this great mission. From the doctors of the Church and the saints, to the priests, consecrated persons and laity who continue to spread like fire the Word of God and the teachings of Christ, all of them have undoubtedly done their part and made a significant contribution. But from time to time, there appears without warning, some who leave a unique, deep, and permanent mark on the history of the Church. They are people who, guided by the Holy Spirit and blessed with a great charism, generate disruptive changes. It could be a Saint Augustine or a Benedict XVI with their wisdom; a Saint Francis of Assisi or a Saint John Paul II with their humility; a Saint Mother Teresa of Calcutta or a Saint Giuseppe Moscati with their vocation to serve the poorest or the sickest, or a Fulton Sheen or Robert Barron with their ability to communicate clearly and convincingly.

Without a doubt, Fr Jorge Obregon is one of these disruptive apostles, one of these entrepreneurs who are leaving their mark. His call has been to work with young people in an era where youth is mostly unbelieving, and materialism and sentimentalism take precedence over the will. It is the era that has seen the most significant exodus of the faithful from the Church in history, and it is precisely the young people who are jumping out of the boat the most. What a great mission God has given Father Jorge! His task is almost as titanic as that of Peter and Paul in the first century.

I have witnessed much of what Father Jorge has built. He inspires me because he works as if everything depended on him, but he prays and trusts as if everything depended on God (St. Teresa of Avila's words). The alliance he has with our Lord and the Virgin

9

Mary as his intercessor has been an instrument for his achievements. God has given him a great mission and has told him, "go and fill the jars with water," (John 2:7) and he has obeyed. It has not been easy, it has involved hard work, great sacrifices, and many frustrations, but the fruits have been beautiful. God has turned that water into wine—into the best of wines!

I could go on to make a detailed inventory of Father Jorge's years of priesthood, but while that is not the purpose of this prologue, credit must be given to the work of this great man. This summary is not exhaustive, but it will give the reader an idea of his capacity to get things done, always guided by the Holy Spirit and devoted to his disciplined life of prayer.

He initiated the "Diplomado de Liderazgo", ("Leadership Diploma") a series of conferences and meditations given by leaders from different sectors who sought to provide tools to young people to help them exercise leadership based on Christian values. To date, more than seven-hundred young people have attended this program, which has been supported by companies such as BMW, Hoteles Estelar, and educational institutions such as CESA.

He has traveled with groups of young people to several World Youth Days, providing spiritual guidance and accompaniment.

He has designed a retreat for young people called SEARCH, which is already present in nine countries and has served more than ten-thousand young people.

Thousands of people listen to his weekly podcast "SEAR- CH-CAST" in which he reflects on the Sunday gospel.

Together with over ten young people, he has created a large Catholic youth community called NEW FIRE, with more than 25,000 followers. It uses digital media such as a world-class website, mobile applications, and multimedia to effectively reach its members.

He is now starting out as an author with this, his first book. Whoever holds it in his hands has a treasure from which he can extract much value. It is an ambitious book since it deals with profound and transcendental subjects, but at the same time it is a delightful and even amusing read.

I have been on the road of faith for about fifteen years and have read many Christian authors. It has not been easy to "taste" the classics of Catholic literature such as St. Augustine, St. Thomas, St. John Paul II, or others. However, by reading Father Jorge's work, I have been able to understand many of the concepts expounded by these great Doctors of the Church and to understand philosophical concepts that I had always had in my mind in the "unfinished business" box.

The book centers around the fascinating story of two friends, Luis (the unbeliever) and Alejandro (the believer), who ask and discuss many of the transcendental questions that we all ask ourselves throughout our lives. They find answers in the Catholic tradition and teachings of the great masters of the Church. Through their story, the reader will learn and understand many of the foundations of our faith. Many times we think that those who come before us have nothing to say to us, but the truth is that we are standing on the shoulders of giants. They have so much to contribute! Let us take the best of the past and make the best of the present to become happy forever. That is what Fr Jorge has achieved with this book.

Each chapter of the story ends with a rigorous and well-documented reflection where the concepts and ideas that are lived in history are deepened. Going deeper into this book will be like simultaneously reading an excellent novel and an exquisite book on the theory of the Catholic faith, one that is a delightful read. In this book, as in that afternoon in the Bogota hills, the fire of the Holy Spirit burns, and you can feel the presence of the Virgin Mary, who has interceded to guide the pen of Father Jorge.

Whoever reads it will enjoy an exquisite delicacy that will feed his intellect and spirit. Finally, I can only say: Enjoy!

Felipe Gómez Arbeláez.

ACKNOWLEDGEMENTS

It's ironic that someone who appreciates golf so much would write his first book and then realize that it has 18 chapters. For years I had a great desire to write, and I thought I could not die without writing a book.

One day, a great friend, Juan Pablo Neira, gave me his book as a present. I opened it and found this sentence: "Whoever reads a lot one day will end up writing." And that's what happened to me.

I want to extend a word of thanks from my soul and heart, first of all, to my Lord Jesus Christ, who has called me to follow Him closely. I am also grateful to his holy Mother, Mary of Guadalupe, to whom I am very devoted. To my parents, my brothers, sisters-in-law, and nephews: they are a great hope in my heart.

And I am very grateful to two great friends, Felipe Gómez and Juan Pablo Neira, who, over the years, have been a source of inspiration, friendship, motivation, and support for me. To all of them, I send a big hug.

Finally, I want to thank my great team at New Fire: Cristi, Fio, Ale, and Arantxa. It's a gift to have you on this team. Thank you for being present. And how can I forget my editor, Hernán Darío Cadena, for his support in this work.

INTRODUCTION

I meet an infinite number of people with no horizon in life—people who easily fall into the clutches of any new theory. They are like dry leaves that fall from a tree and end up where the wind takes them. The men and women of today seem to have no points of support, accurate truths or firm references.

It is sad to see today how many people feel confused about how to live happy lives. Suicides, depression, and stress are constant and frequent news items. There is no solidity to life.

How are we to live today? What kind of spouse should I look for? What should I tolerate in him or her, and what not? Is there some kind of job that will lead me down a path of unhappiness? When I travel, I see in the airports so many books with the latest magic formula, the newest method, the safe process, the new philosophy, seemingly all fresh from the oven. Why?

I think the reason was made clear by the auxiliary bishop of Los Angeles, Monsignor Robert Barron: we live in the age of self-invention. It seems that there were no wise men in the past; that there were no wonderful civilizations that today are still a brick on which we have built our present world.

One day I heard Bill Clinton, in his speech to the nation, say: "We stand on the shoulders of giants." In my ignorance, I thought that was his own quote. Now I realize that it is attributed to Isaac Newton. Whether it's one or the other, it is a wise quote.

How little we realize—especially young people—that what we have comes from an extraordinary Judeo-Christian and Greco-Roman civilization! We could not conceive our present reality without those influences. And this ignorance is partly a product of electronic devices and social media that steal our time from true wisdom.

Central Scheme

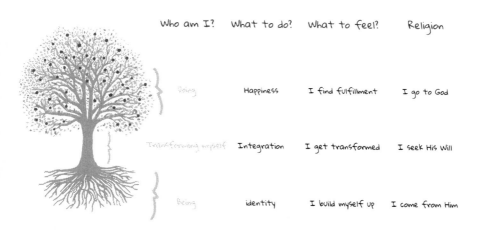

	Who am I?	What to do?	What to feel?	Religion
Doing		Happiness	I find fulfillment	I go to God
Transforming myself		Integration	I get transformed	I seek His Will
Being		identity	I build myself up	I come from Him

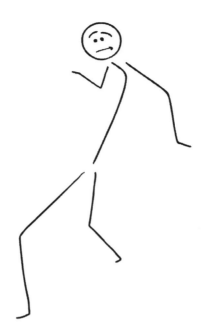

Each man and woman, without knowing it, suffers a spiritual deformity due to a lack of an adequate integration of the different aspects of himself (herself).

Why not follow what has already worked? And why not listen to the one who brought us wisdom from outside our planet? As Ecclesiastes says, "There is nothing new under the sun" (Ecc. 1:9 RSVCE). As a wise friend said: all wisdom can be summarized in a few lines, in four or five fundamental rules. That is enough. Don't get complicated. Less is more!

The Greeks invited us to get to know ourselves. "Jesus said: You lack one thing; go, sell what you have…and follow me" (Mark 10:21 RSVCE). Paul of Tarsus said that "if you do not have love, you are nothing." Augustine gave a basic rule: "Love, and do what you want." John Paul II tirelessly repeated: "Do not be afraid."

For all these reasons, I have tried to write this book covering many subjects, and therefore I do not intend to go deep into each subject, but into them as a whole. Then it is up to each one to go deeper—only if I succeed in lighting in the reader the flame of wisdom. That is my hope and my illusion. "And you will know the truth, and the truth will make you free" (John 8:32 RSVCE).

In this book, you will discover the tree of life on which everything falls. It is not my invention, but a compilation of those giants who precede us, and to whom I owe so much. To them we that live in the West owe so much.

This tree has three great parts: the roots, the trunk, and the branches. Each one corresponds to the identity, integration, and happiness that we yearn for. If I know who I am, and work on myself, then I can easily understand how to achieve true happiness.

I want to be able to open your eyes to the destructive culture that is making us believe that no truth is possible, that we must doubt everything and that there are no solid points in existence on which one can rely on for total firmness and security. I hope that while reading this book, you will shake off the relativism that makes us doubt that there is a truth and that it is within our reach.

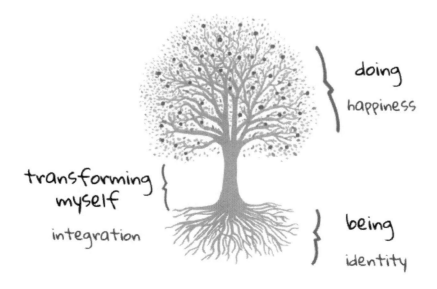

You will not be told again about a reality that seems uncertain—something where you don't know what to expect.

If man, in his observation of the world (metaphysics), does not know the causes of why something exists or the destiny or reason for it, what I see is matter without any meaning. If what I see does not transcend, does not have a touch of someone who created it, that matter is only something I can play with (materialism), or is bad (Gnosticism). Thus, there are only two realities: man and the world, but without God. There is no way to go up from matter to the One who created it, to find the Painter through painting. Hence relativism and each individual has their own truth, for there is no other source of truth. And since man is wounded by sin, he will tend towards selfishness (individualism), and not towards self-giving love. What I have just compacted into one paragraph is the outline of the book.

I would like to capture here what I wish for you, my dear reader, by borrowing the words of St. Paul: "For this cause I bow my knees unto the Father of our Lord Jesus Christ, of whom the whole family in heaven and earth is named, that he would grant you, according to the riches of his glory, to be strengthened with might by his Spirit in the inner man; that Christ may dwell in your hearts by faith; that ye, being rooted and grounded in love, May be able to comprehend with all saints what is the breadth, and length, and depth, and height; And to know the love of Christ, which passeth knowledge, that ye might be filled with all the fulness of God" (Eph 3:14-19 RSVCE).

Miguel de Unamuno said: "Man is born complete, but not completed". Our whole life passes between birth and death. From one to the other, man is developing; he is passing from total need and "selfishness" to fulfillment in surrender and self-giving to his neighbor. That task passes first through knowing who I am, what I must do, and how I can become happy. In this journey, the task is performed—as can be seen in the picture—from the inside out. Just like the instructions on how to use the oxygen masks on a commercial flight, we must first take care of ourselves in order to support others.

We must build ourselves up with virtue and healthy self-esteem, and then transform or build ourselves up in a Christian way. In this way, we fulfill ourselves by being a present and a gift for others.

In everything, we must remember that we come from God, and to God we go. Therefore, if I know my identity as a beloved child of God, and then manage to integrate all that is good in me, happiness will be nothing but a happy outcome.

Our main characters:

a) Luis: he is in the last year of college. He's 23 years old. He is a competent young man, a leader, an inquisitor, and quite far from the faith, without completely rejecting it. He is the second son in a family of five. He and his older brother have a bad relationship. Both of them have similar characteristics, although his brother has already graduated.

He is not convinced by what the Church says, its "stuffiness" and its rules. He already has a job and makes good use of his time. He is a post-modern young man whose mind and ideas are generally left-wing and rooted in the world's way of thinking. He is an economist.

Luis is someone who lives a life that goes between a conscience that barely illuminates him and the desire not to clash with his friends. Although he tends to give himself a good life, he undoubtedly has enough light in the depths of his soul that he does not completely abandon his thinking, feeling, perceiving, and acting. He reads about various subjects, although right now, it is mainly about economics.

Luis has a problem, but it won't be easy to find out. His house has been a dysfunctional home, but he doesn't realize it. He just feels there's no peace in his life. He notices this because he continually has low energy, is restless in his relationships with others, has constant fights with his girlfriend (Sofia) and tensions with his brothers and parents. You could say that his "well-being" is not very solid. The last thing Luis thinks is that he has something to do with these things. All his thinking, feeling, talking, and living are ordinary for him. He doesn't think that he could live better, with a greater sense of peace around him, with himself and others. In this book, we see how his great restlessness in life is born from many unanswered questions that he carries inside himself, questions which cry out for answers. This book will be a reconstruction of his life on the three levels that we propose: to be, to become, and to do. The journey, therefore, will be one of healing and will be built on rock

b) Alejandro: He is in the last year of his career. He is also twenty-three years old. He is a competent and sharp person, a leader, and has well-educated parents. He is someone who has absorbed the combination of a good and solid home along with the wisdom that he has always found in his group of friends. This group of friends gets together to talk about life, truth, and the present world, sometimes accompanied by guest speakers. Alejandro is a confirmed and knowledgeable Catholic and reads many books on contemporary culture. He is an industrial engineer.

Alejandro is quite the sportsman. His girlfriend, Natalia, is a year younger than him; she is an ideal girl for him as a whole person. You could say that Alejandro is a young man like many want to be, and whose parents are proud of the child they have. Football and snow skiing are what he is most passionate about. He also enjoys cooking at home on Sundays for the family. His weak point as a person is impatience, but hardly ever towards others, rather he is demanding with himself.

PART I: IDENTITY

The answer to each person's identity

Chapter 1:
What Do We Think About the World We See?

"Ever since the creation of the world his eternal power and divine nature, invisible though they are, have been understood and seen through the things he has made. So they are without excuse"

Romans 1:20 RSVCE

This time Alejandro told Luis that they would meet in front of the café by the parking lot. Alejandro kept looking at his watch, and his friend didn't show up. About five minutes later, he saw him from a distance. Alejandro pointed to his watch, saying:

"What punctuality."

"I'm sorry," said Luis. "There's a car blocking the entrance to the university. I think it's a student, but I don't know."

Luis and Alejandro have been friends for many years. Luis was happy to have Alejandro in the middle of his ups and downs, so that he would not "get lost" too much. Luis knew that his other friends did not give him views that would provide him with peace. Again and again, something brought him back to Alejandro, to try to discover the enigmas of life.

Is there a truth?

"What did you want to talk about, what's wrong with you?" Alejandro asked.

"Everything, really," Luis said. "I have something on my mind. Sometimes I wonder if there's even a single truth. People at work our friends here and teachers—they all seem to see the world from a different angle. Everyone has their truth."

"And you, what truth do you have?" Alejandro asked.

Luis answered: "Well, the one I am gathering, the one that seems to be more logical to me, is the one that I see that most people see as the one they like. Well, not so much the one they like, but the one I see everyone following."

"Well, that's fine for a start," said Alejandro, "but I don't think that will solve the problems in the medium and long term. Give me an example that's on your mind now."

Luis hadn't thought about it, but soon he said:

"Here's an example. I don't understand how we can get to know if what we think about the most important things applies to everyone, or if everyone has their own way of living. That is, I don't know if there is a way we should all go, or if all roads lead to Rome."

Alejandro looked out over the gardens thinking about what answer he could give his friend, and where to start. Then he brought his gaze back to his friend.

"Look," he said. "I don't pretend to know everything, but here's what I think. If all the paths that each person chooses are equally valid, what happens if some collide with others? For example, if I like a girl and I walk with her, and then you like the same one, and you want her for yourself, what is more appropriate, to respect that we are already together or to take her away? If the important thing for you is to express yourself in whatever way you feel, and for me, it is to respect a friend and his girlfriend, who is right?"

Luis had a giant smile: "They always fall more in love with me than with you—bad example!"

Alejandro replied: "Yeah right, Romeo. That's something you'll have to prove on the field."

Luis continued with the conversation:

"That example is easy because it is something I just wouldn't like, but things are not always so clear. For example, if someone says that the abortion law is fair and someone says that it is unfair, what do we do? Everyone has their own way of seeing things."

"Right. We're going in the same direction. Tell me, what do you do in such cases? To begin with is the most basic question everyone must answer: Is there one truth, or are there many? In my ethics class, a girl from El Salvador said: "There are as many truths as there are heads in the world. That's freedom of speech and freedom of thought. Is there a truth that we can know, or not?'"

Luis looked away and held his fist to his chin. Nothing came out of his mouth but a "hmm."

"I believe in total freedom in all fields," said Luis. "I understand your classmate. But on the other hand, I don't think everyone has the truth on every subject."

"If I'm an economist and I listen to a guy who gives an inadequate explanation of the 2008 financial crisis, I tell him to shut up and not talk about what he doesn't understand."

"Exactly," Alejandro said. It's the same in every field. If someone said something incorrect about industrial processes, with all that we learned about industrial engineering we would have elements to refute. So, what's the deal—is there truth or no truth?"

"Perhaps there is truth, but no one has it," Luis continued. "Or maybe it's better to say that whoever says they have the truth is just plain arrogant."

"Yes and no." Alejandro answered. "If I tell you, 'Luis, I have the truth: two plus two equals four,' am I being arrogant?"

"I think so."

"Why? If science has proven that two plus two equals four,

what problem is there in saying that's the truth?"

Luis kept thinking, turning the question over in his head. Then he replied:

"I suppose, if the truth is already proven scientifically, then that's fine. But if the truth is more human, more of a feeling, depending on each person—there it changes."

"So you mean", Alejandro continued, "that there are fields in which there is a truth, and fields in which there is not? Don't you think there are other areas of knowledge that also have a more and a less "truth"?"

"Like what?" Luis asked.

"The example I gave you," Alejandro replied, "the case of a girl who likes two men. Or in the ethical field, what about an illicit business, or money that comes in through illegal channels... don't you think there's truth in that?"

Luis picked his words with care.

"I think there are fields where you can't get to the truth and others where you can. But something tells me that in morals and ethics there is some truth, it's just more difficult to reach it there. And also in politics and social life... it's more complicated to reach the truth."

Alejandro smiled as if he felt that things were getting better and better:

"I totally agree that it's more complicated in some fields than others. But to think that it is not possible, that it is not true, that seems impossible to me. There has to be a way to get to the truth, both in science, physics and mathematics as well as in personal, human, and social life. Because men and women are more important than things that can be measured."

"I feel that there are thousands of things that we cannot measure, but they move the world more than can be measured."

"Like what?" asked Luis.

"Oh, man, don't be naïve," Alejandro said. "What makes every man and woman happy? You can be passionate about a job or a project, but never as passionate as being happy and about someone else. Things like happiness, love, the details of patience in our house... is what we see at Christmas. Between the gifts and peace, what would we rather have? The poor give us an example every day. There is a quote that I love, and it says: 'The greatest things in life are not things.' And another that says: 'The essential is invisible to the eye.'"

Luis felt a little moved inside.

"Yes, actually my girlfriend and my family are more important than many things," he said.

"Of course," Alejandro replied. "But then another question arises, and it is a very philosophical one. How can we know the truth in all fields?"

"I don't understand," said Luis, confused.

"Yes, THERE ARE THREE THINGS to understand in physics: there is an **object** that we measure, an **instrument** to measure, and a **person** who measures. That's in the classroom, but what about the universe? You can't know anything without those three elements."

Luis looked at him curiously:

"Let's see, go on, go on..."

"Well, the same thing happens in the universe. There are real objects, instruments to measure, and people who measure them. Real objects are of two kinds: those we touch and those we don't touch. We have already given examples: numbers and happiness. Some measure material things; others do not."

"So you think that you can find a truth in every field and that there is a truth in every field?" asked Luis.

"If you can't get to the truth, why does one person get upset by arguing with another? If both opinions are only opinions, if one idea is not more valid than the other, if everything is oppressive and subjective... why live? We choose what to think about life, depending on whether we believe something is worth more than giving our life and time and money for it. You are studying economics because you think it has a higher value than other options".

Luis was thinking, and somewhat agitated, he asked:

"Okay, but don't ask questions to my questions anymore. So, is there a truth or not?"

"There is. But to give a suitable response, we have to build on a secure foundation, okay? Look, every human being, since before the great Greek philosophers, wondered:

'What are the world and all I see made of?' The one who went the furthest on this was Aristotle. He said that everything we see in the world is composed of two principles, which he called matter and form. They are not two separate things, as if there were, on the one hand, a pile of matter without recognizable form and, on the other hand, a form, like a ghost, which then come together, and voilà, there is a man. Rather, they are two principles of what exists. For example, look at this stone in my hand. This particular stone is something concrete and intelligible, right? You can touch it, and you can recognize it as a stone and not as a bird. But, also in the case of the bird, there is matter. Both principles are essential, that is, real. I know it's a bit difficult to understand at first. But what Aristotle saw was that everything that exists has something in common: matter and substantial form, which makes it possible for our human mind to understand. More than a thousand years later, there was St Thomas Aquinas. With the help of the Judeo-Christian doctrine of the creation of the world by God, he saw a more fundamental level than Aristotle, whose works St. Thomas studied a great deal. He saw a difference between what something is, its essence, and the simple fact that something is, that it exists, as opposed to not existing. He called it being. Being is what everything created, the visible and the invisible, even God, has in common—the fact that it is. It is said that the being of creation participates in the Being of God."

"That sounds like religion to me, and it also sounds a little bit like pantheism. Like everything created is a little part of God", answered Luis.

"Yes, it seems so. Let me go on. I'll give you an example: the sun has its own light, it's the light itself. On Earth, we only have light because it comes from the sun. Without the sun, we would have no light.

This way of thinking is a fundamental piece of what we can call the Judeo-Christian tradition that was married to the Greco-Roman culture. Between these two cultural currents, we have a part of philosophy that is called metaphysics. What happens is that now

All things that exist, including all humans, receive their being from the Being by excellence. That is namely, God.

many wise men have used the word "metaphysics" to sell and distort. But, in short: it is the science that studies the fact that things ARE. Not that they are one way or another, but simply that they exist."

Luis, already very interested, had one more doubt: "What is the matter of which the universe is made, then? I understand that there are fire and air and water... Didn't the Greek philosophers say that?"

Alejandro clarified, "that level of knowledge is what Aristotle arrived at. As far as matter is concerned, there are components that make up the whole of the created universe. But the level at which St Thomas arrived is an essential one: everything exists because someone gives it being, like the sunlight to the Earth. So, when Heidegger in the 20th century asked, 'Why is there something rather than nothing?' the answer is because God gives it existence. Let us not get into the manner in which God is in things, but be content to know that it is not in the pantheists way of seeing things, who confuse God as existing in people, animals, plants, and even inert matter.

"If you let me use religion a little bit for this, that's why in the Bible St. Paul says that "In God we live and move and have our being", and in the letter to the Colossians he says: "Everything exists in Christ", that is, outside of God nothing exists. And in the Gospel of John, notice how it begins: "In the beginning was the Word, and the Word was with God, and the Word was God. He was in the beginning with God. All things came into being through him, and without him not one thing came into being."

Luis replied: "Wait. What does religion have to do with matter and physical things? They are different and separate things."

Alejandro shook his head. "No, everything is linked in one way or another. The God of the Bible is the same God who created everything. So, everything is a unity in the wisdom of God and human wisdom, but those things have been lost in an age when we separate everything. And in a sense it's understandable that today we focus on areas of expertise. We specialize a lot to be very intelligent in many fields, but we are unwise in the sense that our ancestors were."

There was a pleasant silence between the two of them. It was as if the conversation had led Alejandro to be able to explain what he had struggled to learn for so long, and Luis to hear for the first time that everything has an existence willed by God.

But restless still, Luis wanted to investigate:

"Well, if that's the way things are, then tell me: Is there a truth or isn't there?"

ANALYZING THE CONVERSATION

Every human needs to know the rules of every game he plays and of every adventure he undertakes. Since time immemorial, man, who is naturally a philosopher, has wanted to know why it rains, why there is fire, what exists after death, why there is pain, why volcanoes erupt, and more.

What we are going to do in the first part of the book is to lay down a firm ground, a foundation for everything that will be said in the rest of the book. That's why we're going through the questions that in all centuries and places man asks himself over and over again.

There is another way to ask questions for this adventure, for the adventure of life. Where do I stand? Where does it begin and end? How do you win, and what do you have to do to lose?

How do I get disqualified? And there are more fundamental questions. Is this adventure worth it? Is it worth not asking questions and just going forward? Is the cause I am pursuing a just cause? The search for meaning never dies. As long as he lives, man will be a being who asks questions, from the most basic to the most profound and enigmatic.

Why is there something rather than nothing?

Focusing on this first stage, the fundamental question of "Why is there something rather than nothing?" has been in the human spirit since the beginning of time. It was how the German philosopher Leibniz expressed in words what all of us humans perhaps wanted to ask.

Let's talk about the world and its matter, but first, let's use analysis of the human body. The medical and scientific community was stunned when DNA was discovered in human beings. This genetic code in the cells that make up a human being and contains information about growth, development, functionality and human reproduction is something that is surprisingly complex and accurate. Through DNA we can find in each human being a certain logic, an ability to be understood, which helps us discover details about them: whose child is this? What data do we find about it? How can we predict its health in the future? What diseases could it contract? And this gives us hundreds of fields of study which bring well-being and progress to the person.

I find it very daring to think of chance when everyone reflects on these things. We use science to measure many things, and then we look at more philosophical questions, those that science cannot answer, like why does this being exist? Or who organized it like this? So much design, so perfectly organized and coded. Left to "non-intelligence", that requires a lot of faith. Every time we see our newly-cut lawn, the mind immediately begins its "cause-and-effect" process. We'll ask: who cut the grass? Disorder can't make order. Chaos cannot bring order. If I don't clean my room in two weeks, what do I tend towards, order or disorder? You've thought figured it out: disorder.

The Intelligibility of the World

You're starting to see where we're going. If that happens in the human person, similarly, we find that same intelligibility in the whole world. Physics shows us how I can measure the world; I can obtain physical and mathematical formulas that "describe" the material reality created. There is a logical code that is repeated, that is constant, that allows us to predict the weather, that allows us to decide whether to build here or not, that gives us information to calculate how to fly a Boeing 727. In short: there is order, there is intelligence, there is constancy.

Physics, therefore, describes to us what a thing is, and describes whether it is this way or that. It answers the questions how, what, and how much. But metaphysics ("meta" in Greek means beyond), describes to us not that something is "this way and that", but simply that something IS, that something exists. It helps to answer the questions: what for and who?

Everything in the world has an origin. By using the laws of God's existence, which both Protestants and Christians have used for centuries, we can come to understand what the world is made of. I will use only one of many tests about God's existence: the law of causality.

Everything that exists has a cause for existence. And what caused something to exist, in turn must have another cause. If I go backwards again and again, to infinity, I have to find a cause that does not have a cause, otherwise everything is absurd. In the words of St. Thomas Aquinas, there has to be a cause not caused by anything or anyone. We call that first Cause God.

Everything we find in the world can be traced back to finding God. But still, at the level of metaphysics, all things exist because God keeps them in existence. If He were to stop thinking about them or giving them "the being," they would cease to exist.

The DNA of Existence

All this is starting to get us back on track. There's a code, a DNA in existence. There is a way to "pass through the created" to reach the uncreated, who is God. There's a Painter who painted the picture. Looking at the Painter's strokes, we can discover and affirm: "Ah, he was here."

We do not need to go any further in this chapter on the implications of this for you and me. The time will come. But it is important to answer this question: In the world, is there a creator? And, is the world intelligible? These answers are obtained with the combination of the physical sciences that measure creation and with the philosophical thinking of those who draw conclusions about creation. It is the combination of the two. It is not for science to answer philosophical questions, and it is not for philosophy to measure creation. Both are partners, co-responsible for "deciphering" the world in which we live. This is fundamental to become wise truly. If not, we will only be intelligent, but not wise. And wisdom embraces and moves the world.

In the picture above, with the sun and the Earth, you can see something very clear. There is a Being whose existence is the origin of the many beings we find in the universe. The metaphor of the sun and the planets helps us to understand this better. From the sun comes all light, the other lights are just reflections. The origin is one, the others are only recipients. The perfection of light is in the sun; in the planets there is light, but incompletely.

Likewise: the perfect way of being (existence) comes from the perfect BEING (person). We are a specific way of being, but in imperfect ways. We do not give life to ourselves, for it begins in Him. He has all the perfection of existence; we have the imperfection of existence. That is why we read in Psalm 104:19-20 RSVCE "You have made the moon to mark the seasons; the sun knows its time for setting. You make darkness, and it is night, when all the animals of the forest come creeping out." And in Psalm 90: " Before the mountains were brought forth, or ever you had formed the Earth and the world, from everlasting to everlasting you are God."

Questions to think about:

1. Is it valid to ask about the meaning of everything? What is an unquestioned life like?

2. What are the three necessary elements for the human being to know the world around him?

3. After reading, how would you explain what metaphysics is? What are you trying to figure out?

Chapter 2:
What is the Truth in Life?

"The truth is incontrovertible. Malice may attack it, ignorance may deride it, but in the end, there it is."

Winston Churchill

Ever since the last conversation, Luis had been turning things over in his head, and he was very interested in digging deeper. Yet he was not entirely convinced about that recent talk, at least as far as the truth is concerned. But the topic of Metaphysics made him feel intrigued and satisfied at the same time.

Once again, they got in touch with each other and met at the usual place. Luis arrived first this time, and he was looking at his watch when Alejandro came:

"Didn't you say something about being on time?" asked Luis, tapping his watch.

"Oops, I guess the tides have turned," Alejandro said, giving his friend a nudge. Luis pushed him back and laughed.

Then Luis started their talk again:

"Let's see. You got me thinking. This idea that everything I see is made up—in the end—of a being that God gives it, I think that this is something I should have known in the past. Everything that exists, in its most important aspect, has a being "borrowed" from the eternal BEING and because of that, it continues to exist. I liked your point and I did some Google searches. You're starting to convince me. But I still have the question: Can the truth be known or not?

How does Each Person Know Reality?

"Let's take it step by step" said Alejandro. "What would you say is the way that you and I know? How does a person know something?"

"I suppose by seeing, by looking at things, and testing them." Luis replied. "The scientific method is the way to start from a hypothesis and arrive at a precise, unquestionable statement."

"Right," said Alejandro. "I see different phenomena, things and situations. Then I collect them and I take them to a laboratory to experiment. This is all that is required to do science and have objective conclusions. I do that by using all my senses: touch, sight, hearing, smell, and taste. All of these are the method by which someone learns.

There was a pause in the talk. A beautiful girl walked by and Luis, as always, stared at her.

When Alejandro noticed it, he hit his friend softly on his head and said, "Ah, you're stupid. You have a girlfriend, fool."

"Yes, but I am not jealous," Luis replied.

Both friends smirked, and Luis continued:

"But we also learn by reasoning, thinking, making formulas, and applying them. How should we consider that?

"Yes, this is true," Alejandro said. "But if you look closely, those steps come from the previous ones we talked about. The first thing that happens is more existential, less scientific. It is a learning that is given by the senses. Saint Thomas Aquinas said a phrase in Latin: "Nihil is in intellect quod prius non est in sensu", which means "There is nothing in the intellect that has not previously entered through the senses."

Luis' look was one of polite rejection. He said to Alejandro,

"Calm down, Einstein. You and your Latin phrases—how much do you think you know?

Alejandro laughed, as if he was embarrassed for having been a little vain, and added: "I promise you that it is one of the few phrases I learned, since it is very important in a subject called Epistemology. Where I live there are five of us who have been have been taking philosophy classes for a year and a half. It is for the sheer delight of knowledge. And by the way, Einstein didn't know Latin!"

Epistemology: the science of human knowledge

5 senses

Universal, immaterial

Singular, material

Human beings with their intellect convert concrete material reality into a spiritual one. This is what we call the process of abstraction.

"Epistemology? asked Luis. "Sounds like science. What is epistemology?"

"It is the area of philosophy that explains what human being can know," Alejandro replied. "In other words, how does someone know? What ability does his little inner machine—intelligence—have for knowing?

"Ok," said Luis, "but go back to the last story. You were talking about the feelings."

Passionate now to explain the details of his philosophy course, Alejandro continued:

"I told you this: the first thing that our intelligence does is to use the five senses to build a scheme of reality in our heads. It is both hard and simple at the same time. I'll explain it to you in a simple way."

Man knows through his five senses

"Material things have information that our five senses perceive, which is processed in the mind and then is kept with a concept that is called a "universal". That is, when you see one, you can see the others. If I see a horse in Madrid and then I see a horse in Santiago de Chile, my mind says, 'Horse.' I did not have to learn again about this specific horse, because the 'I' can connect the universal horse that I have in my mind. Have you never heard this before?

Luis just shook his head. It was like he was listening to something in Martian. Alejandro continued:

"If I have to learn things one by one, since concepts are repeated in reality, it takes me a thousand years. On the other hand, because the human mind can take something singular and make it universal, mankind has knowledge. There are things and processes that are repeated, in the same extent or similarly, here and in China.

Luis asked further, "And who invented this theory? That is to say, who created this process of human thinking?"

"It was the combination of many people," Alejandro replied, "but above all, the same ones I told you last time: Aristotle and St. Thomas Aquinas. One picked up where the other left off. Aristotle was Alejandro the Great's teacher in the third century B.C. and Saint Thomas lived in the thirteenth century. He is one of the most intelligent thinkers who ever lived, among others."

There was another pause in their conversation. It was like the pieces were starting to fit together, both for the one explaining as well as for the one listening.

"Ok," said Luis, "Let's continue. I see that you are leading me on like the good movies without revealing everything. But then, what does this have to do with the truth? It's one thing to experiment with things, to do science, and another thing is truth in every area.

"What we've seen is that men and women have the capacity to know what exists. Last time we talked about the being that gives existence to everything. Precisely now we know that seeing things (material things) is obtained little by little by the senses. Then we pass them on to the intellect, and we do science. But it seems to me that the real key to this is the following:

The world is real and we can know it

"Everyone knows what's out there. That is to say, what is outside, in a way, throws rays of material at the intellect. I'm using very flexible language and images to make it easy to understand. Don't take me too literally," said Alejandro.

"Then, matter 'projects' that 'information' that is like lightning to the mind, and then the mind receives it and says: 'hair' or 'car' or 'elephant.' Do you understand me?"

"Go on, go on," said Luis.

"Yes. Project those rays into the mind, the mind measures them, and there, right there is truth. There the human being, when he says: 'Ball,' cannot be wrong. That is, if our senses see something

It is not man who
creates things.

It is not man who
invents realities
ourside of himself.

They already exist.

and 'measure' it and affirm something, they affirm what they are seeing, there we have truth. That is why the definition of truth in Epistemology is the adequacy between the intellect and the (observed) thing.

"Let me clarify. What is adequacy? It is the identification of the mind with what it is seeing. It is an atunement of the senses to reality. Everything that exists receives that ray, it is perceived by man, then he says something about it, and there we have truth."

"So, can we know the truth?" asked Luis.

"What we are seeing together here is that before anyone thinks, the world around him gives him information. It is not the person who creates things. No one person invents new realities. They are already there. People see the existing world and this existing world already has its rules."

"Where are you going with that?" asked Luis. "It sounds to me like someone in history has said the opposite."

"You are getting at something important. After the fifteenth century in the West, there has been a big crisis in the world of being and thinking, that is, in human life. Why? Because there were some thinkers who did not understand this process of knowing people. They invented other ways of knowledge. They did not understand that things can be known by everyone because they have a being in each one, and that everyone is capable of knowing them. Then, from that time on, and reaching even to our days, there is a big crisis of reason."

Crisis of reason in modernity

Thinkers like Kant, Malebranche and Hegel left us many doubts about what we can know. Then Einstein came along and created the theory of Relativity—which is amazing—but some brought his theory to all areas of reality, which he only intended for a few. Space and time are relative to the person. They took Einstein's findings and extended them to all reality. That, however, is not what he had in mind. That is why it does not mean that we should say 'everything is relative.' No, not everything is relative. And I'm not being dogmatic, Luis. Look at the irony. If I say 'everything is relative,' I'm including that same phrase. And then I am turning the very phrase that I pretend to be true into a lie, not the truth."

"But what made those you mentioned, Kant, Hegel and the other one who started with 'm', not understand?" Luis asked. "What did they say?"

Alejandro had a passion for all these subjects, and he continued with passion:

"What they did was deny man's ability to know. They said that things are not always clear objects of reality. Kant said that in the mind we have some 'categories', as if they were some packaging that we put on things when we see them. Other people spoke of the appearances of things. A crisis of reason was created. And thus the only thing that can be known is what can be verified by the scientific method. On the one hand, there was a big certainty in some areas, on the other side a crisis of reason."

Luis' eyes shone like when someone puts together a puzzle and finds pieces, and the final image begins to take shape. But he still had many questions.

Modern Scientism and its Consequences

"And then," asked Luis, "what consequences do those ideas or mistakes have in understanding how and what people are capable of knowing?"

"Many things have happened," Alejandro replied. "First, that we can only trust what can be scientifically proven. This is not good, because, do you believe that what can be known only comes to us through the senses?"

"I guess not."

"Well, no," said Alejandro. "Last time we said it. Most things loved and appreciated by everyone—our behavior at home, our love, our hobbies, the pleasure of a beer, the happiness of a patient recovering from his sickness in the hospital—well, hundreds of things, do not enter the area of the senses or of the measurable. For that there are other sciences like philosophy and theology. I bet you, Luis, that you have some certainties for which you would give your life and nobody can measure them."

Luis nodded without arguing. Then he asked:

"What other consequences are there to not understanding what man can know today?"

"Second," said Alejandro, "and a direct consequence of what has been said, attributes that are so human and that will always exist such as love, happiness, personal relationships, the soul, as well as the differences between neuroscience, psychology, and religion—they have all become second-rate matters. These are matters that can only be talked about in the privacy of your own room. If it can't be verified with the scientific method, it does not exist. An important thinker of our time, the auxiliary bishop of Los Angeles, Robert Barron, says that we live in a time of what he calls "scientism". He says: scientism is a threat not only to religion, but to every non-empirical mode of knowledge of truth. It endangers poetry and art, for example, both in religion and in the beautiful discipline of philosophy". In fact, he puts a question to those who think like this: "Where did you verify empirically that only through empirical knowledge we can know the truth?"

"This is great," said Luis. "I see this all the time here at the university. Most teachers don't care a lot about anything other than science."

"That's right. It's everywhere. And not only in the university, but in the media, in the mainstream mentality of the people on the street," added Alejandro.

It was almost time for both of them to go to class. But they gave a few more minutes to the matter.

"Is there any further consequence of the mistakes of those philosophers?" asked Luis.

47

"Thirdly," said Alejandro, "yes, we can see how many areas of morality are being questioned, distorted and destroyed. Think about it: If the only thing that counts is what we can measure, and ethics and morals are within philosophy, and that cannot be measured, then everyone is allowed to think as they wish. In morals, everything is questionable. And what was once an aberration is now freedom of expression. What used to be bad for humanity is now not so bad, as long as you don't hurt anyone. This is called moral relativism, and it is also called subjectivism. I will not go into too much detail on this subject, because I have to go now and we can talk about this later, but this has created an idea that there is no natural law in the world and in humanity. This idea is now very widespread in the West. The only thing that exists is positive law, that is, that what is comes from whoever is governing at the present moment, those who people vote for. Things, then, don't exist because there is a being that gives meaning to all things, both to the physical things that we can measure and to the more philosophical ones that we can think about. But we'll leave that topic for later, because I'm late for my class."

With disappointment on his face, Luis looked at him and said, "Okay, but I could never get the answer to my question from you: Is there a truth or not?"

"I think you can think about the answer yourself. You never feel freer in life than when the truth comes to you through

your own discovery. I don't want to influence you. I show you what has been presented to me, and you come to your conclusions. Now, I have a question for you:

Is it arrogant or not for a Catholic or Christian to say: I have the truth?"

ANALYZING THE CONVERSATION

Alejandro and Luis' talk leads us to three major topics. Every human aspiration must be based on something specific. If a person who is at sea wants to know whether he is moving forward or not, he has to be pushing himself from something (water), and he has to have a safe point of reference (an object on land). It might sound like a lie and something basic, but there are many thinkers in the world who instead of having common sense, have non-common sense. Usually, they set their affirmations on beliefs and and a desire to see things in one way, as their own creations, rather than on taking from reality and getting, through it, to the truth.

The fixed point on Earth for man, using the metaphor of the previous paragraph, is exactly what Saint Thomas said. On the one hand, material things have a consistency of raw material that feeds us and gives us life. But the first person replies: "I don't think it exists, because I don't see it". The second says again: "You don't see it because we are inside it." But of course, it exists. On the one hand, material things have the consistency of raw material and form, as Aristotle said. This principle of things makes them have a limit, which corresponds to the matter, and an intelligibility element, which is the form. But that higher level of the conclusion that Saint Thomas reached was that before the thing is in one way or another, a bird, apple, or stone, there is something in common in all of them, and it is that all of them have being and essence. Without going too far into it, because this book's level does not seek to deepen these complex ideas, we simply say that things would not exist without this principle.

This is why it is fundamental for a man to answer: What is the world made of? How do I know what is possible to know? What do I do with what I have known? Mind, matter, word, and action are the elements to live and discover about life.

Since we know that things have something that makes our instruments of knowledge, namely our intellects, able to grasp them, then we move forward comfortably and surely.

The man then comes into contact with material objects, and through that process extracts from them, with his mind, the material and individual part of each thing and form in his mind something spiritual, which we call a universal concept. We said: if I see a ship in the Atlantic Sea, and I see a ship in the Gulf of Mexico,

I don't have to learn again. One concept leads to another. And so, the spiritual being shows to be capable of spiritual processes. Even though I don't have the boat physically in my head, I do have the boat's spiritual concept in my head. Like one brick after another, these concepts together make it possible for a man to progress in his knowledge. He has been able to advance in medicine, engineering, and hundreds of other fields.

But here is where the dividing line is drawn. Is the only way to know something through the senses? That is, are there useful things in man's life that are of another nature?

Reasoning a little will lead us to say "yes". And the fact that many people in the world today do not accept this has given rise to scientism. It is the conviction that only through the exact sciences, we can find the truth. The absence of humanistic and philosophical studies in the West has made us excessively materialistic. We are materialists.

Another way of learning, known and accepted in the Western world, is through philosophy and theology. This world view condemns God and religion to one corner of the intellectual sphere. And if that is so, then God has nothing left to say to the man. Man remains the owner and lord of everything, capable of transforming and destroying everything since God does not exist. There is an image that can help you a lot.

Two twins still in their mother's womb are talking. One says to the other, "Hey, do you think mommy exists?" and the other replies, "Of course she exists. We are inside of her. She is the one that feeds us and gives us life". Without it, we would not have life. Wait a while and you'll be amazed that Mom is the most wonderful thing in existence.

We can already see how, for some people, having faith is a fool's mistake. Someone who has faith is someone who is not a scientist, who is not rigorous, who does not have the same push to bring humanity—through science—to all that it is called to become. And this is really wrong.

It is because two good things cannot be enemies. science and Faith or religion come from the same origin. Intelligible and God-made things contain "matter" that the human mind can perceive. The same God is the God of Revelation, who spoke to Abraham to make him father of many nations and father of Israel, which is the people that waited for Jesus, who is born at Christmas and whose death and final victory we celebrate at Easter. They are not two different ones.

One of the big victories of evil and ignorance in our time is an abysmal gap between the created and the uncreated. But we will talk more about this in the next chapter.

Questions to think about:

1. What do you think is the clay out of which the world made?

2. Can the human mind learn from the created world? How?

3. Why isn't the scientific method the only way to know?

Chapter 3:
Does Truth Come Through Faith or Reason?

"Faith and reason are like the two wings with which the human spirit rises to the contemplation of truth"

John Paul II

The conversations between Alejandro and Luis were getting more and more interesting. And sometimes so much that they both admitted that they were distracted in their classes because they were thinking about it, one about how to better explain or what to do next, and the other one about understanding better. Luis was a little uncomfortable knowing so little about these things, but that's why he had Alejandro.

After the weekend, they met again, this time between the first and fourth periods. This left them with a lot of time to stop by the Starbucks next to the school of architecture and go to the normal meeting place. There nobody seemed to take away their space or time. Luis began the conversation.

Sources of Knowledge: philosophy and science

"You know I was talking to my dad about the truth and what you can know?" he said.

"Oh, really? And what did he tell you?" asked Luis.

"Well, I can see he's kind of torn. You know he is such an engineer, but he does recognize that there are many truths that do not come from science alone. He just couldn't explain himself much to me. So, tell me if I understand correctly: Man has the ability to understand the world around him in two ways: The things he learns through what science can tell him, and also with the ideas that are proper to philosophy. Is that so?" asked Luis, starting the debate.

"Yes and no," Alejandro replied. "As far as human knowledge without the help of God, that is true. There's nothing more than philosophy and science. Maybe some people have good intuition. In my opinion, intuition is a complement of knowledge, but one cannot be sure of what one intuits, or at least we cannot bet everything on this sense. But the part that you left out is Revelation."

"We're going to your religion again, aren't we?" asked Luis, without hiding his rejection.

Alejandro felt a little anger inside, but he had had a lot of training in his philosophy course. He knew well that the one who gets angry, loses, and that there is no point in getting furious. He showed a calm face, and took a drink of the frappuccino. So, they spent a few moments of calm pause, before returning.

"Look. Just like we said last time, there is some knowledge that everyone cannot know. And it's not about my religion. It's about reality. But let's go slowly."

"For centuries, humanity has asked itself many questions, both about God and about the real world. The instruments that mankind had were limited. And it was the Greek philosophers—mainly Socrates, Plato and Aristotle—who spoke most about God. In the specific case of Aristotle, he called God the 'first motionless engine.' Just as I explained that Saint Thomas proved the existence of God by talking about a non-caused cause, there are five ways to explain the existence of God. This is philosophy, not religion. I'm not going to explain the five ways, but you already know one of them. Another of the tests is the one of movement. It's very similar to the issue of causes that we talked about the other day.

Every existing being is moved by another. And if we go backwards, we must necessarily arrive at a source that is not moved by anything. We cannot go on to infinity. Aristotle was clear that this first engine was God. But he knew little or nothing else about it.

God's Revelation to Humanity

Luis, there are things in life that cannot be known except by Revelation. Today, it is clear that we know many things about God, for example, that there is only one God, but there are three persons. No one would ever reach this with science or philosophy.

"Yes," said Luis, a bit angry, "but that's what you believe because you are a Catholic. I'm not so sure about that, because right now I don't know what to believe."

Alejandro patiently related ideas: "I understand. Let me explain it to you, because I trust you will see that everything makes sense. Look at all the religions—but we won't get into a specific one now— the big questions of life have answers that make a lot of sense as the Church's Tradition explains them."

"Let's see; answers like what?"

"What happens after death? Why is there pain in life? What is God like? Who is God? Why do bad situations happen to good people? These questions have been researched by all religions. But really, I can't find better explanations than in the Catholic faith. And don't think I'm saying this because I'm Catholic. In my philosophy course, we had a subject called natural theology, where we analyzed Buddhism, Judaism, Islam and other beliefs."

"Don't tell me you didn't find any truth in those religions," said Luis.

"Of course I did," Alejandro replied. "In fact, now I hold them in great esteem. There are parts of truth in every religion. In all of them I could appreciate lights. But in none as much as in the Catholic religion. What can I say? Let's say I gave them the opportunity to change my thinking. The faith in which I was born won."

They stopped talking for a few seconds while each one took a little sip of their coffee and nibbled at the donuts they had bought for themselves. They looked at the gardens for a moment to think through things.

The gardens of this university are very beautiful. It is one of the things that young people like most. Some students nap in them, others sit on the grass to chat or do Instagram, others do homework or read books with great concentration.

"Well, let's get back to the subject," said Alejandro. "There's a phrase I love from a document I often read, and in that book the question is asked: Was revelation necessary for humanity to know God? Wait, let me think about it, because here I have an answer:

This is why man stands in need of being enlightened by God's revelation, not only about those things that exceed his understanding, but also "about those religious and moral truths which of themselves are not beyond the grasp of human reason, so that even in the present condition of the human race, they can be known by all men with ease, with firm certainty and with no admixture of error."

"What book is that?" asked Luis.

"It is the Catechism of the Church prepared by John Paul II with the help of Cardinal Ratzinger, who later became Pope Benedict XIV. He is one of the most brilliant minds of the twentieth century. If you notice, Luis, what he is saying in my viewpoint is that man has to be humble and realize that in this small head," here Alejandro pointed to his own, "we can't understand everything. We are very foolish and arrogant if we think that anything that can't fit inside our heads doesn't exist.

We are stubborn and prideful if what we are not capable of grasping with our intellects we automatically consider non-existent.

Three Ways to Know

"Well, let's see, go on then," said Luis.

"Yes, what I want to tell you is that we are getting the conclusions that you like and that you are always asking me for. Then, there are three ways to know. Human thinking does it through the external world, with science. It does it through its ability for reflection, with philosophy. And it receives it from God, through revelation. God explains to him what his head cannot understand by means of his two ways."

"Does God explain it himself? And to whom? and how? I have no knowledge of God speaking to me."

Alejandro looked at Luis and he was pleased, and he perceived a little openness at least. "God revealed himself to man through Jesus Christ. The Jesus that Christians follow. He was the revealed Word we find in the Gospel of John; do you remember? "In the beginning was the Word..."

Faith is Reasonable

"In fact, among many out there, there is one book written by a religious American, a convert from Protestantism to Catholicism. his name is Scott Hahn. He has a book called "Faith Is Reasonable." In short, in that book he says that although humanity is not able to understand the depth of many of the things that God reveals, nevertheless we are very able to see that it makes all the sense in the world to believe in what he reveals, because it is logical. It is a logical conclusion of what reason leads you to understand.

Faith and reason cannot fight, because they have God as their source and origin. That is why John Paul II said: "Faith and reason are like the two wings with which the human spirit rises to the acceptance of the truth"[4].

"But surely there must be times when faith and reason come into conflict with each other," said Luis, "and one of the two must prevale. Don't you have to choose whether to use faith or reason?"

He asked his question with a lot of uncertainty, as if he were just playing the devil's advocate to understand better.

"When do you see that you have to use either faith or reason?" asked Alejandro.

Luis thought a little.

"For example, if someone is dying and you have to give them the basic resources to live, such as oxygen, water and food, or you could, as many people say, leave it rather to what God says."

"Ok. You choose that example. How about this? People tend to think with extremes. We think that there is either "this or that". In my philosophy class and in the history of the Church, it is usually correct to think inclusively, that is, "this and that". What difficulty do you find, Luis, in doing both things? Giving food, oxygen, and water, and at the same time, after doing what you can with medicine, leaving things in God's hands?

In fact, if you look at it, faith is not against reason, but above reason. For some people, having faith is a foolish thing to do. For them someone who has faith is someone who is not scientific, who is not strict, who does not have the same motivation to help humanity in its advance.

What they do not see is that faith is the act of trusting in God himself, who cannot and does not know how to deceive, and telling him: from this point forward my reason can't explain things, I believe in you, God. The crazy thing is that we already have it so easy. People of the first century did not have many years of existence of Christianity to trust in. But we have two thousand years of which to say: 'Listen, it seems that God is fulfilling his promises.'

"Remember, Luis. These are levels of knowledge. Both come from God. They do not fight or contradict each other. I can live with reason, that is why he gave it to me. And I can live with faith, which comes from God if I ask for it and do not oppose it.

Luis seemed to be contemplating things. He tried to fit some ideas into others, to find meaning in what was being discussed. He did not say anything.

Then he spoke. "Although I don't get some basic answers out of you, I'll try then to sum up what we've said here."

Mankind's Capacity for Truth

"From what you tell me," Luis continued, "mankind can come to know the truth, little by little. On the one hand, in regard to earthly and material things, he uses science and philosophy. On the side of things of the other life, things that have to do with God and transcendence, he needs to believe in God who revealed himself with the presence of Jesus. Is that your position?"

Alejandro replied with obvious delight. "That's how I see things. And even though we cannot know everything or understand everything—since we must also give place to mystery in life and to God's projects that we understand in a very limited way, we can safely and slowly expect to be wiser. In fact, this is one of the most important messages of Christianity. Jesus said: "And you shall know the truth, and the truth shall make you free"[5].

Faith and Reason are Complementary

"There are many scientists who are men and women of great faith. They do not fight with each other. Again, faith and reason are complementary, like a man and a woman, like a pilot and a co-pilot, like an architect and a civil engineer."

Alejandro paused to see if Luis had a comment or question. But Luis said nothing, so Alejandro continued.

"Luis, there was this picture or reality that was the basis of my philosophy course that can help you. It goes like this. In reality there is a big triangle of existence. That triangle has three realities. Those realities are all good, true, and beautiful. Those three characteristics are called transcendentals by the famous philosophers.

Without complicating your life, we will just say that everything that exists has those three elements. If you are talking about the subjective aspect of whether we like a snake more than a dolphin, that's different. But everything created objectively has those three factors, transcendentals.

"Going back to the three realities, they create that triangle and each one has its own, shall we say, personality,. If any of the corners of the triangle are wrong, the other two are necessarily wrong too. For example: If I think that God is in the created world, and that means a tree is God, I have already warped reality. This is called pantheism (God is all things). On the other hand, if I think that man is just a being like animals and that he has no soul or transcendence, this is called materialism.

God, the world and man is placed at the same level by some thinkers. That is called pantheism.

Men   God   The World

"Also that destroys the reality of the three corners. And finally, if I deify a person, like has been done with some rulers in history, that's called idolatry, which is making God out of someone or something that's not God."

So; do you want to reduce everything to those three realities: God, mankind and the world?"

"Think about it, Luis," said Alejandro. "What other reality exists? Everything fits into these three categories. Either you are a created, untranscendent reality, or you are human or you are God."

"And the animals," asked Luis, "where do they fit in?"

"Animals do not fit in the category of either God or mankind," said Alejandro. "They do not have a rational soul. They do have something spiritual, but not in the same way as human beings."

"And what about the angels?" asked Luis.

Alejandro shrugged his shoulders, as if to say he didn't have a concrete answer.

"Well done!" he said. "Good question. Since we know so little about them, and knowing that they belong to a status superior to humanity, that would be one of the few things that does not fit into this scheme. But everything else does."

"What I find too negative is when a Christian pontificates," said Luis. "In other words, when arrogant Christians—I don't mean you, really—feel that they alone have the truth. How dare they be so arrogant?"

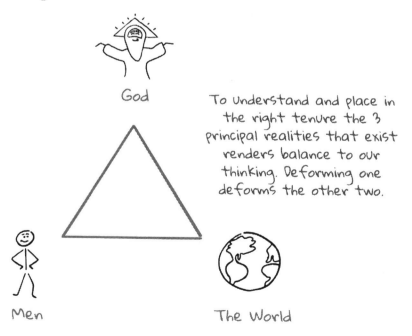

God

Men

The World

To understand and place in the right tenure the 3 principal realities that exist renders balance to our thinking. Deforming one deforms the other two.

"Look," said Alejandro, "no one should be proud. In fact, the Christian is invited by his master, Jesus, to be humble. You can find all typesa book-length interview. It's called "Light of the World", and I highly recommend it. It's your style, because they ask him many questions.

"The author said, "What do you think about Christians feeling that they have the whole truth"? He answered, "We never have it (the truth); at best it has us."

Look at what a great key he gives us. When a Christian says "This is the truth", he is not imposing it on the other person. He is saying: All of us should submit to this truth that we did not create. It already existed in reality.

"In that book he coined a term that became well known and commented upon. He spoke of a "Dictatorship of Relativism". You might ask, what is that? in this day and age, skeptics—those who do not believe that the truth can be known—want to dominate. Anyway... I won't get into that. What do you think?"

Luis felt inside him the special feeling of when someone is advancing in knowledge, like when the pieces of a puzzle start to make up the image. Yet, still doubting, he asked:

"There is still one thing that worries me. There are many atheists, and it seems that there are always more and more. And there is a lot of evil in the world and nobody has a solution for this. I really find it hard to think that God is good, as Christians say, but he allows too much evil. What certainty can we have that God really exists?"

ANALYZING THE CONVERSATION

Among the different forms of knowledge, there are two important categories for humanity: what it can know through reason, and what needs to be revealed.

Humanity can use its intellect to know the material world, as Alejandro explained to Luis. Thus, human beings gradually test the scientific method and can confirm a very important part of reality.

Also, every man and woman can get to know another aspect of the reality through philosophy. Man is naturally a philosopher, and for centuries has asked himself many questions, answering them after rigorous and disciplined work. Man proceeds by concepts that create thoughts and arrive at conclusions.

These two natural ways of knowing for humanity are complementary. They give meaning to what exists and to what is most spiritual in humanity. Ultimately, there are things that human beings could not know in this life if God Himself did not enter the scene and reveal it to them. We call this revelation.

To be precise, the son of God, the second person of the Trinity, Jesus, gave this message. He came to answer the questions we have asked at every historical moment and every place on Earth: Where does everything come from? Who rules the world? What is there after this life? What happens after death? Why is there pain in life? Who is God? What is the value of human life?

As we read in the talk, man would never have reached this knowledge without much help from God. That is why we can see how the times before Christ and after Christ have very different characteristics. Among them, the progress of humanity and its rights which prospered starting with that synthesis that was the Greco-Roman culture and the Judeo-Christian civilization.

If what humanity can know is integrated with what it comes to discover through science and philosophy and this is united with what God wants to reveal to him then it can be said that science and faith are not at odds with each other. Science and faith come from the same place. God is the author of the existing world, the one we see and the one we do not see. To be precise, faith and reason are what made it possible for the important universities to develop within the ambit of Christianity. The first universities were in Paris, Oxford, Bologna and Salamanca. All of them were promoted by the Catholic Church in the eleventh century.

Then, when a person says that this or that is the truth, that person does not try to impose the truth. What he says is that he has reached something that anyone else, in the same way, can reach. It would be as if a person climbing a mountain, upon reaching the top, says, "I am on the top," and when someone hears him says "He's a lunatic." The one who reaches the top and affirms it does not affirm anything false. He simply affirms that his effort has led him to a place where others, with the same effort and discipline, can reach.

In today's world we see a great crisis of thought. On the one hand, there is an enormous pride in affirming specific truths. On the other hand, there is a lot of fear of hearing and saying "This is the truth. The world has made us ashamed, fearful that this phrase is not politically correct. There is a skepticism and doubt as to whether man has the capacity to truly know the world where he lives. And not only that, but there's skepticism that we can say with certainty that something is here and there, today and forever.

Questions to think about:

1. On the matter of truth; what has your conclusion been in life and how do you feel after reading this chapter? Is it possible for there to be truth or not?

2. Have you found people who cannot see how faith and reason can exist together and complement each other—or have you experienced this yourself?

3. Have you ever heard that truth comes from these two main sources: a) What humanity know by reason and b) What does God reveal to mankind? Think of examples of both types of knowledge.

Chapter 4:

Does God Really Exist?

""If God doesn't exist, everything is allowed."

Dostoyevsky.

It was 9 a.m. on Tuesday morning. Both Alejandro and Luis had exams in topics that had consumed a lot of their energy over the weekend.

Once the academic concerns were behind him, Luis told Alejandro to meet him at the same place. They arrived with their coffee and sandwiches and continued their journey. First, Alejandro spoke:

"How did it go yesterday?" he asked. "You told me that the exam was really hard. Was it?"

Luis looked at him, worried. "I don't really know. I didn't feel like I did very well, but it seemed like the whole class felt the same. Let's see if the teacher does a curve, because if he doesn't, I won't pass and it will be too hard to raise my average."

"Well, don't worry," Alejandro said. "Let's hope you are smarter than you think and that you have done better than you feel."

"It's better that way," Luis said, "because my father always asks me how it went."

"Well," said Alejandro, "last time we were talking about a question. How do we know if God really exists? Do you want to explain more or shall I start to telling you my reasons?"

Luis sipped his coffee and took a bite of his carrot cake. Then he said:

"Let's see. I have not believed in God at all for a long time. I am not convinced. And when I listen to my parents or my grandparents talk about God, I never hear anything rational, only faith. And what is clear to me is that there are more and more atheists in the world, and especially a lot of indifference about religion, which is almost the same as not believing."

"Well, to start from some point, what are the reasons you think that God does not exist?" Alejandro asked him.

The evil we see in the world

"Many,' Luis replied. "But I begin by saying that I see a lot of evil in the world. How can they say, especially Christians, that God is good? A good father doesn't allow murder and crimes to take place where his children die. If God is good and sees evil and does nothing, either he's a cynic or he doesn´t exist. There is no other explanation." Luis said this with conviction, and feeling a little anger.

"Okay," Alejandro said, "let me explain. The first thing is that to believe in God or not to believe in God is as old as mankind. Each person must decide whether or not to believe. It does not help much if someone "gives us their faith" or to be "born in Christianity" or "born in Judaism" or whatever religion it is.

In History there have been many attempts to kill God. Atheism is not new. The book of Ecclesiastes 1:9 already states: "There is nothing new under the sun. Frederick Nietzsche tried to kill Go when he wrote: "God is dead". He did not say this phrase directly, but he did as much in his writings, especially in "Thus spoke Zarathustra". And they say that a graffiti writer wrote on a wall: "God is dead", and signed Nietzsche's name. Another graffiti writer wrote: "Nietzsche is dead" and signed with the name of God."

"It is absolutely true that all of us perceive evil in the world, and we have asked ourselves: Why did this happen? Why did God allow my uncle Philip who was so good to leave us? And each one has an example."

Luis interrupted, "Yes. For example, when a child is raped by a priest. How can God allow that? They are traumatized for life."

"Yes," Luis replied, "that example is very recent and there are thousands of examples that we can question. But here's the issue. Many people get upset when something bad happens and wonder why God doesn't do something. The questions are constantly in the mind of everyone: Why do people get sick? Why did my friend have to die? But in fact, I really felt that some people complain when God does something, or they don't believe that it is He who has done it. If he does not do something; why don't you take action? And if he takes action in some way or another it is unlikely that he is God: it is chance.

"For example, if we, the Christians, see something that has no natural explanation, and we call it a miracle, which is an intervention by God, we are told that we are religious fanatics. There are some atheists who read the Bible and are upset because God was involved in specific moments of history by allowing the bad guys to die, such as the Canaanites and Philistines. And in those cases, the atheists cry out, "Murderous God!" They say that because he was involved.

"There are two types of evils that we see. Those ones done by men and those that happen naturally, such as a volcano, a hurricane, etc. In the case of the malice committed by people, God cannot do something. He made us free.

God doesn't always take action because if a father always stops his children from fighting by taking away their Freedom; when do they mature? Is it not with blows that we mature? The father can't always go around solving his children's mischief."

Luis asked: "And when it is something natural, an earthquake and these things; where is God?"

"Good point," replied Alejandro. "The other evil is the natural one. We have to think that nature has its rules and follows its course. The difficulties of life are real. Jesus cried, he felt hungry, he was despised, and surely, he suffered more than once when he preached and would have been drenched by the rain. There is a phrase that Jesus Christ himself said: "God makes it rain on the good and on the bad, he makes the sun rise on the fair and on the unfair." (Mt 5, 45) It is the same for everyone.

Luis disagreed. "I don´t see it correctly. I see bad people everywhere and nothing happens to them. I see good people who are having bad moments."

Alejandro replied, "That is a perception. We all have good things and bad things. Besides, Luis, we tend to see the evils of this world as absolute, and they are not. They are absolute only if this life is all that exists. We are back to scientism. For those for whom nothing more than this life exists, the evil here is not relative, something transitory... Saint Paul speaks of "The good things above" to talk about the treasures of the next life. He also mentions "All the earth suffering...", which means that we feel that our homeland is not here. We are not fully satisfied with anything here. We fill ourselves with pleasures, and then we feel empty.

"To sum up: The evil we see is sad, it hurts us, it annoys us... but in itself it is not a valid or scientific explanation, let alone a philosophical one, to deny the existence of God."

Natural disasters

"And, in the case of tsunamis, earthquakes and fires; what does God say about that?" Luis asked. "Why doesn't he do something?"

"That is also a question," Alejandro replied. "The coach in the philosophy course led us to understand one thing. God is not controlling every little piece of the universe. The world has its way, and in a world where original sin entered by the free choice of man, God allows the forces of nature to work. Many of them represent a joy for man, others are dangerous. The seasons, the rain, the snow, an erupting volcano...all are great events of nature and have a reason. But also, our fragility makes it so they are so powerful they claim our lives too."

"And so it's right when I ask, and God; where is He?" said Luis.

"God is still where he always is, which is in every place." Alejandro replied. "What happens is that in what has the appearance to us of being the big tragedy of losing one's life, because it is the only thing one person knows, we forget that for God it is not a problem really. Yes, Luis, I know this is hard to hear in a time when this life is everything. But God did not make us for this life that lasts seventy, eighty or ninety years. We are made for ever. That is why Jesus said: 'Do not lay up for yourselves treasures on earth, where moth and rust consume and where thieves break in and steal, but lay up for yourselves treasures in heaven, where neither moth nor rust consumes and where thieves do not break in and steal. For where your treasure is, there will your heart be also.'" (Matt. 6:19-21 RSVCE).

"Then, although God is all-powerful, he does not control nature. God put laws in all existing things and lets them follow their course."

Luis sat there, staring. For the first time, he felt that someone was giving him more serious explanation about things.

We cannot see God

Then he added:

"Why is it so hard for God to show himself?" he asked. "No one has ever seen God. If he is so interested in us believing in him, why not make himself visible? You already said that the way to know about mankind is through the senses."

Alejandro smiled. He knew the answer to this one. "Yes, it is true, we cannot see Him. And we do know through the five senses, but we also talk about the fact that we do not learn through the senses only. Also, there is philosophy and Revelation. Do you remember the saying: The essential is invisible to the eyes?"

"First, right now there are cell phone signals passing through here, and we don't see them. Are they less real? You're crazy about your girlfriend, and we don't always see her. When we don't see that you love her; doesn't that love for her still exist?

"In my experience there are, however, other ways of looking at God. The world focuses on the evil in the world. But let us list the many expressions of God's love. Look at the green fields, the eternal seas, the blue skies with clouds, the smile and miracle of a baby, a couple in love who are recently married. Whoever believes in God knows that He is in those things. Why is it so easy to get angry at the evil we see, but there is no gratitude for the good we see? Why do we attribute evil to God, and good to chance?"

Luis thought about it and identified that this is how it is, that his lazier and more liberal friends blame God for the bad things, but when everything goes well for them, they do one of two things: either they think they are Superman or they think it had to be that way. He looked at Alejandro as if to ask him to keep talking.

"Another thing that I am often questioned about—in fact, someone said it in the universal values class—is that religions have brought only wars," Alejandro said. "Religion has been a real disaster. The divisions in the world we live in are because of the hatreds that come from religion.

That is a possible interpretation that is subject to questioning and testing. I have another opinion. Religion per se is not bad. Some aspects of it are bad. It's like politics. Can you rule without politics? No. Whats bad are just some elements of politics. There is medicine, and there are bad physicians. We don´t end litigation because there are some bad lawyers who take advantage of it."

Luis liked this and said, "But the truth is that I do agree that religions have caused many problems for our planet. Especially during the Renaissance and later centuries."

Alejandro continued, "Conflicts have been made by religious men or women, but not by religion itself. And of course, one should not deny that there were some situations for which one had to apologize, such as during the time of the Crusades. Not everything was bad, but there were wrong elements. But Luis, if some people see that in the name of religion bad things happened; what do you say about things that been done in the name of Atheism? According to some historians, the Second World War left thirty million dead. In general, the Communist regime has executed more than those killed in centuries of wars. Current self-proclaimed socialist regimes which in real life are Communist without respect for the God or God's laws, allow thousands of deaths a year. Not only in Asia, also in Latin America."

"We should see how much good has been done in the name of Jesus, who is God. Thousands of hospitals, schools, colleges, orphanages, nursing homes, universities, and nursing homes around the world have been built in the name of Jesus. Works respected by the whole world, such as the Missionaries of Charity of Mother Teresa of Calcutta, are all done in the name of God. Is it possible that there is no God?

Where then do they get that level of commitment and love for the poorest man of the poor?

"One way of seeing God is the testimony of billions of people throughout history. From the first century until today, very intellectual and academic people are great believers. In my opinion, two examples are Karol Wojtyla and Joseph Ratzinger, who later became John Paul II and Benedict XVI. They are very intelligent men who are among the most brilliant intellects we had in the 20th century.

Science and Faith

Luis looked for another area in which he often felt uncomfortable about believing in God, which is how faith opposes the advance of science.

"Well, what about the issue of why the Church opposes science? It's as if it were afraid of the advances of men."

"That's a very common topic," answered Alejandro. -But once again, my opinion and what I have studied in my philosophy course explain how that would seem to be the case. Let me explain to you what I know."

"It is amazing how many world-class scientists are big believers, or at least, believers. Important people like Copernicus, Kepler,

Boyle, Galileo (by the way, there's this black legend about him that is a total lie), Newton, Faraday... all of these were strong supporters of what call science today."

"More modern scientists, such as Francis Collins, wrote this."

Alejandro took a manual out of his backpack and thumbed through the book until he got to the chapter that is about these topics. Once he found the quote, he read it aloud:

" 'There is no problem in being a rigorous scientist and a person who believes in God.' "Therefore, he concludes that 'Those who choose to be atheists must find some other reasons for having that opinion.'"

"Here I have a quote from Robert Jawstrow that mentions the limits that science has in knowing everything—which is what we talked of the other day about the ways of knowing man. Listen to this:

"At this point, it seems that science will never be able to lift the curtain on the mystery of creation... Now we see how astronomical evidence leads to a biblical view of the origin of the world. The details differ, but the essential elements and the astronomical and biblical accounts of Genesis are the same; the chain of events leading to man began suddenly and abruptly at a definite moment in time, in a flash of light and energy.8'"

"Again, as we said, Luis: there is no contradiction between science, which comes from God, and faith, which also comes from Him."

Luis was a little confused and humiliated. He felt that what he heard from his friend was very rational but it was humiliating. He wondered why no one had explained these things to him. He was angry that someone his own age had taken advantage of his extra academic time to research all these things. Then, like a boxer who hits less strongly, he continued:

How do we explain order in the world?

"It's fine if God exists and some scientists believe in Him," said Luis. "But there are also many scientists who do not believe in Him. In fact, many physicists and cosmologists deny there is a god," said Luis.

Alejandro answered patiently: "It is true. It is true that each human being decides whether to believe or not. At the same time, Faith is a gift, and an act of the will, as we said before. Whoever is put in front of the evidence of something is not forced to accept it. He is still free to blindly say that God does not exist because the human senses cannot be correct. It is still an act of Revelation and philosophy more than a scientific one."

There was a silence between the two, then Alejandro said:

"One element that I have read a lot about and that gives rise to many scientists confirming the existence of God is order in the world. I mean the order of the seasons and of the planets, and of their rotation around the sun. NASA has said for years that they deserve scrutiny. Their argument—with which I agree--is that it is ridiculous to believe in all that order as something that comes out of chaos."

Alejandro took out a book in which he had highlighted a quote from a great contemporary scientist and he read it to Luis:

"In the early expansion of the universe there has to be a balance between expansive energy (separating things) and the force of gravity (bringing things together). If the expansion were to dominate, matter would separate too quickly for it to condense into galaxies and stars. Nothing interesting could happen in such a scattered world. On the other hand, if gravity were to dominate, the world would collapse in on itself again before there was time for the processes of life to get underway.9"

Luis stared at Alejandro with a quizzical look on his face, as if he wanted answers.

Alejandro continued, "What this guy is saying is that the macro universe is so precisely and carefully structured that if the initial explosion was stronger, the universe would have expanded without any limit. If it had expanded with less force, it would have compressed and went back to being just the same, making life impossible."

"And you know, Luis, all you need for someone to become a fan of these things is to start reading more, and the whole physical and cosmological topic becomes very interesting. Here I will only tell you what little I know, what we have seen in the course."

Luis was beginning to feel that his friend was showing him that perhaps he, Luis, was in the habit of making his conclusions not really based on scientific thinking or what serious people, had thought out, but based on public opinion and political correctness. He asked:

"Alejandro, I feel a little strange. Have I been learning from the wrong places in all that time at school? I mean high school and university; wouldn't it be good if we were taught some of these things us by the teachers? I don´t agree with everything you're saying, but it really makes me feel very interested in finding out and reading about these things.

Alejandro felt that he was beginning to gain a little ground in his friend's mind. Their conversations gave him a chance to find out how much he was taking advantage of his hobbies and reading.

"You are right," Alejandro said. "Why do you think I was interested in taking a course with friends in my house on philosophy and science? Sadly, there is little enough educated thought in today's society. We spend hours eating junk food, consuming gossip and more of the same. It can't be. You can see why I am so passionate about these subjects."

The Bible lies

Luis continued, "one more topic. I don't know if you really know about the Bible or not, but I think." Luis was silent and looked at Alejandro knowing that maybe in this area he was also dealing with common opinions and not serious thoughts-that the Bible, which some believe to be the word of God, lies about creation and has non-credible data. Isn't it supposed to be a guide of truth for living?

Alejandro answered, "Look, Holy Scripture is not a scientific book. The intention of the Bible is not to answer the questions 'how?', or 'when?' Those are scientific questions. It is a book written by men of faith for men of faith. Mainly, they used it to for worship in the first centuries. They used the Bible to celebrate the first masses."

"The questions the Bible wants to answer are; 'why?' and 'who?' These questions are not scientific, Luis. They never will be. They are philosophical and also belong to Revelation. As we have said before, if Jesus had not told us about his Father, the Spirit, and himself, we would never have come to this knowledge. That's what the Bible means. The bible is not a scientific book, but a theological one. But you will see that it never goes against science. Reading the Bible is something that requires taking courses as well. Look at what a prominent twentieth century scientist and mathematician says:

'No scientific analysis of this planet we are on will tell us why it was created if the Creator did not decide to talk. The great thing is that He has spoken and what He has said is called Genesis.

"I, when I read the Bible," added Alejandro, "need not be precise in those areas, for the intention of the Bible is not to make science. It is to take you to Heaven and teach you about God the Creator and Father who calls you to be happy."

Conclusion

"On this topic of having faith in a God or not, I love a quote." This time Alejandro took out his cell phone. "I have it here in a note. This is by C.S. Lewis, who was a great Christian author that I recommend you look into for all that we're talking about:

"If you are a Christian, you don't have to believe that all other religions are simply wrong. If you are an atheist, you have to believe that the main argument in all religions throughout the world is simply a big mistake. If you are a Christian, you are free to think that all those religions, even the strangest ones, contain at least some hint of truth. When I was an atheist, I had to try to convince myself that the majority of the human race had always been wrong about the question that mattered most to them; when I became a Christian, I was able to take a more liberal view.10"

"Luis, please let me also read you some words that Pope Benedict XVI said very recently about the existence or not of God. With this I am leaving you because I will have to go; okay? He took out his cell phone and read:

'Let us try to explain a little more this essential content of God's revelation. Then, we can say that the first important gift that faith offers us is the certainty that God exists. A world without God can only be a world without sense. Otherwise, where would everything come from? In any case, it has no spiritual purpose. Somehow it is only there and has no purpose or meaning. So, there are no standards of good or evil, and only that which is stronger than anything else can assert itself, and power becomes the only principle. Truth does not count; it does not really exist. Only if things have a spiritual reason do they have an intention and are conceived. Only if there is a Creator God that is good and wants the good, the life of man can then have meaning.'"

Already in a hurry, both of them grabbed their backpacks, and Luis said to Alejandro, "This is very good. But soon I would like to discuss a little about us. That is, about who are we as humans?

We've already talked very much about what exists and about God. When can you do that?"

"I can't do tomorrow," said Alejandro, "but send me a text to see about Thursday; is that OK with you?"

ANALYZING THE CONVERSATION

It deserves repeating that until the world comes to an end, we humans will naturally be Philosophers. The important questions that man asks himself always have to do with God. Perhaps it begins with himself, but ends with God. First, he says: who am I? Why do I exist? What destiny do I have? And this voice that speaks to itself finds that it does not have the answers. He needs other Voices to answer him

Although there have been atheists and agnostics since the beginning of Christianity and for the last two thousand years, never have things been happened as quickly as now, nor in such an aggressive way. As Luis and Alejandro have discussed, **scientism** tries to convince mankind that he can solve everything with science. And yet, in the depths of the heart, there follows a heartbeat that seeks more. It seeks because it feels a wish, a vocation and an intense drive for transcendence. Questions about God never stop.

As we have read, the reasons for not believing have been stated: the evil we see; not being able to see or touch God; specific questions about the Bible; the apparent clash between science and faith, death and disease... We have tried to answer to each of these areas that come from an atheistic generation. These and many more reasons can be discussed. But there's also the testimony of thousands of men and women in the world who, despite their great intelligence, continue to seek to withdraw, to speak to the "Beyond", to a being who is there. But they see things in a different way. They do not expect a God who is similar to men. They know that He is not caught and limited by matter, space or time. He is the cause of all those things, and without Him they would not exist.

Cardinal Robert Sarah, in his book "The Power of Silence", states:

"I am convinced that the problem of contemporary atheism lies first of all in a wrong interpretation of God's silence about catastrophes and human sufferings. If man sees in the divine silence only a form of God's abandonment, indifference, or powerlessness, it will be difficult to enter into his ineffable and inaccessible mystery."

It was once said: "For those people who have faith, no explanation is necessary; for those who do not have faith, no explanation is possible." Faith will ever be something that man has to accept. God does not fail to comply with the freedom of humanity. He wants to be accepted, as a lover will not love his beloved if she does not reciprocate. This goes both ways.

C.S. Lewis, an author known for his arguments in favor of the existence of God, said:

"Atheism turns out to be too simple. If the whole universe has no meaning, we should never have discovered that it has no meaning: just as, if there were no light in the universe and, therefore, no creatures with eyes, we should never know that it was dark. Dark would be a meaningless word."

You don't need to believe in God overnight. God is not in a hurry. He has plans, but always gentle ones. I encourage you to live one week

with this attitude: believe in God for one week only. Give him the opportunity. Tell him to make himself present. Open his door. This is what He is waiting for, and even if you do not perceive it, your heart is too. There are more logical reasons to believe in God. As we have said, it takes more faith to think that from nothingness, from higher non-intelligence, from chaos and pure matter, we could come to a world with such a design as the one we find ourselves in.

But then comes the most beautiful part, and that for which our heart is made. Above all, it is not a matter of many reasons—although these cannot be absent—but of a Presence that can be felt. Pascal said, "The heart has reasons that reason does not understand. It is at this level, on this plane, that the yearning of every human being is placed." Never so much as now can we quote St. Augustine, who said: "You created us for yourself and our heart will always be restless as long as it does not rest in you.[13]"

Questions to think about:

1. Why do you have trouble believing in God?

2. Why doesn't the fact that there is evil in the world not proof that God doesn't exist?

3. Why don't science and faith oppose each other?

Chapter 5:
Who am I?

"We are not the sum of our weaknesses and failures; we are the sum of the Father's love for us and our true capacity to become the image of his Son..[14]"

John Paul II, Toronto 2002.

It was Thursday morning and Luis received an early text. He was surprised that someone was awake at that hour. He had gotten up at 5:30 in the morning to go for a run and then shower before going to class. The text was from Alejandro and said, "So, will I see you today?" Luis was clueless. He had totally forgotten that they had agreed to meet today. He picked up his cell phone and said, "I have (class) from 8-9 and 9-10. How about 10 at the same place." Alejandro answered, "yes."

As he did every day, Luis drove his car about 4 miles to the university. He arrived, had his first two classes and went out to look for Alejandro. The day was beautiful. Spring had already come, with bright sunshine and none of the cold of winter. Both guys arrived with their drink, their snack and with the same level of interest.

"How's it going?" asked Alejandro, as he pulled out his sandwich.

"All good," Luis said. "Some stuff with my girlfriend who is too jealous. But nothing to worry about for now. And you?"

"All good. My girlfriend is pretty happy. The company she applied for called her back and it seems she only needs one last interview and they will accept her."

They both ate their sandwiches and Alejandro asked: "So, last time we talked about the existence of God. What were piqued your interest?"

Alejandro knew well that Luis was interested in talking about humanity, its identity, and its value. He had taken some time to do a review of his philosophy course so as to be ready for the conversation.

"Like I was telling you," said Luis, "we have talked enough about God. The truth is that I found the topic interesting, and I will think about it little by little. There's a lot to chew on there. But whether God exists or not, that has less consequences for me than knowing about myself, and about mankind in general. I feel at times that I am an enigma to myself."

Alejandro looked at Luis, and said: "Well, there's no way the existence or not of God does not have an effect on us. Whether God exists or not is of huge importance. Maybe we can talk about that in the future. For now, let's talk about humanity. Where do you want to start? What is it that worries you the most?"

Luis paused in thought for a moment. He was pondering where it would be best to start. Soon his eyes lit up and he said:

"I don't like how humanity seems so superior to animals."

"In other words, let me explain: I love animals. I know that mankind is more intelligent, but why do people sometimes care a lot about humanity and don´t care about animals? I hate to see them treated badly."

"I like animals a lot too," said Alejandro. "But I would certainly never compare an animal to a man or a woman."

Luis continued, "In my opinion, I sometimes feel much more sympathy for animals than for some people who are more animal than they are. People are abusive and unfair. Animals do not take advantage of each other. They only follow feeding instincts, but I don't understand how among men there is fighting, war and death. Animals have never had a single war."

"Look," said Alejandro, "like I was saying, there is no reason for someone to treat an animal badly. That is certain. But in nature there are levels of dignity that were put there by God. Plants were made to feed animals, and animals to serve and feed humans, and humans are are similar to God. In fact, in many constitutions of nations it is written that "all men are created equally," or something similar. Animals accompany the life and existence of people, but they do not have an immortal soul that lives on after death."

"The other day I talked to you about the first chapter of the Bible where it is clear that God gives people the mission to conquer the whole world around them. That means that God creates it for us. It is with other humans that we find happiness. It is with men and women that civilizations are created. It is above all to them that legislation is addressed."

Alejandro realized that he would have to go slowly here. His friend was open, but didn't understand what was already well known and researched by Alejandro: The dignity of the mankind.

The Dignity of mankind: the image and likeness of God

"Look, Luis," said Alejandro. "Your thinking isn't wrong. It just seems to me to be incomplete. The dignity of man is infinite. It is something we cannot measure. For example, you and I are worth more than all that money can buy. Even a Philosopher like Kant, who in many ways was wrong in his way of thinking, said that man could never be used as a means."

Alejandro took out his cell phone where he had written some basic notes and said, "The phrase Kant used was this: 'Work is a way that you use humanity, both in your own person and in the person of anyone else, always as an end at the same time and never just as a means.' He is saying that man can never be used. However, animals can be used and we're not destroying any right of theirs. We use horses to transport us, or dogs to watch over us, and we should never allow unnecessary suffering for them, but they are there, to be of use to people."

In 1948 the UN wrote the letter of human rights that spoke of humanity in very different terms than any other creature. In fact, it is men who come together to think about how to live better. Animals don't do that."

"That's because not enough time has passed," Luis replied. "But there are studies that show that the capacity of animals is very big, immeasurable."

"Try to understand me," Alejandro said. "I'm not saying they don't have intelligence, but let's not be naive. Millions of years have passed and mankind is mankind, and animals are animals. There is no comparison. Man is the homo sapiens who has progressed and evolved to create civilizations, rights, family and society. Humanity has also committed serious historical errors, such as the failed example of Communism, but his dignity is immense. Humanity is made in the image and likeness of God."

Luis stopped him, saying, "Let's see, where does that phrase that I like, the one so often repeated, 'in the image and likeness,' where do you get it from? Who said that?"

"Luis, look," said Alejandro. "There is an important and monumental document that was created by many very skilled people during the Second Vatican Council, which was called Gaudium et Spes. It means 'joy and hope.' In this document the following is written:

"God, who cares for all with fatherly concern, has willed that men should constitute one family and treat each other in a spirit of brotherhood. All are created in the image and likeness of God, who made of one man the whole human race and made it possible for all the earth to be inhabited (Acts 17:26 RSVCE), and all are called to one and the same end, namely, God himself. [16]"

Luis objected: "Yes, but that is a Church document. What civil institution has spoken of this?"

Alejandro replied, "Yes, the Church talks about this because it is interested in it, but not only the Church talks about it." Pulling out his philosophy manual, he said:

"Look at this quote from the Charter of the Universal Rights of Man."

'Considering that freedom, justice and peace in the world are based on the recognition of the inherent dignity and of the equal and inalienable rights of all members of the human family.

'All human beings are born free and equal in dignity and rights and, endowed with reason and conscience, should act towards one another in a spirit of brotherhood.[17].'

"Luis, In the Bible, in the book of Genesis, which talks about how God made man and what his reaction was, it is written: "Then God said, "Let us make man in our image, after our likeness; and let them have dominion over the fish of the sea, and over the birds of the air, and over the cattle, and over all the earth, and over every creeping thing that creeps upon the earth." (Gen 1:26 RSVCE).

"The European Charter of Universal Rights also mentions the issue of human dignity and the freedoms and rights that flow from it. Do you understand me, Luis? It's not just a religious issue."

Luis took a sip from his cup and nibbled at his apple pie. He listened attentively, but he still wasn't connecting the pieces and he still had many questions.

"Well, how does the issue of being in the image and likeness of God affects me?"

"Okay," Alejandro replied. "Here I'm going to get into the religious area, because I can't help it. When I say religious, I don't mean without reason. As we said, faith and reason should not compete against each other. They are complementary."

"The first thing this implies is that your value is not given by people or governments. It is not given to you by the state. You already have it before there are rulers. So, as Kant said, a human being or a government can never use a person for any purpose. The person is an end in himself. The person has infinite dignity. Jesus said, "What does it profit a man if he gains the whole world and loses his own soul?""

Man's value: unconditional love

The second thing, Luis, is that your value and that of every human being does not depend on other people. What each of us is worth does not depend on achieving things, on big triumphs, on academic or moral excellence. You are infinitely valuable to God. That is, you are really loved by God, no matter what you do. Moreover, there is nothing you do that causes God to love you less than he does."

Luis felt a thorn in his side as Alejandro talked of being loved by God. No one had ever told him this. In his home he used to be undervalued by his family. He had to strive for the approval of his siblings and parents, but most of all of his father. The issue of what he was worth, even if he did nothing, was burning inside him, but he kept his attention on his friend.

Loss of personal identity

"Listen: today there are many people suffering a lot because they don't know who they are. They don't know that they are loved by God. They don't know that they are worth their weight in gold and much more. We are in a time when we have put what we are worth in the hands of others, in the hands of likes on Facebook, Instagram or Snapchat. We let others tell us how good or bad we should feel. We also put our own worth in the hands of people who have their own challenges, difficulties and insecurities.

"Today, so many people are so weak because they don't know their worth anymore! Why do you think there is so much suicide, depression and stress in our time? Why do you think good psychologists are so necessary now? Why do you think spirituality, meditation and yoga are so fashionable? Because man is crying out that he is spirit, that he needs spirituality and transcendence. He;s tired of everything material."

The two fell silent. Luis was pensive. For the first time they were talking about more humanistic, more intimate and heart-touching issues. He felt that unlike the previous topics, such as reason, this time his whole body was moved. Alejandro looked at him trying to figure out what was going on in his mind. Finally, he asked him:

"What do you think?"

"Nothing," Luis replied. "I'm just Thinking." Then Luis asked:

"So, what makes one live in peace, what makes one feel good?

"This is where my faith comes in to answer," Alejandro replied. "And this is because faith, unlike science, answers the important questions. It responds to "who?", and "for what?" The faith of the Christians is one and very clear. We were created for happiness. We were created to be God's adopted children. This is expressed by St. Paul in the letter to the Galatians. Here let me show you," Alejandro said, taking out his cell phone.

'But when the time had fully come, God sent forth his Son, born of woman, born under the law, to redeem those who were under the law, so that we might receive adoption as sons. And because you are sons, God has sent the Spirit of his Son into our hearts, crying, "Abba! Father!"' (Galatians 4:4-6 RSVCE).

Created for family and happiness

"We were created to be part of God's family. That is why we can say 'Our Father' and not 'My Father.' That's why a person of faith should be able to not depend so much on what men say, but finds his worth through Someone who loves him unconditionally. This is just like a father loves his child, even if the child has all kinds of problems."

89

The Creator disposed that each human being would be born in a family. It is there that each one should find their identity and security.

Luis, excited now, interrupted. "Alejandro, what you are saying sounds good but very unreal. I believe that in the world people love you if you have money and if you are successful. You don't find real love in Hollywood movies. I don't know if there is a single home in the world where there is this love that you talk about. It seems like a fairy tale."

"When we are not loved unconditionally," Alejandro continued, "man and the woman are incomplete, broken, fractured. A Catholic psychologist in the United States said something beautiful:

'If he does not receive this identity [as a beloved son] and come to know and contemplate it, mankind will make decisions that reflect a search for the Father's love, rather than making decisions in the light of that love'[18]

Luis was curious about the first effect Alejandro talked about, and said:—"Let's see, tell me more about the first effect of being created in the image and likeness of God. You said something about governments and dignity. What about it?"

"Yes, I told you that for centuries it was clear to mankind that any manmade law would have to be subject to the laws of God. In other words, the basis for legislation in any society was natural law, that which pre-dates the society. But with certain philosophers and scientists from the fifteenth century on, a decline in human knowledge started. So, for many people what matters is what the masses of people say, what the ruler of the moment thinks. This brings us back to the European totalitarianisms of that time, where the king thought he was almost God. So, instead of natural law, we now have a vision of positive law. That means, the one set by the government of the moment. This is Democracy."

"Not only that. We also see how in many countries, especially in the United States, they have an obsession with surveys. But I assure you that if at the beginning of 1945 they had done a survey on whether dropping the atomic bomb was a good idea or not, 95 percent would have said, "Yes, it's a good way to end the war". Today nobody would say that."

Luis interrupted, "Then, do you disagree with the Democracy?"

"I agree with it," said Alejandro. "But it is not perfect; it is the least risky of the power systems. But Democracy can also have negative consequences, like abuses, as we unfortunately see happening today, and it happened extensively in the twentieth century, with two world wars and other wars. What most people say is not necessarily correct in the face of objective truth."

Luis, already beginning to accept his friends way of thinking, asked a question

Who is man?

"Then, how do you sum up who man is and how he lives well?"

"Mankind, you and I, we are a special creature in the eyes of God, made in his image and likeness. Also, man is not only body or only soul. We are the indivisible union of body and soul. We are incarnate beings, with bodies, but also, we are spiritual, immortal beings."

"Let's see, let's see," said Luis, "What did you say? Immortals? Incorrect! We all die."

"Yes, sorry. I didn't clarify," said Alejandro. "Our body will die here in this life, but not our soul. It will either die or go to eternal life or to eternal damnation. I'm clarify this about what we are because recently there are some people who say, in regard to love: "I fall in love with souls, not with bodies". They say it because they are attracted to a person of the same sex or because they do not know that soul and body are indivisible in this life. I am not getting into that now. But you have to admit that we are body and soul. And the body is not a cage for the soul. The body that we have is not ours, we don't just have it. I am my body. And in my body is all my soul. The area of philosophy that studies this—and is part of what we have seen in my course at home—is Anthropology."

Luis thought a little and said: "How is man to live well, as I see that there are thousands of ways in which many lead their lives? There are some who get married, others who don't, others who wait until too late to see if they are born to live together. Some travel and have fun, others live only to work."

Alejandro continued: "Look, later we can talk about more adequate and healthy missions in people's lives. But if we want to talk now about what is the place and the environment where every human being will become as healthy as possible, there is no other place than the family with a mom and dad. For every child, having a mother and father who nurtures them according to their personality and sex, that is healthy. This has been studied and proven in schools and sociological studies. The healthiest and most active citizens are those who have had a correct attachment to their parents. When we hear the word 'attachment,' perhaps it can be misinterpreted. I am referring to John Bowlby's attachment theory that points out that how close our parents were in life plays a decisive role in the social and emotional development of each person. If there is love and understanding at home, you will have people who are good for society."

Luis objected: "Aren't you generalizing too much? I know bad people from good families and good people whose parents were a disaster."

"Yes, obviously I'm generalizing. But generalizations are not purely invented: They are real and reflect a good part of life. We speak in generalities because it is a common trend, not because it encompasses a hundred percent of the cases. We know that for every principle there are exceptions. But experience and studies show that there are families that are good and there are families that go bad. A criminal offender has often suffered so much that one could understand why he or she committed crimes."

Do you know something my dad always tells me? Obviously, it's not exact, but he usually says: 'Do you want to find a good wife? Find yourself a good mother-in-law.' That goes for a girl too.

'Do you want a good husband? Find a good father-in-law" You need to understand the wisdom of the phrase, not take it completely literally."

Luis was enjoying this part a lot, but it was getting late. He kept thinking about the fact that there are families who are good and others who get sick. Again, he felt a thorn inside him. Those feelings that he was having prevented him from paying full attention to the rest of the conversation. In his home, these topics were not discussed that often. He told Alejandro:

"It sounds logical to me that when there is a stable, ideal home, there are more possibilities to be good and healthy people. But we should not blame the parents or the home. I'd love to talk about what I can expect as a human being. In other words, what can we do for ourselves, regardless of the home we're in?"

"How about we talk about it tomorrow. Our time is up."

Yes," Luis replied, "this sounds good to me."

Both young men said goodbye, took their things and left in opposite directions. Luis felt that his time in college was being very productive because of his degree and because he had a close friend who could clarify these issues in a caring, logical and quite intelligent way. At the same time, he felt very ignorant about humanistic issues more focused on the person, and not his specialty of the activities of the business world.

But this time, after talking about family issues, he left the place very thoughtful. How was my family? Do we children have a good relationship, according to the attachment theory, with mom and dad?

What can I do to become a good guy? He paused for a moment, took out his cell phone, and opened a note so that he could then talk to Alejandro about these issues. He got into his car, got inside and drove home.

ANALYZING THE CONVERSATION

Every human being needs to know who he is, where he comes from and what he can achieve on his own. I remember reading a great book when I was only 15 years old. It made a big impression on me. It's called "How to Educate Children with Positive Attitudes in a Negative World."

What did this book teach me in a nutshell? It taught me that what our parents gave us is extremely important, but that I must transform my life with my effort, and with the help of the grace that comes to me from God.

A very illuminating definition of maturity is: Maturity is the opportunity that life gives you to give yourself what your parents could not give you. That's right. What happens in the home is important, but it is not determining or definitive. Mankind is open to the infinite, to an endless number of possibilities to grow within himself. Recently, neuroscience gave us incredible news: the brain can be modified. But that will be addressed later.

A person's identity is the important aspect on which all his life rests. Your subsequent transformation will necessarily have to look at your identity, see how healthy it is, and build on it. If you have had a good childhood, surrounded by the security that the presence of a parent can give you, life will be simpler. In addition, if in your daily journey you have managed not to be wounded substantially, there will be a big personal, emotional and social stability. That is to say: you will feel very good about yourself; you will feel the ability to face life with solidity and freedom and your relationships will be a source of abundance and wealth.

If, on the other hand, you were not so lucky in terms of your home and your childhood and adolescence, there is news full of hope and light: God and this life give you a chance. Healing is possible. There is confidence in a true and good future. But there is more work to be done. Using a metaphor, if a dog was raised by owners who gave it everything it needed from when it was a puppy, it will people mistreated him, the road might still be luminous, but it will require putting in a lot of effort.

One thing can't be forgotten. The reason why every human being, be they Christian or not, exists on earth is because of an act of infinite love on God's part. Every being was a thought full of God's love, and we do not exist except by that love. God did not create us because he was bored or searching for himself. God can be defined as 'the one who has everything,' and therefore we do not give him anything. He gives everything to us.

Therefore, we are those who exist to have a relationship with Him—a very intimate relationship. This is what Jesus, the Son of God, says: "I came that they may have life, and have it abundantly." (Jn 10:10 RSVCE). We are called to be his adopted children, as we read in the conversation between Luis and Alejandro.

What you believe
about yourself
in your heart
becomes your
identity, which in
turn shapes your
whole life.

Identity is so important in life that it determines your general level of satisfaction. Bob Schuchts said it in this way:

"What you believe about yourself in your heart becomes your identity, and it creates everything in your life.[19]"

John Paul II said at World Youth Day 2002: "We are not the sum of our weaknesses and failures; we are the sum of the Father's love for us and our true capacity to become the image of his Son [20]"

We want to have a clear identity. The trunk and branches need that root, the root of a healthy and safe identity that makes our life inspiring and beautiful. When a person suffers a lot because of being insecure about himself, because he or she feels that everything affects him or her, because he or she constantly feels that the world is unfair to him or her, we have to go to the roots and see what or who is saying, "You are good, you are beautiful, your life is a blessing to the world." Depending on who I give that power to is the key between happiness and unhappiness. That is why we have been created. And this happiness will be discussed in detail later.

Questions to think about:

1. How do you feel about your identity today? Where did you come from? What kind of childhood did you have: healthy or problematic? What's your level of personal confidence?

2. In real life, what does it mean that you are made in the image and likeness of God? How does that change your life every day?

3. Talk with someone about the fact that each of us is body and soul, without separation. What mistakes in daily life do you think are made because we don't have clear who we truly are as men and women? You may reflect like this: if I am only a body, then _____ but if I am only a soul, then _____.

PART II: INTEGRATION

What can I aspire to in life?

Chapter 6:
Get to Know Yourself

"The heart of man is like deep water.""

Prov. 20:5 RSVCE

It was Friday. Yesterday's conversation had moved things to new heights. Alejandro and Luis were getting into issues about the person. Luis was worried. He felt that his humanistic side was disorganized, but he couldn't give a name to the conflict. His desire to know himself better and to know how he could make himself a respected, successful person took away his peace.

They both arrived at the normal bench, again each with his own snack. This time Luis came in shorts and sweats, since he didn't have time to take a shower after going to the gym.

"How are you, my good Alejandro?" asked Luis, shaking his hand.

Alejandro gave a half hug. Their friendship was growing.

Then he said: "You smell horrible!"

"My sweat doesn't smell like roses, I can tell you that much," Luis replied, chuckling.

They both sat down and Luis began to be somewhat vulnerable and open:

"You know, Alejandro, the truth is that I was very intrigued by the last thing we talked about. The identity that comes from the family, the families that get sick and the families that help their members—all of that worries me because I feel like I don't know much about these things. No one talks to me about them."

"Yes? Let's see, what do you want to talk about most?

What do you feel?"

Luis answered: "I've been thinking about this for months: How do you build yourself? How can I become a better person?"

From the phenomenon to the foundation

Alejandro felt it was the perfect opportunity to talk to his friend about what had been the most memorable lesson of his philosophy classes.

"Luis," he said, "why do you have so many questions? Rather, why do you think you have all that healthy restlessness?

"Because I am curious," Luis replied, "or because I want certainties that go beyond my own opinion. But why do you ask me that?"

"Because I also want to know where your curiosity comes from. You want to know the answer to everything."

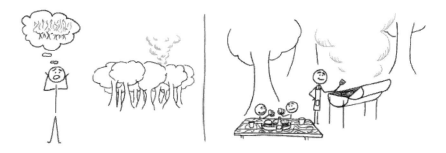

We must move from the phenomenon (what appears to be) to the foundation of things (what is really happening). In the drawing, a young man sees smoke and thinks: "forest fire", while the reality is that a family is grilling burgers.

"Would you rather I have doubts or what?" Luis asked him.

"No," said Alejandro, "in fact, it's perfect. I have to keep answering all these things, which forces me to find answers myself. Do you think I know everything? Not at all. In fact, I have had to look for the answers to many of the questions you have asked me. It helps me if you ask. But do you realize there's something behind your questions?"

"I don't understand," answered Luis. "You got all philosophical."

"Let's see, what is it that worries you the most?" asked Alejandro.

"Among other things, how do I live well?" said Luis. Another question I always have is, how or where is happiness found?"

Alejandro started carefully: "If you notice, men and women in our time often ask about the 'how'. How is this, how is that? We have become more scientific, but less wise. We know a lot of little, and little of the most important. There are much more important, more basic questions. And those are 'why' questions. For example: Why do you want to have sex with your girlfriend?"

"Because it feels good, because I want it," Luis replied. "Why?" Alejandro asked.

Luis said: "Well, because I like her."

"And, why do you like her?"

"Because I like her, I don't know! What kind of questions are these?"

Alejandro calmly said, "Be patient. Look closely. The question 'why' is much more important than 'how.' The men and women deepest in life are the ones who respond to why.

In fact, I don't know if you've seen Simon Sinek's21 video in which he says that the most successful companies in the market are those that start with the 'why.' If they have meaning, they'll find the how."

103

We must move
from the
phenomenon to
the foundation
of things.

Luis said: "Oh, yes, the guy who puts a circle on a board and talks about how Apple is the perfect example of this."

"Right," said Alejandro. -Look, there is a very profound writing by John Paul II and Joseph Ratzinger from 1993. It's called "Faith and Reason", and says: 'We must move from the phenomenon to the foundation.' It is another way of saying: Don't stay in what things seem; go to the causes, to the why."

"If you notice, science doesn't just look at phenomena, it researches until it reach deeper explanations. For example, when humans saw an apple fall from a tree to the ground, they gradually felt the need to reach not only what is seen, but also what is behind it. They came up with the law of universal gravitation. In the medical area, if some people were aging faster, they investigated if it was linked to geographical regions, or food, or habits, and today longevity in the world is much greater. We have to go to the causes."

"Well, what I want to do with my life, and I am trying to explain this to you, is to go from the phenomenon to the foundation. We must not stay with what seems, but with what is underneath what I see.

In the human and philosophical area, it is the same. Why am I a being who needs to answer questions? Why do I want to have kids? Why do I want to have sex with my girlfriend?

Why do I feel sad? And we shouldn't just stay with the apparent, with what everyone says, but we should stop being hollow and become more reflective people. I'm sure that when you say you want to live better, to live happier, part of that is discovering the answers to the meaning of everything. Of everything!"

Luis was satisfied they were getting to the bottom of things. He said: 'Perfect. So, let's start with what I told you yesterday.

How can I expect to become a better person? Why should I become a better person?

Knowing oneself, accepting oneself, and improving oneself

Alejandro clearly saw that the subject matter was just what he wanted to get at. He knew the difficulties Luis was going through in his life. His questions about truth, about God, and about man's mental capacity were symptoms of something deeper. So, with the big heart for which he was known, he began with respect and determination:

"Luis, in life we all have a spiritual mountain to climb. All of us. To seek one's own perfection is the task of life. One day I heard this phrase: "Not to demand from the beloved that he be the best (that he can be), is indifference, which is the opposite of love". Therefore, a way that I have learned in my house and through the formation I have received is that one must learn to do three things: to know oneself, to accept oneself and to overcome oneself."

Luis immediately asked: "But accepting oneself and improving oneself, don't they contradict each other? If I accept myself, how can I ask to outdo myself? Either I accept myself or I improve myself, but you can't do both."

"Yes, you can," Alejandro replied. "Look, acceptance means knowing what I can and can't count on; what matter and which qualities I have. It includes not wanting to be like others. That can become spiritual greed. In short: with what I am, what can I do? With the things I have, what type of house can I build?"

"To improve oneself is to work on oneself, to work on one's defects and to perfect one's qualities. This is just like a sportsman when he says: this is what I bring to the table. How do I improve on what was originally given to me? I propose to see the three parts separately, because this is a giant issue.

Luis just looked at him and nodded, as if waiting to get into it deeper.

Know yourself

"There are three ways to know yourself. I analyze my world or the people of my time. Then, I analyze my family or circumstances and I also analyze myself."

Family

Own decisions

Generation

Each human being acquires knowledge about himself
primarily through his family, his generations and the
decisions that he takes in life.

"Let's analyze the first thing, which is our generation. I am going to explain to you what I humbly observe is an x-ray of what we are, and of how we are. Well, you know that the time we were born and the decisions we make shape human beings differently in different times."

Characteristics of today's young people: the four big holes

"The first thing I see is that we have a very weak **personal identity**. That's what we were talking about yesterday. We don't really know who we are, where we come from, and where we're going. What meaning is there to life? And with a generation of parents who went from one pole to another in authority, and now overprotect their children, there is not so much personal safety. There is an important insecurity in making decisions and commitments. That insecurity leads us to always be aware of what others are saying about us. Even from feeling so much pressure that we do everything to fit in with what we am told, even if we don't like it. Correct me if I'm wrong, but some of our ways of dressing or plans we make in a week come more from imposed fashion than from our own decisions."

"As a generation, Luis, in many areas we have a great **fragility**. I don't know how our grandparents did it, but I don't think we can tolerate a third world war. I don't want it, but you understand me. We are weak. We sink more easily. This is partly because all the advances we were born with, the technology—it has actually made us insecure."

Luis interrupted: "But there you are generalizing again. There are many exceptions."

Alejandro replied: "Yes, remember that for every generalization there are exceptions. Don't sweat it. We agree, but it is not just my opinion. It is already common to identify certain traits for us as a generation. There are many findings in this respect, about the workplace, schools and society. There are studies on this."

"All of the above leads to a second hole in us: the **fear of failure**. Our fragility and at the same time our desire for success makes us live between two poles: success and failure. We want success, but we are afraid of failure. Then, we do not dare to do many things. We don't like big commitments. We are afraid of marriage. In dating, we go through all kinds of stages that never existed before.

From friends we move on to 'being right' with someone, or special or entitled friends, but there is still no commitment. We are more volatile in the workplace than all previous generations of the modern era. Today, staff turnover is higher than ever before. There is a paralysis in many areas for fear of failure. Perhaps the entrepreneurial spirit is as alive as ever, but commitment is not made. That is why Pope Francis has described this generation as the generation of the provisional."[22]

"A third characteristic I see is a **great fluidity** in the way we see the world."

Luis stared at him with a strange look on his face. Alejandro, upon realizing that he was asking for an explanation, said:

"By fluidity I mean little rigidity, little severity in the way of conceiving reality. As we were just saying: we know little about the foundation of things. Do you remember that the other day we talked about how in the world there is a type of clay, there is a code in nature? There is a DNA that is in it, one that man must respect and that we must learn and can learn from what previous civilizations learned. Now it seems that there is nothing solid, that what was true yesterday is not true today. And what today is, tomorrow could change. We question everything. Moreover, precisely because of this, we distrust authority, because they tell me this today, but tomorrow it may no longer be true. Do you see how this is due to the relativism of which we speak? Do you see how this depends very much on the fact that legislators and governments have nothing to hold on to in nature, but that each ruler governs according to what he thinks? Everything is connected."

"This obviously explains why we are so **self-sufficient** in a bad way, and this means that we do not see that it is good to learn from those who are older than us. Not only that, but in the ethical and moral area, we are extremely **self-indulgent**. Since there is nothing fixed, and since there is no objective morality, it seems that we say, 'I did nothing. It is a weakness that is in me, but it is not me.' In fact, many simply think that evil is determined by each person."

Luis bit into his sandwich while listening attentively. He wondered again how Alejandro knew so much about these non-engineering topics. His eager eyes showed that he wanted Alejandro to continue.

"And a fourth clear characteristic is a confusion between **happiness and freedom**. Many people think that freedom is absolute. If you don't hurt others you can do whatever you want. Freedom has no rules or principles to follow. I will simply be happy if I am free. If you want, we can go into this subject further later. I am interested in finishing the topic of the holes in the people of our time."

Luis had already listened for quite a while. He felt he had to intervene, since he could not understand everything at once. He interrupted:

"Okay. So, do you think those gaps are what describes our generation?"

"There are other ways to classify it, but in short, I think so. I would say: weak identity, fear of failure, fluidity and confusion between happiness and freedom. That's where the external factors come from that let us know who we are today."

"What other factors are important for knowing oneself?" Luis asked.

"Well, the things that come from outside. It's the world around us, and it doesn't mean that we all suffer from it, or in the same way, or to the same degree. We are not conditioned. But we are strongly influenced by our time. That's why what the Spanish philosopher Ortega y Gasset said is true: 'I am me and my circumstances.'"

"But we must also take into account what we were talking about yesterday and what I just mentioned."

"What you said about the family, right?" Luis asked.

"Exactly," Alejandro replied. "Understanding what role the family has and how the environment has been, will always be decisive. You see, it is said that 'the apple never falls far away from its tree.' This means that the influence of our family is always there. Sons tend to look like their fathers, and daughters like their mothers. Every time in marriages a husband says to his wife: 'You are just like your mother,' and vice versa, she says to him: 'You are just like your father.'

The Family

"The other day you mentioned something about family, and the author is an American who talks about attachment, right?" Luis asked.

"Yes," Alejandro said. "Yesterday I was telling you that we have our family inside us. Look, our past is not just something that is in the past. We carry it within us. John Eldredge, in one of his books, says this:

'Each child, on his journey to become a man, takes an arrow in the center of his heart, instead of his strength. This happens because the wound is rarely discussed and even more rarely healed, every man has a wound. And the wound is almost always given by his father.' 23

"Let's see," said Luis, "how can that be? I don't understand. In most cases, A father doesn't hurt his son."

Alejandro replied, "Yes, this is true. It's not something the dad does with bad intentions. But experience says that there are elements in the son that have to be healed in order for him to be whole. They are the wounds of life that come from those who love you most. And you know, girls suffer from something similar. John Eldredge explains it like this:

"The wound hits right in the heart of your heart of beauty and has a sad message: No. You are not beautiful and no one will really fight for you. Like your wound, hers almost always comes from her father's hand. 24"

"Luis, with this, the author is not saying that every man and woman, without exception, has a wound from their father. Generally speaking, he is saying that there is a big neediness in men and women, and in many cases one has to heal from the shortcomings of one's parents. It's part of life. It happens to everyone. It's more or less intense for each person. But it is something real that the insecurities, imperfections and real mistakes of our parents, who have no one to teach them how to be parents, affect us negatively, and this shows itself many years later."

"Also, remember that in a world with so many break-ups, divorces and new relationships, society can't help but be quite wounded."

"The family is the by far the greatest source of what we become. We must consider this to answer your question of how to become a better person."

There was a silence between the two men. Alejandro took the opportunity to sip his drink and take a break. They both left a moment of somewhat prolonged silence. Alejandro wanted Luis to lead the discussion. And he did.

"Circumstances, family... these I understand," Luis said. "If I understand the times in which I was born and how people are today, and I understand my family; is that enough to get to know myself?"

"Yes," said Luis, "but one more element is missing. Three elements matter: circumstances, family and the decisions you have made, and your experiences. At the same time, what you have done also has an effect, positive or negative."

Your decisions and experiences

"How does that work?" Luis asked.

"Well, we've all done things," Alejandro replied. "Those things leave a mark on the soul. If a person steals once, and then again, and again, what do we call him?"

"A thief," said Luis in a low voice.

"And if someone gets drunk once, and then five times, he's a drunk. Our actions make us and shape us. There is a big connection between the body and soul. The things we do with the body have an effect on the soul and vice versa. The decisions we make affect us and can be for better or worse."

Getting to know me in the other

Alejandro continued: "Yes, and there are many ways to know yourself better. One of the best ways is through others. It's clear that, psychologically speaking, we know ourselves in the other. An author writes it in this way:"

'First, the mind we see in our development is the inner state of our caregiver. The baby makes a noise and he or she smiles, the baby laughs and his or her face lights up. We know ourselves first in the measure that we reflect ourselves in the other.'[25]

Examination of conscience

"Another way we get to know ourselves is by examining our conscience. Each day, many people spend time reviewing how their day has been, what moved them to act, what things went wrong, where they got it right, and what feelings and inner drives were guiding their whole day."

Luis, feeling curious, interrupted: "Do you examine your conscience?"

"Yes," Alejandro replied, trying not to intimidate his friend. "I often spend time in silence doing just that at the end of the day. It helps me a lot to discover things."

Alejandro paused to see if there was any reaction from Luis, who was engrossed with the snack he was eating.

"There are all kinds of psychological, skill, strength, character and teamwork tests that you can take," said Alejandro. Companies use the Myers Briggs and DISC tests a lot so that you can see things in you that some people already know and others that are blind spots for you."

Luis said: "Yes, I've done some of those tests—you mean those long ones they made us take before we went to the university that seem to ask you the same thing in different ways?"

"Those are more psychological, but yes." Alejandro replied. They are tools to help you get to know yourself you better. In some organizations there are some very good ones that are called 360, because you are evaluated by people who depend on you, by your colleagues, by your bosses and by other people. This way, you can see how you are with the different types of people around you."

Luis had enjoyed this conversation. He started to think about whether it would be good for him to start knowing himself better, too. Although he knew he knew himself, he also sensed that many times he didn't understand many elements of his own thinking and acting.

"We have to go, right?" he asked, looking at his watch.

"Yes, it is time to go," Alejandro replied, smiling as he thought about all their conversation had touched upon that day.

"Do you think that on Monday or Tuesday we will talk about my question?" Luis asked. "I mean how accepting and improving oneself are not contradictory?"

"Of course," Alejandro replied. "On Monday let's meet and figure out our schedules, because I have a team assignment for the industrial processes course. What do you think?"

"Ok," said Luis.

Both said goodbye and headed to their cars.

ANALYZING THE CONVERSATION

We all have the question: what do I have to do to succeed in life? The words we use may be different, but that question is in everyone's mind. In the gospel it says that a rich young man came to the Jesus and asked, 'Master, what must I do to have eternal life?' This is the most important question for every person. Each person knows that his own effort is necessary to make life worth living. He looks at his neighbors, at those passing by, at the one who succeeds and at the one who fails, and he feels a desire for transcendence. He makes his own conclusions and wants to choose the best for himself. But do the best and the worst exist?

How do I transform myself? How do I take advantage of every minute of my life? We find in our current world much wisdom in a very fragmented way. The variety of sciences and specialties has made knowledge about the spirit and human wisdom scarce. Technology and science rule over the professional and commercial world.

We see in this part of the book that the key to all work on oneself is integration—integrating the various parts of the human being and the different factors that influence him. A helpful example could be the muscles of an Olympic athlete. What do they look like? They're not dispersed or flabby. They are all concentrated towards one center, the center of the bone. They have a healthy tension and are strong and aligned. This very limited image helps us to think about how one person works on the beautiful sculpture that has been given to him, which is his own personality. The various parts that constitute us must all work in the same direction. This requires many things:

1. Knowing yourself (who am I?)

2. Having a mentor (who guides and advises me?)

3. Having a good direction in life (what is my goal?)

4. Motivation (why do I want what I want?)

In this chapter we have made two concepts clear. The first is that the superficiality of the world, due in large part to sloth and the advent of technology in our lives, has made us stay in appearances, in what is seen on the outside, which we have called the phenomenon. To have depth in our way of perceiving and living life, we must go to the foundation.

There is a second concept needed to accomplish this beautiful task of becoming someone who lives his life with purpose and transcendence. It is the threefold task of knowing, accepting and improving oneself. We have started with the first of the three parts.

Men and women aren't not born for loneliness. They are born for community. Since childhood we are weak. We get to know ourselves at first through our mothers, and then also through our ourselves through the reactions that others have to us. That is why, without being totally conditioning, the family we come from determines a lot of what we will be.

It is also important to know the characteristics of our time and of the people around me who have developed a clear opinion of the world according to the time in which they lived. The classification of generations is something that helps sociology to understand how to better know the necessities of each generation.

Finally, we know each other by analyzing our own decisions and experiences. We get to know ourselves through the other and through frequent examination of conscience.

Although there are several other means to get to know oneself, such as tests, spiritual direction or coaching, going to a good psychologist, and going to the sacrament of confession, we have tried to summarize it here in those two points mentioned above. Let's be clear, however: self-knowledge is a lifelong task. No one is exempt from continual self-revision, for no one is exempt from losing their way at times. This is what Jesus meant when he said, "Watch and pray, lest you fall into temptation."

Questions for thinking about

1. Today, in general, the world does not go from the phenomenon to the foundation. In what aspects of your life do you feel that you stay in the phenomenon and do not get to the foundation?

2. Can you see how the four holes of today's generation are connected? Think of specific examples of people around you who have each aspect.

3. Do you know yourself well? In your case, do you think you could identify essential elements that have built you up in all three areas: family, circumstances and your decisions?

Chapter 7:
The Inner Ocean

"I know of no more encouraging fact than the unquestionable ability of man to elevate his life by conscious endeavor"

Henry David Toreau

It was Monday. Alejandro and Luis hadn't talked during the weekend. There was a friendship developing between them, but each of them had other friends, and those friends didn't have much in common. Some of the things Luis and his friends did over the weekend weren't the healthiest, and weighed on him.

But he had been thinking about all their conversations. Alejandro realized that when he touched on more humanistic matters, concentrating on the human being, Luis was keenly attentive. He knew that his friends didn't have the most ordered of lives, and because of this he understood that they had their own restlessness inside themselves. His own eyes showed a complete lack of peace.

When Alejandro arrived at the place they used to meet, he noticed that his text message to Luis had not even been seen yet. He thought this was something quite strange, but assumed he'd see it within a matter of minustes. He waited fifteen minutes and tried to call Luis, but he didn't answer. The cell phone seemed to be dead. Alejandro decided to abandon this plan for today and went to the library because he had some time before class. The industrial processes assignment was meant to be done as a team and it was important for it to turn out well.

In the evening, around 7 pm, Alejandro received a message from Luis. It said: "Sorry I couldn't make it. I need to tell you something urgently. Can we meet tomorrow at 9 am?" Alejandro, now curious about what might be happening, said yes.

Luis got there before Alejandro.

"What happened yesterday, Luis?" Alejandro asked with a smile and with an attentive attitude. "Must have been something important to keep you from coming."

"I had a rough weekend," Luis replied. "In fact, Alejandro, I'm getting a little sick of it."

Alejandro was surprised, not knowing what his friend was talking about.

"What happened?" he asked, noticing that Luis was down.

"My parents are sometimes very stubborn and fight about everything. They say very harsh things to each other and make the atmosphere at home uncomfortable. Then I go out to avoid being there and when I come back home, Sofia is the one on whom I take out all my frustration. Then she and I get into these arguments and it becomes a vicious circle."

"What do your parents fight over?" Alejandro asked.

"Honestly," Luis replied, "they fight about everything. They fight over the stupidest things, like if the food is not on time, or if the club membership was not paid on time, or if vacation should take place on one date or the other. You can't even imagine, man! It's like a soap opera. And my siblings and I always get trapped in the middle of all this crap. My parents don't know how to control themselves and find solutions."

"How long has this been going on? Is it recent?" asked Alejandro.

"It's been going on for as long as I can remember. Sometimes it gets better, sometimes there is tension for a whole month. It's unpredictable. In fact, when you told me that day that there are

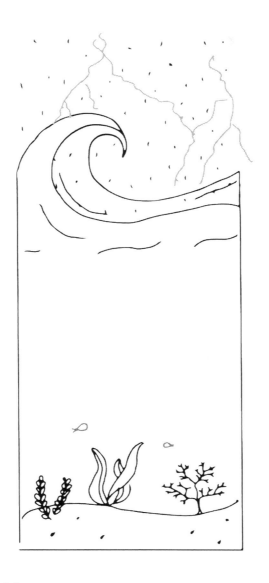

We all suffer at one point or another in life. At the surface it is felt, but in the depths of our inner ocean, calm should reign.

healthy families and others that are toxic, it was like a bullet in the stomach. I felt you were describing me."

Alejandro could see was going on. Luis was struggling with problems that were not easy. There was something dysfunctional, but he could not have imagined the extent of this issue. He noted the restlessness, a restlessness that was evident in many other friends.

"Look, in case you need help with anything, I'm here for you," Alejandro said. "In fact, don't wait until the end of the week. Give me a call or we can meet up when things get too tense. All the same, let me tell you: it's incredible that what we've been talking about has been so timely. Now I can understand why you have been asking me about how to transform your life into something good."

"Yes, I would like something better for me than what I am experiencing at home," Luis replied.

"Ok, that's totally possible," Alejandro replied. "And it's simple, but not easy. I mean, it's simple if you have clear ideas, but it's not something you can do without a fight. Life is like that, it's hard and it requires effort."

"Alright, let's start with you," Luis said. "Do you have these same problems at home?"

"Not really," said Alejandro, "and that doesn't mean there aren't problems, but both my parents seem to set an excellent example of getting to know, accept and improve each other, like we talked about last time. That's how they talk to us. They are very good at handling conflicts. In fact, I think that's one of the keys to why we have a lot of peace in my house."

"Oh, so they never fight? Never yell at each other?" asked Luis.

"I'm sure they have things they don't agree on," said Alejandro, "but I notice that they go into their bedroom, and sometimes I walk by their room and get to listen. They talk to each other with the upmost respect about whatever issue they have going on, and I see a lot of empathy between them."

Gardeners of life

"Luis, our life is like the work of a gardener. The good gardener goes through life watering the plants and trees in his garden, and he knows that it is not enough to set up the garden and make it look nice once. He regularly goes around watering the plants, checks them and removes pests. On the other hand, he needs to have the pruning shears always ready for when the plants start growing to the wrong side or disproportionately. That is his job."

"In my house it seems that all the bugs and all the pests arrived at the same time. The gardeners—my mom and dad—are each playing tennis while the garden is getting all screwed up."

"Well, I don't know if it's so, but I see from your discouragement that something is indeed not right. This is where the two topics I told you about come into play: getting to know oneself and accepting oneself. Let's talk more about these two."

Luis held his cappuccino in one hand and his sandwich in the other. He listened intently and didn't interrupt.

Alejandro continued. "I'm going to talk to you about two realities that you and I will discover little by little: effort and trust. It is true that in life, the effort that a man puts into things determines what he will achieve. But on the other hand, we have a guarantee that we are loved by God, just as we are."

Luis objected: "That seems complicated to me. It seems to me like a contradiction. How can I on the one hand strive to achieve things, but then at the same time trust none of that matters since I trust in the fact that God loves me?"

"You're right, Luis," Alejandro replied. This is not an easy subject. Like many things I have been learning in the humanistic and philosophical fields, you have to go slowly and then everything falls into place. I will begin with the first reality: our effort."

Effort

"By effort, I mean that whether we use our God-given gifts or not really matters. Man did not go to the moon by trusting God alone. Nor did he invent the internet just by trusting. It took serious research over a long period of time. Christians say that God is a God of the living, not of the dead. That means that what we do counts, because Christ also became incarnate and His effort was indispensable, but not sufficient, to sow the seed that is still alive in us. Let's divide this into separate parts."

"We all have an inner ocean. And it has a kind of sensor. When something is disturbing us, when we feel some heaviness in our stomach or a knot in our throat, we have to ask ourselves questions. What is it that is making me so restless? Why am I restless? What am I afraid of?"

"The soul and the mind are that inner ocean. At the bottom, they are calm and at peace. But on the surface, they are uneasy. There are always thoughts, feelings, emotions, and questions running through it. And that's where all our acts come from. Everything begins in thought, then passes into the body, either somatically or by words. And this is how we come to be: we form ourselves."

"What was that word you said?" asked Luis.

"Somatic?" -asked Alejandro. Luis nodded.

"It's about how the body receives and is affected by the activity of the mind. This is as old as mankind. I'm talking about being aware of what's going on inside yourself. In own our times much of that has been lost, because we don't know how to have spaces of silence anymore."

"St. Ignatius of Loyola, without speaking of the desert monks or the monastic tradition, spoke of discernment as the act of 'seeing myself by seeing' myself from the outside. But this requires leaving behind devices and distractions. One cannot gain self-knowledge while there is noise in the background."

"What are the advantages of knowing yourself?" Luis asked.

"Phew!" exclaimed Alejandro, "everything! You may know that on the porch of the temple of Delphi, the Greeks had the phrase 'Know yourself.' We also hear a lot lately about self-awareness, being attentive to oneself. If we don't, we have a lot of things that cause us problems and become blind spots in our lives—things that generate conflict, like the ones you are having at home. I don't know, but maybe your parents don't know themselves. Maybe that's why they're in conflict, because if they knew themselves, and they knew the other, they might understand a little better why they do what they do and think the way they do."

The two sat in silence as Alejandro's words sunk in.

"Nowadays he continued, "many are calling it mindfulness. It's being aware of oneself. There is an excellent book by a modern-day psychologist who established another term. He uses mindsight, which he defines as "the basic skill that underlies everything we mean when we talk about having social and emotional intelligence.[26]"

Integration as the goal of "self-help"

"Look, I want to summarize something that seems fundamental to me now that we are going to be talking about the question you asked me before. You asked me, 'how do I transform myself into a great person?'"

"One of the things that the universe always seeks, both in nature and in each human being, is balance. If there is no balance, things begin to go astray. There are many people who have some strong characteristics, and some weak ones. They lack balance."

"We will see how when we are attentive to who we are, to those movements that occur in our inner ocean, we begin to be aware that we can lead a life of effort, a life of achievement. And there are many fields that we will not be able to talk about today. This applies to the whole human individual. That is, we all have a will, intelligence, emotions, passions, and instincts. All these are the various parts that make us up. They are not separate within the person. They are united, but it is possible to separate them in order to work on ourselves little by little. This is where knowing and accepting oneself comes in, so that later one can improve oneself."

Luis chimed in. "Let's see if I'm getting what you're saying, Alejandro. So, to answer the question of how I become a great guy, or how I live a worthwhile life, there are three big stages: getting to know myself, accepting myself exactly as I am, and then overcoming myself. Is that right?"

"That's it," said Alejandro. "Please, keep going."

"So now we are talking only about knowing and accepting oneself, and then you talk about those two; you tell me that there is a reality that is divided into two, which is effort and trust. With the first one, the human being puts what is on his side; with the second one, that is, with trust, he leaves things in God's hands."

Trust

"Yes, you're getting it," Alejandro said, "but for now, we will not be talking about leaving things in God's hands. Rather, I want to talk about knowing that God is the best mother or father who loves you just the way you are. And that He doesn't want us to be stressed out by going through life like someone who has to accomplish things. Yes, to a certain extent what He wants is that we accomplish everything that we strive for, but never in an anguished way. Simply put: there's nothing you can do that will make God love you less. Man has to go through life doing his part, collaborating with God, who in the end is the one who decides whether things come out in one way or another."

"That's so complicated," Luis replied. "How does man cooperate with God? Thousands of people don't ever even think about God!"

"That's true, Luis. Thousands and even millions, I would say. But that does not mean that in what they do they are sowing for eternity. When Christ came, He said: "But seek first his kingdom and his righteousness, and all these things shall be yours as well." (Mt 6:33 RSVCE). Among various interpretations, one could be that God wants to walk with us. He wants there to be, of course, a human effort, but also a great peace in our knowing that His love is unconditional. Unconditional means just that: not conditional. God is not a tyrannical father who demands that we be distressed in order to please Him. We are interested in living in intimate union with Him, but not obsessed or living as spiritual 'workaholics'. That leads to many frustrations in life."

"So," aske Luis, "is it like a collaboration? Man puts in what he can and God puts in what He wants? How do you know when God is acting? How does that collaboration comes into place? Things that mix faith are too complicated, and that's why I find it hard to believe."

Alejandro made an effort to slow down the conversation to ease some of the obvious tension that was being created. He waited a moment, while he bit into a pear and took a sip of his drink.

"Yes, it is a collaboration," he said. "Do you know what 'Emmanuel' means? That is the name with which Jesus was known in his time. It means 'God with us'. Never doubt that God collaborates with us, especially with those who are paying attention."

"I believe, however, that the most important thing is this: you are enough. You are sufficient in the eyes of God. What you do, the gifts He gives you, the effort you make—all of them are taken into account; you are enough for Him. Yes, we make our own efforts, but always with the certainty that we cannot earn God's love: we already have that love. Like the son who knows that even though he comes home with stained clothes, or the girl who knows that even though she got in trouble at school, she is very much loved. Yes, her mother will talk to her, maybe even punish her so that she learns her lesson. But one thing is how much she is loved, and another is the disciplinary measure, which comes from love."

Luis looked into the distance, and Alejandro seemed to see a glow in his eye, as if something had fallen into the right place.

"Let's see," Luis said. "I think I see things clearly. Summarizing what you said about effort and trust, God tells you: Luis, Alejandro, Poncho, Monica... invest all your gifts into life, and do everything you can. If there is something you can't do, that's okay. I know you are limited. I know that you fall and will fall. I still love you, as long as you are always open to putting in the effort."

Luis stopped talking and looked at Alejandro, hoping he was making himself understood.

"That's right, Luis," Alejandro said. "Just like that. Look, this thing we've talked about here is relationships. It's a relationship between a creature, a human, with the creator, with God. This is at the foundation of every human relationship. Men, as we saw last time, will measure and judge us with the lens they have on. But they are imperfect. We humans, stress each other out because we see each other with a distorted, limited lens based on our own experience and all the limitations that we have. God sees you with the greatest love there is. And I began by clarifying this balance between effort and trust; the greatest well-being that a human being and his mind can achieve is when he knows he is loved. All our actions to become a great person, to transform oneself, to make the hours of my day and the days of my life more enjoyable must be built on rock solid. It is the Rock of God's true gaze, which is the only truly objective opinion about what we are and what we have to become."

There was a silence that created a haven of peace. Luis suddenly felt like all the parts of his body were getting hot, because no one ever talked to him about these matters like Alejandro did. He felt the great difference between the demands of his parents and what Alejandro told him God sees and how God thinks. He looked at his friend, and said:

"Wow! This really sounds good. I feel a little more peaceful than I did this whole weekend with the problems at home."

Looking at his friend, he continued with sincerity, "Thank you, man. You'll never know what good you're doing me with these conversations."

"Hey, well, these conversations do me as much good as they do you," Alejandro replied.

Luis continued: "When you talked about integration, what does that have to do with the matters of knowing and accepting each other, and with the matter of effort and trust?"

"Yes, I digressed a little, but that's okay. We'll talking about how to transform ourselves, Luis, like the work of a fine watchmaker. I mean, there are many pieces in the construction and perfection of the human being. Similar to training a team or tuning a car or taking care of a garden, the gardener has to be careful with excesses. He has to avoid going too far to one side or the other. And for this reason, the tree trunk of our construction as people must come together slowly."

"Again, integration is all the pieces pointing in the same direction. It is the balance in a human being. It is the growth of man's virtues and faculties in harmony. It's like everything that has harmony: an orchestra that plays a piece of music with skill; a tennis match by Federer; or a well-coordinated team like Real Madrid or Barcelona."

"Yes, it's like nowadays man lacks harmony, right?" Luis asked. "I actually realize that. He has too much knowledge in some fields and absolutely no family harmony. Or he's a great sportsman, but a failure in his family life."

"That's right," Alejandro replied.

Luis looked at his watch. What seemed like only five minutes, had actually been more than forty.

"Hey, well, it's getting kind of late. You've got class right?"

"Yes, now I have to go to industrial processes. What about you?"

"I have to go to accounting right now. See you tomorrow?"

"I have a class the frist two periods. Are you free at ten?"

"Yes," said Luis. "See you at ten. Do you know what question I've had all this time? Let's see if you can tell me."

"Which one?" Alejandro asked.

"How do we know what to put the effort into? In other words, who decides what are and what are not virtues?"

"That's a good one," Alejandro replied. "Let's talk tomorrow, shall we?"

"Great. See you, Alejandro."

ANALYZING THE CONVERSATION

I want to give you a message that seems to me to be essential in every person's life. It is sad to see how many people spend their lives suffering in order to maintain an appearance. From the hundreds of people I get to know and help in their lives, and also from my own experience, I see that man is at risk of not finding his center. What do I mean by his center?

It's another way to say his identity. We have seen in previous chapters how fundamental it is to know who gives me my value and how much I am worth. Those seem to be very simple concepts, but just knowing about them has proved to be insufficient. The whole world would affirm that it is not good to base your identity on what others think of you, and do you know how many people manage to actually implement this in their lives? Every person would admit that they do not have to put their self-esteem or value themselves according to the academic and professional successes they achieve, so why has there never been so much stress or so many suicides as in our times?

In the process of getting to know and accept each other, which we will continue to do together, we have to be gardeners of our lives. We must always have the pruning shears in our hands. Specifically and without metaphor, that happens by being attentive to that inner ocean that we carry inside, and that we will never completely understand. The path of self-knowledge never comes to an end. The blind spots we have in our personalities, from the most superficial to the most hidden and deep, are features that do not cease to surprise us. Recognizing the act of knowing oneself as a continuous process is fundamental. If not, the big problems in adulthood or later ages, the marriage and personal crises in the late thirties and forties (and beyond), will continue to create very painful seasons in people, in couples and in society.

If we study ourselves sufficiently and are always attentive to that knowledge coming to us through others, we will be able to respond adequately at each stage. We will not be stubborn and blind. I will not think that others need help, while I do not.

This work of integration of which we have spoken is the harmonization in each one of the aspects that, due to the fall of man and to the original sin that we all experience daily, is not easy. It requires effort.

And here comes into place a fundamental, precious element that only Christianity knows how to harmonize with man's weakness. I'm speaking of the patience and mercy of God who is a father and loves us. I'm referring to the fact that although we must be gardeners, guards, fighters in life (as the Bible says through its books of wisdom, of Jesus and St. Paul), there is a reality beyond everything which only comes from God. The thing is that He already loves us without us doing much. It is not easy to explain. That is why Luis and Alejandro have discussed it in the form of a metaphor of a father's love for his son.

God does want us to use our talents well. He was demanding with Himself, with His disciples, with the rich young man, with those who followed Him. In Matthew's gospel, especially, we see how He sets a very high standard for those who wish to follow Him. He says, moreover, that following Him requires abandoning oneself, taking up a cross and following Him. But at the same time, He clearly shows His disciples that He only asks us to give what we can. The long history of saints shows us that God binds up wounds, that He is a good Father, and that he forgives everything when there is even the slightest desire to be forgiven. There is no sin, however severe and dark, that God is not willing to forgive, like the father of the Prodigal Son. He only requires that we turn towards him, repent, and desire to make amends.

Having said this, man can know in life that both his effort and his trust in God are the attitudes he needs to be able to answer his great question: what can I aspire to in life? What is this seeking perfection all about? In what sense can I be as I am, without having to prove anything to anyone in an anguished way?

In later chapters we will complete the picture. We will be talking about the multiple parts that we have to integrate. It is slow work, but it requires knowing who man is, what he was made for, and what aspirations he carries in his soul, whether he recognizes it or not.

Questions to think about:

1. What do we mean when we say integration?

2. How do effort and trust work?

3. Why would you say that we have to be gardeners of our inner self in life?

Chapter 8:
What is Man's Ultimate Goal?

"... since the ultimate vocation of man is in fact one, thedivine."

Gaudium et Spes #22

It was Tuesday. At 11am, right after his class, Alejandro arrived at the usual place. He waited a few minutes and Luis did not arrive. He texted him. He could see that Luis , but Luis didn't reply. Alejandro waited a few more minutes. "Maybe Luis stood me up again today?" he wondered aloud, Then he looked up and saw Luis coming at a really slow pace. "Perhaps he had had another problem at home or with Sofia, his girlfriend," Alejandro thought.

When Luis arrived, they shook hands, and Alejandro could immediately tell something was wrong.

"What's going on, Luis?" he asked.

"Something always happens in my house," Luis said. "Yesterday my parents were very rude to each other. My brother got impatient and he also shouted at them that he was tired of so much nonsense and fighting. He also complained about the fact that the perfectionism at home was becoming tedious, and that the constant tension was suffocating his environment. I was not in the right mood either. I went into my room and started watching pornography. You know how it is. One thing leads to another, and I've made up my mind to stop watching this, because even though I like it, it leaves me empty. I don't know why. It frustrates me that in life, no matter how hard you fight to eradicate things, you never succeed. It's like you try over and over, only to fail once again."

Alejandro remembered that Luis had asked him the previous day about virtue, about what to work on, and about how to know what real purpose is in life. He thought this could be the direction of the conversation. "Let's see where it leads," he thought to himself.

"Luis, don't be so harsh with yourself. I understand that you feel bad. Pornography and problems in the house make you feel bad and it's not like they are separate elements. In fact, they are intimately connected."

Luis raised his eyebrows, surprised. Alejandro's comment left him astonished.

"What do you mean by that?" he asked his friend. "How can pornography and the fights and tensions in my house are the same?"

"I didn't say they were the same," said Alejandro, "but that they are intimately related. Pornography is nothing else than empty spaces produced by lack of what the soul desires so much: love. But we can talk about that some other time, Luis. If you'll let me, I want to answer your question from yesterday."

"Man, you have a great memory! What question did I ask you yesterday?"

Yesterday you asked me about what to choose to to transform one's life. In other words, you asked me how one knows which virtues to work on first in life? Do you remember?"

"Yes," said Luis, frowning.

Life is a struggle

"Well, I want to tell you that according to my little experience and the many things I've read, plus what I hear from someone like my dad, life is a struggle. You don't have to worry about it, you just have to deal with it. It's very normal that we get a little desperate in life, because we see that we fall into the same thing again and again. We try to improve ourselves in something, and that doesn't go away. Those who have a tendency to be rude and sour with people, without realizing it, is no longer that way the next day. In the case of the one who is vain, if a person who loves him points that out, he can recognize it. But, does that mean that for the next day he's not like that anymore? No way! And the one who has a tendency to drink too much, or the girl who loves to kiss every guy that walks by needs to navigate strongly in the opposite direction to stop acting like that."

"Where are you going with this? What should I understand by this?"

"Oh Luis, it's very simple. That you don't have to torture yourself just because you might appear weak. Your parents' quarrels, your brother's impatience, your weakness with pornography... you have to identify them, and get to work improving. But don't expect to end up with bad habits just because you know you have them. It's a process, it's a path, and it's also a discipline, thanks be to God."

"Look, a very enlightening phrase for me from my philosophy classes goes like this:

'We are in continuous development; therefore 'to know, to accept and to improve' are not static goals to be achieved once and for all, but a constant vital process, which has a very concrete field of application in the attention to the inner movements: the emotions and passions, the sensibility and the affectivity, etc.'

"Look, we have been talking about knowing and accepting yourself. Later we will talk about getting better, but the interesting thing is that we do not change from one day to the other. You have to achieve what is called inner freedom. You have to learn to accept the times of nature. To go little by little. Life is a gift, but it is also a task. It's a gift, but it's a path full of effort and full of peace."

"What are talking about when you say full of effort, and full of peace?" Luis asked.

"Yes, it is an effort, because love asks the beloved to be the best he can be, but it is also full of peace, because it's not a competition. It is an effort that has trust [in God], don't you remember?"

Luis responded by nodding. Everything was going great, but his gaze still reflected anguish. He needed to continue reflecting, listening to Alejandro.

The what and the why of man

"There is an explanation of concepts that we saw in philosophy that has made a lot of sense to me in everything I do. Look Luis, it's about the "what" and the "what for" of things. This also includes man."

"In everything that exists, there is the "what is" and the "what for". An example: I understand what a chair is, if I understand what it is for. So what is the chair for? To sit on. So I understand what it is. I use a chair properly if I understand what it's for."

"Take a table. What is it for? It's to put objects on. So, I understand what a table is if I understand what it is for. Am I being clear enough?" Alejandro asked.

Luis shrugged his shoulders. "And how does this relate to what we have been talking about?" he asked.

"Oh, well, a lot. You ask: how can man know how to transform himself? To know what to do, or in which direction to head, he has to understand why he exists. Excuse me for inserting a philosophical concept now, but St. Thomas Aquinas calls this the final cause. What is man for? Where will he end? Where is he headed?

"I can use a table to sit on, but it wasn't made for me to sit on it. So, even though a table will hold my weight for a while, since it was not made for that, one of two things will happen: either the table will break or I will get tired of being on something so unergonomic, and pretty soon I will be looking for a chair. Now let's apply that to man.

"What is the 'what for' of man? It can be expressed in several ways, all of them intimately related. Saint Augustine says that man is made to rest in God. Christianity says we are made for the waters that spring from eternal life, which is nothing else than God. John Paul II always reiterated that man is made for love. Aristotle and Saint Thomas Aquinas both said that man and woman were born for happiness. And finally, the Bible says that we are made to aspire to and reach eternal life. Which one of them sounds right to you?"

"Luis hesitated for a few seconds, before answering. "All the answers sound reasonable to me; I suppose there will be some more accurate than others. But ultimately what Aristotle and Saint Thomas said seems to me the truest: we are made for happiness."

"Yes, exactly," Alejandro said. "Actually, all of them are right. All are saying the same thing in another way, because those who aspire to eternal life, aspire to be happy there, where God is, which is pure happiness. And where God is, there is pure love, as Saint Paul also said: "The greatest gift is love" (1 Cor 12:31).

Well, then, if what we have said is that the purpose of man is to reach God, it would not be a bad idea to ask God, or to try to find in God, how to live in order to understand the "what for" of man. How are we to live? We to live so that the direction of our lives is towards the destination of love and happiness is guaranteed."

"And why do we have to ask God and not determine it ourselves? Why bring God into this question?" Luis asked.

"Let's see," Alejandro replied. "Can a lamp ask other lamps what the lamp maker created them for? Maybe you'll say: yes, why not? But no one will answer the question as well as the one who created them. And he will say something like: to illuminate a space. In fact, without God, man has made man, again and again throughout history, a slave either to other men or to their passions. And the world has been on a pendulum over and over again. What has most stabilized man is when he, centered in God, has valued his fellow men because he has regarded them as brothers, who are all on a journey to another country, one that is not on this Earth. That is why it is necessary to ask the one who 'made' things: what did you have them in mind for?

Luis seemed to find a lot of logic in this, again. His intuitions that his friend's accumulated wisdom was still very beneficial to his own problems were solidifying. Then he asked a question:

"Alejandro, the subject of knowing the 'what for' of man, which you later told me some call the final cause, how important is it?"

"Very important," said Alejandro. "Take a good look at why, because we talked about this the other day. The cause, the reason why in this world there is not much intelligence in how we live and how we transcend, we said that it is because there is superficiality. I told you about that phrase from a document by Pope John Paul II that says that people stay in the phenomenon, but they do not go to the foundation. They stay in the smoke, and they will not investigate the fire itself. Well, the same thing happens with man."

"I'm not quite understanding what you mean." said Luis.

"Sorry. What I mean is that the key to knowing what man should do and what he should not do in life is to know his whole purpose. That's how you answer the 'why' of man—how to know where he comes from, what he comes for, and where he is heading to. If I do not know what the final destiny of man is, what his whole being and soul longs for, I shall make of him an object to be used. Think of two examples:

"If I meet a girl in a bar, I get to know her, and I like her, but I just want to hook up with her, she will be my object of pleasure. But if someone managed to show me a movie of her, and I saw when she was born and the baby she was when she was little; then they show me when she almost died because she had a very serious case of chickenpox at age six; then they show me how she won a social service award for helping sick people at her school. They even show me her crying with joy the day she delivers her first baby and how she is happy with her husband for that miracle. And finally, I see her as a seventy-five year-old with terminal cancer, surrounded by all her children and grandchildren around her bed in a hospital, a few minutes before she dies… Do you think I would treat that woman in a less superficial and selfish way? Having the complete picture, being aware of something or someone makes us act differently.

"The second example is if I see a marathoner suffering at kilometer thirty-two of the marathon, and I don't see at all the inner goal he has of finishing the race, I might think he is suffering because he wants to. In other words, looking towards the finish line, towards the final destination, makes everything make sense. Even though his face only reflects pain, and I from the outside say 'what an idiot,' it's all because I don't see his goal, his dream, his aspirations, his whole story. Am I being clear now?

"In short, Luis, seeing the final goal of something or someone changes everything. We do not live only for this life. We are transcendent beings."

Luis now felt somewhat humiliated. Not because of what his friend told him, but because he realized more and more that there was an abyss between him and his friend. "Why don't my parents tell me any of this at home?" he thought to himself. "Why aren't there classes at the university with these contents? It all sounds logical to me, but why are these treasures in the hands of only a few? If Alejandro didn't have the patience to spend this time with me, how could I learn these things? It seems to me too important to be a coincidence."

As all these questions piled up in Luis' mind, Alejandro watched him until the silence was broken:

Wow," said Luis, "it's incredible that we don't have space to talk about these things. None of my other friends ever talk about these things, Alejandro. You cheer me up."

Alejandro looked at him with compassion. He didn't want to break this moment of silence and reflection without first giving Luis a few moments. A few more seconds passed.

"May I touch on one last topic that I think is a foundation for your question on self-transformation?" Alejandro asked.

"Yes, of course.' Luis replied. "Go ahead."

The "Central Trunk" of a Person

"A while ago," continued Alejandro, "I mentioned a term to you: inner freedom. Many people live for others. They always have an eye on what others do. It's the famous FOMO (fear of missing out). Not only young people, but also adults, sometimes exaggerate the need we have for the world's approval. It is the addiction of approval: to be approved, to be valued, to be applauded."

"Is it wrong to want to be loved?" Luis asked.

"It is not wrong to be loved, because in the commandment of love is 'love your neighbor as yourself'.' Alejandro said. "From that we can conclude that one must love oneself. But one must be free. We must not be attached to the opinion of others. And today there is a need to belong that is sometimes unhealthy. This has increased a lot with social media. If we don't get 'likes', our mood crumbles. There is an addiction to approval. I would say that there is a big difference: it is not wrong to be loved; it is wrong to need to be loved."

"I see," said Luis. "Is that what you mean by inner freedom?"

"Not only that," Alejandro replied. "Listen, the key to building ourselves, to making ourselves, to strengthening the trunk of our identity, is to build a strong trunk in ourselves. That is, knowing that we are worthy by ourselves, regardless of the opinion of others.

"Two sailboats go out to sea. On the dock they were both just as solid, just as strong. But when the storm comes to the sea, a sailboat endures high waves and strong winds. One of the sailboats, sadly, capsizes and is shipwrecked. Why, Luis?"

"Because the mast is weak, or the keel is badly set, or because the hull of the sailboat is weak."

It is not wrong to want to be liked; it is wrong to NEED to be liked.

"Right. That last one is especially important. In other words, the trunk is weak. As humans, we have to find that inner freedom, which includes—but does not conclude—the issue of not depending on the opinions of others. As they say in Spain: 'Fight for God, not for the stands.' What a slavery, what an anguish, what a bond those who live for what others think!

"Jesus said it like this: 'I am the Vine, you are the vine shoots.' It is the same as saying: 'I am the trunk, you are the branches.' As a branch, do not look at or feed on the other branches. You are attached to the trunk, and that is where solidity and strength come from. Not from constantly comparing yourself to the other branches: if the others are longer, shorter, thicker, thinner, or if those have more or less fruit. It's about solidity, Luis. Having a strong central trunk."

Luis was now connecting ideas and thinking about the impact of yesterday. He had questions, but at the same time he was looking for answers on his own to apply what he was talking about with his friend. Then he set out to unify everything:

"Alejandro, do you think that not having heard and applied these concepts contributes to the difficulties in my house? Because with Sofia I never talk about these things either. I believe that neither she nor I know much about all this."

"Maybe," Alejandro replied. "What do you think you need to connect in this case?"

"Well, the fact that life is a struggle and you don't have to be perfect, that's enough peace. The purpose of each man, the 'what' and 'what for' which we discussed earlier also makes me have a broader and more humane vision, more transcendent, I would say, of each one. In my house these things are not part of the equation. At least not in a fashion in which I could recognize it."

"Luis," Alejandro asked. Do we agree that in many homes, although these ideas are not spoken, they are lived? That is, there are people who bring these ideas as a habit of life—homes where

Sometimes we hear that this or that person is rock-solid. We must aspire to solidity and fortitude of our personality.

they do not speak of these subjects, nevertheless, they live them. Of course, it is better to know how to directly refer to these things, because otherwise, it seems luck that there is more peace and harmony in a home, but not every home is very philosophical, and yet they live in relative harmony."

"Yes, Alejandro, but you will agree with me that you cannot depend only on luck or chance that in a house that they live well without knowing why. Because when it comes to bigger difficulties, they won't know how to find the solutions either."

Alejandro felt this time that Luis was right. In fact, he was trying to give him windows of light so that he wouldn't be crushed by the situation at home, which was affecting his girlfriend as well.

"You are absolutely right," he said. "Building yourself up as a person cannot be by chance. You have to have a little more wisdom."

"Alejandro," Luis said, "it's time to go, but if you are free on Thursday, can we meet me here? I would like to focus a little more on the concrete. These tips or principles are really good. But I would like to deepen more into the practical and applicable details. I wouldn't know, with what I'm discovering here, where to start. In other words, what things in a person should be solidified? In what fields? What parts of the person should be 'brought to the gym'?

"Alright," Alejandro replied. "Yes, let's meet on Thursday. But try to think through your questions now that we are going to go more to that concrete aspect. For example, look at how you are living each moment of the day, or how you are handling the distress in your home. Try to generate questions so that you can go through them to the applications. How does that sound?"

"Perfect," replied Luis, taking his backpack and leaving after shaking hands with his friend. Each went to their own classroom."

ANALYZING THE CONVERSATION

Alejandro is getting to know Luis better every day. He realizes one thing: he has not been exposed, either by his family or by the world, to much of the wisdom accumulated in centuries of humanism. In fact, Luis is not to blame. There are thousands who have not received this and he feels indebted to God for the gift that he has.

Alejandro is discovering that Luis' difficulties and doubts are nothing else but a product of a world focused on material things and what money can buy. In the lives of great people there are usually three things that help them become what they are: 1. a very big dream; 2. many difficulties along the way; 3. the presence of parents and mentors who played a fundamental role in getting there. When we listen to these people tell their stories, they immediately highlight the main principles with which they came to build what we see today.

That is why Alejandro, who is putting those main principles into practice, wants to share them with Luis. Foreseeing that in life there will be many struggles, that there will be people who will not understand and that one should not pay much attention to something that every man and woman should take into account. The hope of winning a race without the sweat, the sacrifice, and the doubts that come with it is not a good teaching.

On the other hand, there are many people who want to quickly grasp at those achievements. This is not possible. To build upon principles that make us understand the "why" and 'what for' of our lives is fundamental. Without understanding man in his complexity, but also in his reason for being, every person will be tempted to always look for things that are only triumphs that time and rust corrode. A person will be moved by goals that, although they may require effort, do not lead to the way of the 'what' and 'what for'. They do not satisfy the soul. They will give joy today and tomorrow will cease to be interesting. This is because the deepest desire of man is not to be halfway through his 'what for'. If he was created to reach the summit of that high mountain, to proclaim triumph in the middle is only deceiving oneself for a while. Then the truth emerges and the soul feels boredom. To use an image that summarizes everything, an American soccer player cannot reach the seventy-yard line and shout 'touchdown!' because in football, it's only a touchdown if you reach the hundred-yard line.

If these principles or foundations are solidly in place, then people will quickly know that they will need clear goals, discipline, and perseverance. That is what we will see in the book now. What parts does man have? How am I to work on myself? What areas of life are there to be polished and which cannot be left to chance?

That is what we must now analyze. First we had to lay down solid principles, since in the modern world it seems that what is an objective and universal good is not clear, and thus every goal seems equally valid.

Questions to think about:

1. In life, when do you think people have stopped knowing, accepting, and improving themselves? Why?

2. What is the final cause of man as we have defined it here? Why is it important to know what the human person was created for?

3. How important is it to strengthen the trunk of a person's identity? What if that is not done?

Chapter 9:
Starting with the Man

"The first thing we have to do to change the world is to change you and me.".

Saint Teresa de Calcutta.

Wednesday ended, and on Thursday Luis and Alejandro met again at the same place. This time it did not seem that either of them had any difficulty at home. In fact, Alejandro rarely did. But Luis was in a humanistic and spiritual awakening that was making him see things from another angle. Moreover, he felt the need to answer so many questions he had. Many of them had taken him away from the faith he professed when he made his First Holy Communion. Why had he not preserved the values of that special day?

The simple answer is that nature is ready for us to seek new answers at each step of life as it corresponds to our age. Just as a young man of eighteen years cannot wear the jeans he used to wear when he was fourteen, a young university student must look for the reasons that convince him at that age. What can be explained about faith and life to an adolescent must be related to his or her age. A baby eats baby food first, then starts with foods that children like, and as an adult changes his tastes. However, at all times you have to give the stomach what it needs and not just what tastes good.

Alejandro arrived a few minutes late, because once again the parking lot was full.

"What's up, Luis?" he asked.

"All good, Alejandro. Did you have to park in the back?"

"Yes, the number of students continues to grow and the parking lot spots stay the same," Alejandro said.

Alejandro had not had a chance to buy anything at the store. Luis took out his coffee and a sandwich. He offered these to Alejandro, but he said that he wasn't hungry.

Alejandro began: "Luis, well, I think I'm anxious to start talking about more concrete things. We have talked about many principles that serve as a foundation. I wanted to do this more than anything else because I am applying what I have learned in my philosophy courses. You don't have a clue! Every time we have them, on the one hand, the five of us who are in it enjoy it very much. On the other hand, I realize that I know very little."

"One of the areas of life that I find most difficult—and I discuss it with Sofia often—is the subject of everyday decisions, from the simplest ones like what to wear, to the most complex ones like love and career. Every day we find ourselves, at least ten times, with an 'and' or 'or', and we think: "Do I go left or right?" On many other occasions, not only do we have two options, but they multiply. How do we make safe decisions, Alejandro?"

Without giving his friend a chance to reply, Luis continued: "I am interested in knowing what to choose between two or more options in life. And I realize that no one knows what is better than what."

"What do you mean nobody knows what is better than what?" Alejandro asked.

I mean that for some what has to be done is different than for others," Luis said. "What a Muslim should do does not coincide with what a Jew should do. And what a Jew should do does not coincide with what a Christian should do. And those of us who are more openminded and do not close ourselves to a religion, we also have our way of thinking."

Alejandro felt like he had swallowed a hot pepper when he heard about that openminded thing, but he bit his lip, and without Luis noticing anything, he ignored the comment.

"Look," he replied. "Since you touch on the subject, let me share with you what has worked for me. I am totally convinced that the Christian proposal of good living and of how to decide is the clearest and most convincing. What I have been discovering day by day makes this more and more clear."

"Of course," said Luis with an ironic smile, "how can you not defend your faith if it is yours anyway? It's not like you're dumb. Each one defends his own."

"I know it can be seen that way, and it's true that it's mine," Alejandro said with as soft and convincing a tone as he could muster.

"But do not think that I have not studied other religions," Alejandro continued. "Pedro, the teacher who accompanies us every week, just Led us for three months through the different religions in order to analyze all of them. With each religion, we asked about who founded it, what they think about evil and about death, and about whether they think there is life after the current one. Within the many studies we made, each one presented a religion to the others. And we fought hard against each other's ideas, due to the fact that Pedro asked us to really play the devil's advocate for each other."

"And what do you see as negative about Christianity, for example?" Luis asked, trying to push Alejandro with a hard question.

"The negative things I found in Christianity are above all the misuse of Christians' freedom. The lack of conviction. But not Christianity itself, because I am actually convinced that Christianity is not a religion."

"How so? Then what is it?" Luis asked.

"Christianity is the way God made things. And we Christians have a responsibility, once we discover it, to be even greater light in the world than all religions. I would call the others religion, understanding that they are a way of understanding the world. Christianity is not just a way of understanding the world. It's not just a question of how I think about it at the level of the mind. It's how the world is in reality, regardless of how the whole world thinks about it. Let me use other words:

"Christianity is the way of life that results when you have met God, the only one alive and true. The other religions have much, much good. We saw clearly that they have truths, but not the Truth. They are lights, they are not the Sun."

According to the nature of creation

"Luis, I got into this topic of religions, but right now let's not spend too much time on it. We said that we both want to go to the concrete part of transforming ourselves, of the trunk of life, of knowing, accepting, and improving ourselves."

Alejandro continued. "I was impressed by the wisdom of God, how God creates man and how all that man has and is, is made to be oriented towards God. That is, man does not have to decide arbitrarily, out of the blue, what he should do, what he should promote in himself. We were talking about wanting to know how to make good decisions, right? That's done. We return to what I like to remember and that is that the centuries of wisdom and learning of humanity already give us a path to follow. Do you remember that a few weeks ago I told you that we believe that we can invent theories out of thin air as if we were not standing on much wisdom that we already have? The wise auxiliary bishop of Los Angeles, Robert Barron, calls this the age of 'self-invention,' the age where everyone re-propose the laws of nature."

Luis just nodded his head, hoping to decipher Alejandro's words. He still couldn't see where all this was going.

"Well," continued Alejandro, "Let's get into the specifics. When I say the concrete, I mean the part you are most interested in, in the person, in each human being. Let me read you this paragraph about man and his ultimate purpose which is God:

"Since God is the purpose of man, all human faculties have been created so that, through them, man can be oriented and united to Him. The intellect is made to know Him through the sensible world and His Revelation, the concupiscible appetite to desire Him and love Him, the irascible appetite to fight evil, to move away from temptations and to be protective for things of God; the will is made to embrace filially His good will for us, the memory to remember Him and His works of love, the senses and imagination to serve as a basis for His contemplation in all things. So, all faculties or powers are by their nature spontaneously oriented to the possession of God and to the exercise of virtues. That is why the Fathers say that a virtuous life is 'in accordance with nature.'"

"Wait, slow down," Luis protested. "Can you summarize what you just read a little? It wasn't very clear."

"Sure," Alejandro replied. "In short, this paragraph I just read to you says that because of the image and likeness of God in man—and this is a fundamentally Christian principle—man and his parts are made to feel good objectively, to elevate themselves, and to find fulfillment in God. So for example, Luis, my intelligence is pleased when I learn something new and I understand it. Also, man feels good when he does a good and generous act for another person. Some say that these feelings are a social construct. It is good that they think so. But when humanity has experienced it for centuries and millennia, that theory crumbles."

"I'm following, but not completely," Luis said. "I understand that man and his faculties feel good when he does good. However, why is this important?"

"It's important, Luis, because now you can connect what we talked about—the fact that all of nature is created by God and has some God-given rules. All creatures have a law that makes them logical and intelligible. It's natural law. And the natural law is also enjoyed by human beings. So, if man simply studies himself and observes himself, he will see that he has in himself many of the answers to his questions. If you allow me another way to explain it, natural law is that common thing in the heart of every man and woman that makes us know the most basic aspects of the actions. That basic thing is to know to avoid evil and to do good. And even if Christianity did not exist, man has this internal code, this sensor that knows what to do and what to avoid."

Luis thought about it then asked: "I understand. How would you say that this is the right way to put my life in order? How do you do it? More importantly, why are you explaining this to me if what I want is to learn how to make better decisions?"

"Good question. If I understand that there are laws inscribed in man that are like an instruction manual, if he reaches that point of comprehension, then he will make free and very safe decisions. When I say free, I do not mean a way of being absolutely free, without moral rules. I mean true freedom, which is doing what will make me happy. But this, which is getting into ethics, is something we'll talk about another day. Now we'll get off topic, okay?"

"Okay," said Luis, "but I'm interested in talking about ethics later."

"Look," Alejandro continued, "I'm really far away from getting where I want to go. But thanks to my parents and to God, I have been able to use a mental model they gave me one day."

From the inside out

The first thing to realize is that all change in life is done from the inside out. If I really want to change or improve something, I cannot blame it on the thousand things that surround me. They can influence, they can hinder, they can even tire, but they are not the cause of my problems or challenges.

"How sad it is to hear of people who are unsuccessful or living an unhappy life, who say that everyone is to blame but them. The easiest and most effortless thing is to complain about everyone and blame everyone except oneself. Therefore, change begins with oneself. How am I thinking and living today? And so, when you start by changing yourself, you will be able to make better decisions."

"In fact, that's what happens in my house," said Luis, "there's a lot of complaining and criticism of circumstances and people. My parents constantly blame each other for their dissatisfaction."

"I understand," Alejandro replied. "So we have the potential to work on ourselves now, without delay. And the scheme I give you is three steps or concepts: convictions, attitudes, and behaviors. This same scheme, if you look closely, goes from the deepest to the most immediate and visible.

Convictions

"Convictions are the deepest beliefs about life that we have. Examples of these are hard work, confidence in the value of effort, the conviction that every human being has a heart that we are capable of making vibrate, and the value of virtue in life. These and many more are examples of convictions with which many people live."

Convictions are the deepest beliefs in our lives

153

"I see, "Luis replied. "Please give me a concrete example."

"For example, the conviction that there is a truth that can be known by every human. That is, the fact that for the human to get to know the truth is something possible, am I being clear enough? Now, let's go to the second concept."

Attitudes

Mi attitude in the mental decision that
I take right before my actions.

"Attitudes are my favorite. It refers to the decisions we make right before an action. For example, putting a good face on things, being positive, being friendly, avoiding bad moods, and having everyone put up with us, perseverance in what we started. Attitudes are what differentiate some people from others, those who achieve a lot in life and transform their environment, and those who complain about why this or that is not possible.

"The attitude that you put to every project will be definitive for you to achieve what you set out to do or not. It is unbearable to live and work with someone without a positive and harmonious attitude."

"Tell me about it," said Luis.

Behavior

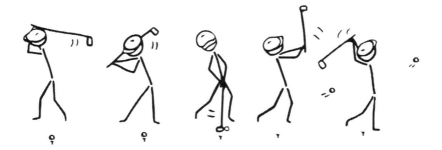

Behaviors are the external actions we all see in others.

"The last one is the behaviors. It refers to the action itself, to what others see on the outside. Behavior is the putting into action of that which was previously intended.

"Behaviors derive from above. My convictions and attitudes lead to the behaviors or actions I do. If I have clear convictions and appropriate attitudes, my behaviors will be very good.

"Sometimes it makes me sad to see how some film artists, and especially many athletes, make decisions that we all see and that do not set any example. It is clear that they did not have that formative structure. They go through life inventing what to do, the example to set, and doing things that are not polite at all, things that detract from the great dignity of the human person.

"In fact, I just read a book by a golfer—you know how much I love golf—who has already died. I don't know if you remember him: Arnold Palmer. In his book he says this:

'It is not enough to simply provide the basic needs and perhaps some comforts to your children. A parent must offer firm direction in attitude and behavior, which I can say my parents did for my siblings and me.'

155

Luis was left thinking by these words and then said: "How can I easily remember all three?"

"I like the image of some sport like golf or tennis," Alejandro replied. "I'm going to take the one of golf. In golf, to succeed, to hit the ball properly with those clubs that are so hard to use in order to hit the ball as you should, first, you must know the most fundamental principles of the golf swing. Second, you must be convinced of the technique for you to be able to swing. Third, you must hit the ball."

Luis' eyes were wide open. This scheme that Alejandro had just presented to him sounded logical and clear. He found it simple to follow and to live. He asked:

"If I understand correctly, this scheme leads us from the deepest ideas to perform acts that are in accordance with those convictions. Is that how you see it?"

"That's right, Luis." Alejandro didn't want to add much to let Luis ask more, if he wanted to.

Then he continued. "In fact, I do agree with what I once heard a TED speaker say: that the actions we take are proportional to the ideas we have."

"And look, it's something so natural and ancient. There is a Latin phrase that Pedro always mentions in our philosophy classes, which translated into English says 'doing follows being', that is, the way we act is nothing other than the result of what we are. The thief steals, the player plays, the virtuous does acts of virtue."

"I suppose," said Luis, "that what you have to concentrate on—using your image of the golf—is mainly in principles and conviction. If I have that, I will hit the 'ball' quite naturally."

"Exactly. Because remember that if the mind understands well what it has to do, the will is determined to put in its effort and the attitude is positive, the person achieves what he or she sets out to do with ease. This is called virtue. But if you want, we can talk about virtue another day, when we talk about ethics. For now, let's go step by step."

There was a pause in the conversation while Luis shared some of his sandwich with Alejandro. They both took a bite out of their respective parts and continued what they had started:

"Alejandro, where do I start, then? You know about the current hardships in my house and the ones that are created with Sofia. I have the impression that my parents don't talk to us much about this. Also, I have no idea how to improve myself, to use the word that you use."

Taking action

"The first thing is that I would like you to have a lot of trust in what we are going to be talking about, Luis, and that is what I have been learning and then applying. If you want to live better, if you want to bring order and light into your life, you have to trust everything we have said and we will talk about. I can tell you that it is a treasure that comes from two-hundred years of Judeo-Christian culture."

"It is also important that you see the essentials of having discipline and perseverance. 'Discipline is the bridge between goals and reaching them,' said Jim Rohn, a very successful American entrepreneur. If suddenly I suggest you do something and practice something in your relationships with others, do not see it as a small thing. I will not give you advice that does not have a purpose for you or leads you to perform useless tasks, only what I see that really works."

"Oh, now you're going to put me to work," said Luis.

"Not always, and not unnecessarily. But take our conversations seriously. What is only heard, but not practiced, is useless. You know what they say about us capturing 10% of what we read, 30% of what we hear, 50% of what we see and hear, 70% of what we explain to others, and 90% of what we say and do."

"Yes, the truth is that when we get involved with something—it happens to me in every subject in the career—we get much more out of it than if we stay static."

"Okay, let's do one thing," suggested Alejandro. "Since we have been here for a while and we can't get into the first concrete thing about the person and how to make a change from the inside out, let's leave it here and we can continue tomorrow, Friday. Does that work for you?"

"Yes, I only have a class on Fridays from ten onwards. What about you?"

"My schedule on Fridays coincides a lot with yours, so I'll see you here at nine. A while ago I didn't want to mention it, but you talked about the open-minded stuff. And I want to clarify something for you regarding that. For a while in the past I thought very similarly. If you believe in this doctrine or that, you are pigeonholed. Especially I, who come from a Catholic home with parents who know these things thoroughly, thought: if I think as a Catholic, I am stuck, restricted. It is very closed, because there is no freedom to think differently than the Church."

"Let me tell you that it is an apparent truth. Those who do not believe in anything, or those who say they prefer to refrain from defining whether they think this way or that way, in fact this is also a doctrine. To believe that it is not important to conclude what to think, that in itself is a doctrine. Call it what you wish: self-thinking, agnosticism, laziness, modernism... But it is not free from being a doctrine. It is the doctrine of 'I do not decide so I cannot be pigeonholed.'"

"You don't have to worry about being pigeonholed. It's as if a young man is super in love with a girl and says: but I don't want to commit myself to her, otherwise I lose the possibility of having all the others. You may feel freer not to commit to one, but it's actually a very selfish life."

"The thing is that I detest the Catholic dogmas that say 'this is so and it is not discussed.' It seems to me that this is idiotic," Luis said.

"I don't doubt that you have found people like that. But these have not gone deep into their faith. Clearly their formation is only to repeat what they have been told. We, unlike the Protestants, do not believe anymore in the doctrine of 'faith alone,' but we believe in faith as well as in reason. In other words, by going again to the example of the young man who is falling in love with the girl: he does not decide to propose to her because he knows everything about her. He knows her, he is attracted to her, he does some research, they go out for a few months... and with what he sees of her, he decides to commit himself and continue to know her."

"Excuse me for saying so, but those who say they are very open-minded are then very closed-minded to the one who believes in something seriously, and take away the right to believe in their faith. Those who say they are open-minded do not leave alone the one who has clear ideas and morals and says: 'Don't take me to a table dance or cabaret. I don't want to go.'"

Luis realized that perhaps Alejandro had been offended by his comment earlier. He asked him:

"Alejandro, were you offended by what I said earlier?"

"No, man! It bothered me a little, but I didn't feel offended. But I do hear it often from those who have taken the route of not believing in anything and calling themselves open-minded, and then labeling those of us who have decided to follow our faith after we have researched it. That's it."

"I see. Well, don't worry, I wasn't saying it about you. But I have met many very closed-minded Catholics."

"Yes, I know there are many of them," said Alejandro, "but there are also those who aren't that way. I think the distinction has to be made more in the individuals than in 'the Catholics,' because you put them all in the same bag."

Luis nodded. They both looked at the clock. Alejandro was hungry now. He had hardly eaten any breakfast. They said goodbye and went their separate ways.

Luis didn't want any more theory. He felt like he had to start making his life much better. His problems with Sofia his girlfriend, and the tensions at home were already taking a huge toll on him. He asked himself: where will we start tomorrow on the subject of improvement?

ANALYZING THE CONVERSATION

So far we see that Alejandro has been trying to lay a firm foundation. This is before laying the foundation stone for the construction of the whole person and before seeking a healthy integration of our faculties.

As they have said, we are in a world of self-invention. Everyone believes that one can invent the way in which he realizes himself. They do not realize that creativity and seeking alternative ways to make the most of life are good, but within the framework of a reality that is already given to man. This is what is known as human nature.

Just as in the physical field we cannot decide whether to take into account the laws of physics, such as gravity or the laws of thermodynamics, because we necessarily obey them, in the moral field it is the same. God has put a nature in everything created. Although it is not so easy to detect this, we already have a lot of history and human ethics and humanistic sciences that direct us towards the good, the beautiful, and the true. That is the challenge. Dig up the wisdom that past generations have already given us. A dog cannot learn from previous generations, but we humans do have history as a great teacher. Hence the saying that those who do not learn from history are condemned to repeat it, along with mistakes.

In every human being, action requires deep convictions, positive and confident attitudes, and correct behaviors. With these three concepts, we have recognized the way in which the winners and heroes of history have reached the heights of human existence. Socrates, Jesus Christ, Augustine, Erasmus of Rotterdam,

Leonardo, Churchill... all of them, whether they left it in writing or not, had firm convictions, which became attitudes that later led to behaviors. That is why they are known today. There are also thousands and millions of hidden heroes, mothers, fathers, and religious people who have lived this, whether they know it or not.

Now that these foundations have been expressed, we have to begin to live according to them. The human being first conceives something in his mind and then lays the bricks for its construction. That dream is a building that begins with oneself. Mother Teresa was interviewed once, and asked what it took to change the world. She responded: 'The first thing we have to do to change the world is to change you and me.'

Questions to think about:

1. How do you understand the idea that things are according to the nature of creation? What does that mean in man?

2. Why are great changes in a person made from the inside out?

3. What is the first thing that must be solidified in a person so that their behaviors are right? Do you act according to your answer? How does it show?

Chapter 10:

Improving Oneself: The Lofty Heights in Man

"There is no deficit in human resources; the deficit is in human will."

Martin Luther King

It was Friday. Luis was walking quickly, wanting to get to the appointment. He was beginning to feel excited about this friendship, about what the conversations were bringing him. It was a strange sensation to feel that in the rest of his environment the conversations and ideas were something that seemed meaningless. With Alejandro he felt the joy of wisdom. He was beginning not to fly so low in his aspirations and desires. The whole subject of getting to know and accept each other had been of great interest to him.

Upon reaching the site, he waited for Alejandro. He kept reflecting on how much of what they had discussed was shedding light on his problems at home. His parents, the little training at home, the tension he felt—it all made Luis come to the conviction that without clear ideas to apply, without convictions that become attitudes, there is no direction in life.

In the distance, Alejandro was already coming at a calm pace, with a serene and peaceful countenance. He stopped to greet him:

"What's up, Alejandro? How are you doing?" Luis asked.

"I'm doing great," Alejandro replied, "what about you? How is everything going? I'm a bit sleepy today. I slept less because of the Barcelona match yesterday. It was great, but it ended late. They lost by two goals against Manchester. We'll see how they do the next time."

"Are you a fan of Barcelona, or of Manchester?" asked Luis.

"Barcelona, of course," said Alejandro.

Eager to start the conversation, they each took out their sandwich and their drink and started right where they left off last time.

"So, now, how have you managed to transformyourself, to bring the best out of yourself?" Luis asked.

Higher powers in man

"OK," Alejandro said. The first thing to know is that man has two levels of action. Those two levels of action are the highest and the lowest in each of us. You know that sometimes we want the noblest and dignified thing, and sometimes we just want to give free rein to all our passion. Sometimes we feel a pull towards spiritual things, and sometimes alcohol, girls, and money exert a force like kryptonite on us."

"These two levels have powers or faculties that can regulate them. The superior powers are intelligence and will. In the Christian faith, we say that because we are beings with souls and oriented toward God, reason or intelligence, illuminated by faith, can also strengthen our actions even more. But now let's speak only of intelligence and will.

"The intelligence of man is made by God to desire the truth. In fact, I have already told you the phrase of Christ that says: "And you shall know the truth, and the truth shall make you free" (John 8:32). Then there's this phrase attributed to Cicero: "Nature has put in our minds an insatiable desire of seeing the truth." So, Luis, the first thing to do is to cultivate the truth.

"And how do you cultivate the truth?"

"There are many ways. The first thing is to want to get away from lies, gossip, and unsubstantiated information. There is so much falsehood out there. In the field of journalism, it is incredible how easily they take phrases out of context just to sell and generate scandal and fear. The other day there was a story about Zinedine Zidane and something he supposedly said. It was on the cover of two sports sites. I went to see the actual video of how he said it, and there was a huge difference between what he actually said and what was being said about him. That's slander, that's defamation. That's not even considered serious in today's world. But living a lie is serious. It's deforming the truth."

Luis paid intense attention to the conversation.

"A second way is good readings. When I go to the book fair, I see that I could spend my whole life reading many things. There is so much content that is so valuable. Reading classics like Shakespeare, Cervantes, Victor Hugo, the Russian authors—knowing how to access real culture, and not junk content."

"In life we will not have time to read everything we want, and so what we do manage to read, we must make worthwhile. This also applies to not being cheated."

"What do I mean? In every place, in every city, in every social circle, I observe that there are people who penetrate beyond the headlines and people who stay in them. There are people who truly believe that the world is as it is presented by the daily news. It takes education to be well informed. One cannot be informed about everything, but we can at least be informed about a little beyond common ignorance. There are many people who are very misinformed."

Luis, wondering if he was part of that which Alejandro called the uninformed, told him: "What do you mean by common ignorance?"

"I mean that news agencies, newspapers, and magazines have an agenda. They don't always give you the news as it is. There are some more tendentious than others, and some that are more objective and real. Others twist things a lot.

"If we don't learn to read news with more judgment, we can be very ignorant."

"Give me an example, Alejandro," said Luis.

"Luis, tell me what you think: What's your opinion on Barack Obama?"

"Oh, Obama seems like a great guy to me. He is someone who is very graceful and has great charisma. Besides, he gets along great with his wife and seems to seek the good of the underprivileged. I have a very good impression of him."

"I imagined a probable answer like that, Luis. I think Obama has some good things, no doubt. I'm not going to judge his performance on economic and international policy matters. I understand that he had successes and failures, as foreign policy is not easy at all. I am going to touch on a much more serious and profound subject. It is incredible that many people say that he had good looks, good appearance, and that Michelle is also an elegant lady, and to jump from that to say: 'Obama was a great guy.' So little is known about how Obama created situations of violence in Syria and Afghanistan and contributed to the growth of the Islamic State. Many have no idea that he promoted the entire gender ideology from the White House, which promotes the marriage of people who are attracted to the same sex, as well as the adoption of children by same sex couples. In the field of abortion, he promoted the murder of many innocent children simply because of ideology, because of his political party or to be re-elected. In fact, he told Planned Parenthood, the world's largest abortion organization, 'I am committed to you. Thank you, Planned Parenthood, and God bless you.'"

"It is as if there were the world of the apparent and the world of complete and synthetic information. I say synthetic because it gathers all the data and takes into account various aspects that are fundamental, especially ethical and moral aspects that make the fabric of a society have virtues and values that promote the good of all. I'm not talking about the apparent good, but the real good."

"I had no idea about that Obama stuff," said Luis.

"But let's move on from Obama. That was just one example. In many fields that protect the needs of the most affected, in fields of protecting the family, which is where a child grows up healthy and safe; in fields of justice and not what comes from ideology, there are many people who do not cultivate their intellect."

"And how else, or in what other fields should intellect be cultivated?" Luis asked.

"Well, a third fundamental field is that of ethical and moral truth," Alejandro replied. I refer to the fact that there are fundamental ethical principles that the intellect of man must come to know. We all have engraved in our hearts an inner law, which we call the natural law, and which you have already heard me mention, that must be cultivated. We can call it the formation of consciousness. Sometimes we can have a good conversation more focused only on the conscience, because Pedro has told us a lot about this."

"Alright, but you talked about intelligence, and then you also talked about will. I can imagine what you will say to me, but what do you mean by will, to see if we are on the same page? I understand will as the strength to do something. Is that right?"

"Will is that," said Alejandro, "but I believe it is the spiritual faculty in every man to choose the good. We said yesterday that everything we do is in accordance with the nature of man. Well, if we do not do good, the will begins to become unbalanced. There are many people out there who do not know how to use the intellect properly in conjunction with the will. In reality, man is one. That is, whenever there is one, there is another. But they also work separately, because to give you an example, a sportsman may have had a lot of knowledge about how to play, but if he never practices, it is useless."

"The will is strengthened by having projects, dividing them into mini-projects, then these into tasks and finally into concrete actions. You know that nowadays efficiency is fundamental. If we do not know how to take dreams and projects from conception (in the mind), to execution (with the will), it is useless. We know the saying: it is useless to know what is good if we do not have the strength to pursue it."

"Wow," said Luis, "you're giving me a lecture and I need all those things. I do achieve things, but mostly those I like and those that I am forced to. I have not been very constant in life. In fact, I feel that I need to polish one as much as the other. I don't always feel confident in my actions. I ask myself: am I doing good? I'm not always clear on whether something is cheating or not, whether obtaining illegal copies of software is always wrong or only sometimes or never. Whether kissing with a girl in a bar isn't wrong if you don't have a girlfriend, or if it is actually wrong."

"Don't worry," said Alejandro, "that is why we are talking and advancing in the knowledge of the whole person, Luis," said Alejandro, with a tone of understanding.

"Remember one thing," Alejandro continued patiently. "What we are looking for in life is to form the trunk of the tree well so that it bears much fruit. So in everything we are doing we are seeking to see the parts of man and his capacities, separately, and then to integrate everything. The aim of everything is integration. A good man or woman who has achieved an integration of all that constitutes him or her, is one of those people whose personality attracts and enchants. Have you ever met someone like that?"

"Oh, of course. My uncle José Alberto is a great guy. He's my dad's brother. If you could see how he handles himself, how people love him, including his children... But, besides, when he is present at family gatherings, his presence inspires serene authority. In other words, he has everyone's respect for the peace and control he shows. Most of his business is done with many partners who simply trust his integrity as a person."

"I have an uncle like him," said Alejandro, "but I basically find that in my dad. There is no one I look up to more in life. My dad is all that I described to you."

"Alejandro," said Luis, "we have already seen the higher powers. And in order to understand how to achieve integration, we lack the other thing you mentioned: the lower powers. The question is not easy, as it requires discipline. In fact, I would like you to give me tips to advance in these two fields, but what are the lower powers?"

Emotivity and passions

"Ok, Luis," said Alejandro, "unlike the higher powers, these are the powers or faculties that can also be a super effective ally in life. But at the same time, they are the ones that, if you're not careful enough, cause all the havoc we see in today's world. There are many people who live as the song says: 'If it makes you happy, it can't be that bad.' It is incredible that some people think this way, but thousands live this way because they have lacked training. They have lacked good examples like your uncle José Alberto and my father. They are people who live fulfilling a duty and not doing what their bodies ask them to do."

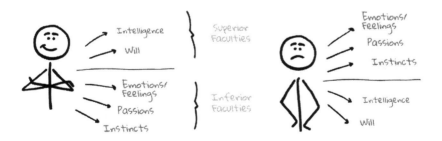

It is good to be aware of our superior and inferior faculties. It enables us to act with prudence and justice.

"Yes, wow," said Luis, "today the degeneration is total." I will not argue about that. But isn't God supposed to be love, love us, and want us to be happy?"

"No doubt," Alejandro replied "but the point is to know how to reach happiness. Happiness for some is to be free of any restrictions. Happiness is drinking all the bottles, smoking all the marijuana, and hooking up with all the girls. And tell me: do you think the world is happier today? Do you think there is a reason why there is so much depression, so many psychologists and so many suicides? People are not finding happiness through the path of misused freedom, which you know is called debauchery. Luis we can talk more about true happiness another day. I don't want to digress."

"Digress about what?"

"Well, we are talking about the lower powers of man. So, it is those faculties of man that require a boss, a manager, someone to guide and motivate them. They need to be directed rightly. In essence we can talk about three: emotions, passions, and instincts. You have to know how to educate the passions, emotions, and impulses or instincts."

"Emotions are usually temporary. We feel them now and not tomorrow. Sometimes we wake up very emotional, other times we are dry. The image that I have been given many times is that of emotions like a dry leaf on a tree that falls and is carried by the wind to where it blows."

"There are people who give much more importance to their emotions than is necessary. There are times when they cloud the mind. Sometimes they feel strong emotions and don't know what to do with them. They even act in such a way that if they feel this or that emotion, it is surely happening. Without realizing that sometimes what we feel is not only subjective, but that the person feels it because he or she is going through a bad time. That is to say, we cannot be carried away by emotions as a factor of decision."

"So, is having emotions or feeling emotions a bad thing?" asked Luis.

The person that does not build her character with a strong and decided will is often times prisoner of her own desires and whims.

"No, not at all. Neither instincts, nor emotions, nor feelings, in themselves, are bad. The only thing to remember is: they must be governed by intelligence and will. Otherwise, they can be bad. Think of these two sentences: 'The husband loves his wife passionately' and 'the killer used all his passion to end the life of his victim.' Two facts, both with passion. In the first, reason or intellect is telling him that using his passion to love his wife is a good thing. In the second, the person is using a passion of anger, a temporary emotion, to brutally end the life of his enemy."

"Alejandro, what differences do men usually have with respect to women in emotional matters?" asked Luis.

"Well, because of the difficulties you have with your girlfriend, you already know something about this. But in general, you can say that the woman has a very diverse and very comprehensive emotivity. They give to every human being something that a man hardly gives. They are the ones who bring every human being into the world. Their emotional world is wide, and they themselves say that this plays against them. They feel things in such strong ways that it can sometimes cloud the most rational thinking. But there are women who control it a lot and have reactions that are very similar to those of men."

"In the case of us men, you know how things work. We are generally less emotional. I am not saying that there are no emotional men, though. But we do tend to be more rational, we look for ideas and reasons for what we do and think. An emotional situation is usually less likely to bring us down. At the same time, this is why men need women so much in every home, because they bring the tenderness and detail that nourishes us so much. We men are more frugal and dry. We can therefore create less of an environment of unconditional love, since the woman is very relational and the man is more entrepreneurial and focused on concrete results. As I say, Luis, all this is generalized, with variations in each culture and place."

"And what difference do we find between the passions and the emotions?"

"There are passions that both men and animals have. Saint Thomas Aquinas, in the Summa Theologica, says that passions in man derive from his appetites for anger and sensuality, that is, from getting angry and sexual debauchery. And he says that wise men resist them, that is, they manage to control themselves."

"Let's see. These are the things that shock me about the Catholic Church. If God put them there, why does He then forbid us to use something He gave us?" asked Luis.

"When He originally gave them to us, the passions were not under the effect of original sin. With the sin of man, there was disintegration. That is why all the work of man, as we have said Luis, is to work to achieve integration in himself. Each person must struggle to reach a healthy integration of all that he or she is. A divided person is like a divided company, army, or team. He will lose for sure."

"In other words: sin brought confusion and weakness. Confusion occurs in intelligence and weakness in will. See how interesting this is? Our decision weakened the two higher powers, and these—we see it in the history of the Bible—are always being challenged by the lower powers. The one who is on a diet feels the instinct and passion to eat apple pie and has to work against it so as not to eat it. The sensual woman is willing to hook up with the guy who fascinates her and has to say with intelligence and will: 'no! I can't give myself to anyone like that any more.'"

"Luis, summarizing your question: God created us much more capable of doing good, but original sin has us in a kind of civil war. We are divided between what we should be and what we want to do. That is why St. Paul says in the letter to the Romans: 'but I see in my members another law at war with the law of my mind and making me captive to the law of sin which dwells in my members.'" (Rom 7:23 RSVCE)

"I will tell you this: passions can be used in thousands of directions in ways that do enormous good. Think of the passion of thousands of athletes, the passion of thousands of mothers in their work with their children, who are everything to them. Think also of the passion of hundreds of thousands of new inventions and businesses, projects, and advances that are made at every moment in time."

Luis felt again the coherence of what Alejandro was telling him, of how he was explaining with a lot of common sense all this knowledge. After a pause, he asked:

"Okay. You talked about a third lower power. What was it?"

"Yes, there is a third power which is instincts. Let's say that it is the most animal thing in man. It is the greatest primal impulse, without much resistance made by reason or will. Animals also have instincts."

"Let's see, Alejandro," said Luis. "Sometimes it is said that someone has a good instinct for tennis, or for business. You hear it a lot. Is that the bad instinct you're talking about?

"No, that's not it. Like many terms in life, there are different ways of speaking according to context. What I am referring to is instinct, better known as a very primary, very spontaneous impulse that often has to do, as with passions, with anger, the conservation of the species (use of the reproductive capacity), or self-defense."

"Oh, okay. So they are two different ways of understanding. I see."

"Yes, and that is why the important thing, Luis, is to know that when we talk about these three realities in each one of us, a question arises. In some people, especially in the past, like our grandparents, desires were considered a bad thing. It was thought: 'You don't have to live based on desire,' or 'desiring something is bad, it's a sin.' Some thought that desire should be suppressed. But there is something wonderful that John Paul II came to teach us."

"Desire is a sign of the greatness of man and woman. When you have a desire, it has been put there to satisfy it. A desire shows that there is a longing for greatness and eternity. Just look at what the Bible says in a psalm: 'And there is nothing upon earth that I desire besides thee.' (Ps 73:25 RSVCE). When the most common desires that we see in people, Luis, like having sex, eating, drinking, gambling, or dominating, appear, there is something about them that is very good. There is something about them that shows the appetite for the good, for what pleases, for what satisfies. The problem is that because of our limitation in knowing what is good in reality and in the long term, we want to satisfy our desire in the wrong way. When someone wants to have sex with someone else, or when they want to drink four or five beers, what they are looking for is something that someone put into their being: they are looking for connection, ecstasy, happiness, joy, and forgetting about problems. And all that is not bad, it is good."

"There it is. You are saying it. So why did you insist on sin, if all that is good?" asked Luis.

"Oh, because of something quite simple. Because there is a time for everything, a circumstance and a suitable person. Because man is not only instinctive. Not only has he received instincts, but he has received—."

"The higher powers," interrupted Luis, helping Alejandro respond.

"How did you know?" Alejandro said with a smile of satisfaction at the fact that Luis finished his sentence.

"That's right, Luis," Alejandro continued. "If everyone simply goes around letting emotions, passions, instincts and, with them, all desires come out of them without filter, then you already know what's happening. Those are called sick people. They have one vice after another. Man's nature was made to be guided by his reason. In the animal it is pure instinct. The dog does not commit a crime by biting, the shark by hunting, or the snake by poisoning. They only follow what they have been programmed to do. We do not."

The winds that blow

Luis was left thinking, restless, and with a feeling of being trapped. He felt again an annoyance because of the intrusion of this morality in his life. He didn't want a morality that he felt was imposed on him. He said:

"I don't know. I feel all this is too structured. As too artificial. I don't feel that the world agrees with many of these things. And the world can't be all bad."

"I understand your doubts, Luis. You don't have to agree overnight. You don't have to push the process of everything taking shape in you and making sense. We all take time to process new ideas. And I of course don't want to fight against your current thinking. Just think about how much we talked about in our first conversations about the truth. Is there or isn't there truth? And it doesn't matter that thousands of people say that white is black. All it takes is for the color expert to arrive and say, this is white."

"What I want to tell you is that yes, indeed the world today is not the most humanistic world there is. As I told you before, scientism has made us think little with wisdom and much with only science. And both have to be combined, because both come from the Creator."

"This generation has been criticized for its 'culture of the provisional'32. It is that culture that thinks that morals change, that what is worthwhile today, will not be so tomorrow. And in some things it is right, but in others it is not. I had thought that we would touch on issues of morality later, but at least now I am telling you that one cannot decide to make one's own moral reality."

"Alejandro, what if I say that there is no morality or that I don't agree with this scheme you are proposing?"

Alejandro was left thinking. Sometimes answering the most basic questions requires quite a bit of expertise. Then he said to his friend:

"Luis, you can feel free to think what you think. You know that in all these conversations I am only sharing with you my lifestyle and what I have been learning with Pedro in these classes. I feel like maybe it's not that your mind doesn't find truth in this, but rather that there are other reasons. Like there is resentment inside you and you resist understanding these things because of the rage it provokes in you that your parents didn't teach you much about this. But maybe they are not to blame. Don't blame them. Forgive them for what they didn't give you. But you and I are too young not to grow up on our own."

"Look, Luis, it is well known that sometimes we men do not accept what people tell us, not because we do not agree, but because humility is required to learn as we advance in life. Or because 'we don't want to accept to think differently, because it implies living differently.'"

Alejandro filled his words and his tone of voice with such patience and kindness towards his friend, that it was almost irresistible not to agree.

We don't want to yield to thinking differently, because it entails living differently.

There was a silence in both of them, and Luis made every effort to fathom with his mind his friend's well-constituted explanations. Everything seemed logical to him, full of truth!

"Look, Luis. We can't deny it. The current world brings us winds that blow in any direction and we are here to understand reality and ourselves."

"The winds that the world brings require discernment. It is like an obstacle course: I run freely on the track of life, I find obstacles or fences, I jump them or leave them aside, and I go on.

"There is a Calvin Klein ad that relates a lot with what I say: 'I speak my truth.' This way of thinking, which reminds us again of relativism, is not appropriate and is leading to enormous mental confusion. Again and again, we have to affirm that if there is no one way that is right, if all ways, all mentalities, all people have their own truth... it is useless to argue, to agree on what is good for everyone.

"Okay, okay... I think I'm moving forward and agreeing with you on that," said Luis. I do realize that sometimes I'm very stubborn and I get into this macho persona, and say things out of anger that sometimes I can't live up to as I would like to. But yes, I understand you, Alejandro; the world's trend in terms of thinking seems to be meaningless."

Both stayed silent for a moment and there was a sort of consensus that it was getting late before the next class. They had been talking for a little over forty-five minutes and Luis felt more structured in his desire to be able to work on himself, to become more human and more rational in solving the difficulties he was having at home.

"Well, what do you think I can start to do to apply some of this?

"I believe," said Alejandro, "that for now, begin to look for two things: the first, to have a clear mind as to what is the objective good that every person should live, and avoid evil. Get into habits of thinking and speaking well of others, and you will see that you will begin to see more and more clearly what is convenient, what is good and uplifts every human being. And the second, every Sunday, write down the three or four big tasks or goals that you want to finish in the week. Get them done, Luis. Don't be easy on yourself. Discipline, constancy, and clarity of mind. Thus. you will be forming your two higher powers: your intelligence and your will. And by the way, you will be defeating the lower ones."

"Remember that feelings can be good, and they can be bad. Let your actions be guided by these weekly goals, and keep them on your desk or with an alarm that reminds you of them on your cell phone. Everyone finds for a way. But it's about starting to do more of the good things in life, with discipline, and you'll see many other parts of life begin to fall into place. Do you like the idea?"

"That sounds great. I like it," said Luis.

"What are you doing this weekend?" Alejandro asked.

"I think we'll go to the farm. My cousins and grandparents are going too. So, quite a normal weekend."

"And is Sofia going?"

"No, she's going with her family to the beach. Besides, currently we are not on very good terms. We could use a weekend of rest."

They both took their things and headed for the exit, towards the parking lot.

ANALYZING THE CONVERSATION

These two friends have outlined a structure that is not new. The knowledge of the passions, emotions, reason, will... is as old as mankind. But the Greeks had a strong, forceful contribution.

Man has been seeking perfection since ancient times. Sometimes he seeks it in very suitable ways that have served as a basis for the construction of Christian civilization. Sometimes they have sought it with all kinds of excesses and deviations that have harmed the human being.

Alejandro made it clear: man must always act according to his reason. A quite solid conscience formed in accordance with the principles of right reason dictates to him what in fact he already has in his heart. Intelligence, like any human faculty, does not reach a point and already know everything without the possibility of discovering and going deeper. With God's light, one can always go more to the source in order to see with new eyes, with greater wisdom. This is what the Catholic tradition has called reason illuminated by faith.

Along with reason is the will. We will not repeat what Luis and Alejandro have already said. But we will say that these two faculties work together for the good of man. One can have one without the other. And in both cases, this is a great danger.

If a man or woman has an acute intelligence, a straightforward knowledge, but no strong will, he or she will know what to do, but does not have the right engine to carry it out. An image is that of a rider, an elephant, and a road. Reason represents the rider. Having it is important. But if the rider can't make the elephant which is the will, move, what's the point?

On the other hand, the elephant may be very strong and ready to move, but if the rider doesn't tell it to, it will stay still. This paralysis is a danger to everyone. Sometimes there are people who have an iron determination to box or to play billiards, but are unable to distinguish the right moment to do so.

And, finally, the road represents the truth and what is appropriate for each human being. I think we can agree that man's actions either nourish him or weaken him.

If I choose to study or work intensely, or decide to put it off until later when time runs out, it makes a difference. It makes the elephant fat and lazy. If there is no road better than another, you cannot get to a place that is worthwhile. It doesn't matter. It is indifferent. And that sadness is what we see around us. Well, sometimes we don't see it, because Facebook, Instagram, and Snapchat only show smiles. But we know. There are so many lives lost and floating so aimlessly in the vast sea of life.

Questions to think about:

1. Are you consciously attentive to strengthening and cultivating your higher powers? How do you do it? Where can we see that work?

2. On a scale of 1 to 10, how much does your week go by in the midst of feelings and passions?

3. What is missing for the world to recognize that not all theories and ways of living can be correct? Why is it difficult for it to recognize it and live according to a common line of good and evil?

Chapter 11:
The Power of the Mind

"Your mind is your greatest power. Use it well.".

Aneta Cruz.

It was Monday, and Luis and Alejandro always arrived with weekend experiences. Alejandro sometimes feared that Luis would arrive upset by things that had happened between him and his girl-friend, Sofia, and if not with her, because of his family where Luis' parents clearly did not have much wisdom in running a functional family.

As usual, Alejandro arrived at the meeting place, to the usual benches, the ones that were not even at a few hundred feet away from the 'Starbucks university.' This time they had both gone to get their coffee and donuts, and Luis could already be seen in the distance.

"Oh, oh!" Alejandro thought. He did not like the face Luis was making. He must have had some kind of argument with someone.

"What's up with that face, Luis?" Alejandro asked.

"Why do you think I have this expression?" he answered emo-tionless, as if he already knew what was going on.

"Problems with Sofia, or something?"

"Yes."

There was a silence between the two. Alejandro was quiet, drinking his coffee. He gave Luis some time to settle.

"It's just that there's no weekend without trouble, man! Women are such a hassle!"

"Calm down. Tell me what happened," Said Alejandro.

"She arrived unsure on Sunday, because she says that perhaps I was too comfortable with my cousins and her friends at the farm. I came back at her by telling her that she was probably dancing with someone on the beach. And from there we just kept the argument going and the thing escalated. We started to say things to each other that later hurt and we talked about how, if we keep this up, we'll have to give ourselves some time."

"Oh, boy. How often do you guys fight?"

"Every Monday that I have a talk with you," Luis smiled to diffuse the anger a little. "Because at the beginning of the relationship, the conflicts were not often. But recently, we fight a lot. I don't know, maybe once a week."

The strength of the mind

Alejandro had just started reading a book called 'Feeling good', by a psychologist of the behavioral area, a guy named David Burns, who has sold over four million copies. It was helping him a lot.

"Luis, I want to tell you about a book I just started. It is in synthesis a book that speaks to us of the power of our thoughts. It says something like: we seek to feel good. To feel good, we have to think well, because we feel in accordance with what we think. If we manage to tame the powerful force of the mind, we will be able to feel very well."

"I don't know," said Luis. "I think we can't fool ourselves in life. If something is going wrong, if I don't get along with Sofia, I can't do a magic trick and pretend nothing is happening."

"It is true. I don't think it's about fooling the mind. I would rather say that it is about acquiring a power to think more rationally, because we all have—in Dr. Burn's words—cognitive distortions. We all allow the mind to defeat itself. This is very evident."

"Have you noticed how in sport there is a very mental component? In games like tennis or golf, did you know that there are players who earn a lot of money and are dedicated to the mental part of the game? There's a guy named Bob Rotella, who in his book 'Golf is not a game of perfection', says: 'People in general become what they think of themselves.'33 In fact, Luis, this is part of the ideas we were talking about on Friday. The attitudes we have, which come from convictions, are the way of behaviors. Do you remember or have you already forgotten?"

"Now that you tell me, I might find it helpful to memorize it," said Luis. "I do remember that you said that the order is: convictions, attitudes, and behaviors. And I think I'm just getting good about how to make better decisions. Decisions would be the equivalent of behaviors, and so my focus has to be on convictions and attitudes."

"Wow, that's awesome!" Alejandro exclaimed. "Exactly, wow! Ben Shahar, a Jew who has been very successful in talking about happiness and how to think about our daily experiences, states the following: 'One of the most significant findings in psychology in the last twenty years is that people can choose the way they think.'34 He says that one day he was feeling very depressed and had two options: to feel depressed or to get passionately involved in his work. And this idea came to him: 'Once I made a choice, I changed my approach. By changing my focus, my whole mood changed.'35 And that's right, Luis. In every moment of life, we can choose."

"Henry Ford once said on this very subject: 'If you think you can or if you think you can't, you're right.' You decide. Choice is creation. To choose is to create. Through my choices, I create my own reality.

People in general
make of themselves
whatever they
think of themselves.

Both were passionate about the subject. They were very into it. Each one was eating their sandwich and analyzing the subject. Luis was smiling as he looked at the horizon, as he saw a new world opening up to him. A world more within his control, and less at the mercy of his feelings that come today and go tomorrow.

"One of the things I have learned from the book 'Feeling good', Luis, is that there are people who create hell for themselves in their daily lives, and others who find ways to be happy. A Mexican psychologist said it like this: 'There are people who have everything to be happy, but they are not happy.' He says it's about self-sabotage."

"What do you mean with self-sabotage?" asked Luis.

"He explains that it seems that in some people there are elements of their past, needs, wounds, and traumas so rooted that they don't see them, but they make people uncomfortable in life. People who seem to need to be victims, need the attention of others."

"Why does this happen to them? How can they prevent it?" asked Luis.

"There are multiple reasons," Alejandro answered, "but there are people who have not learned about the power of their mind. They have not learned that what impacts the level of satisfaction, peace, and serenity in their lives is how they use their mind to think about their experiences."

"Yes, but surely they don't want to be like that, Alejandro."

"Of course, no one is saying that they are necessarily to blame. In many, many cases, what happens is that they have blind spots. And they are called blind because, precisely, for them, that way of acting is normal. There's nothing wrong with that, there's nothing sickly about it. But let's leave that—because I love it and we can go into it so much deeper—for tomorrow."

"Now I want to show you something that has been a huge awakening for me. It is this reality that Dr. Burns says: 'It is not what happens that impacts us in life, but what we think about what happens to us.'

"No, no, no. I don't agree with that at all," replied Luis. "The problems that happen to us are real, not imaginary. If something is happening to us, you can't pretend, as I told you. I don't see that part the way you do."

"Look, let me put it this way. The way in which we interpret things is what makes them one way or the other. Of course, there is a fact, but we can control and guide how we interpret it or not."

"Imagine, for example, that a boy breaks up with a girl. If she doesn't have some confidence in herself, maybe her mind will lead her to depression. She will tell herself thoughts like: nobody wants me, nobody loves me, my friends are more attractive, I will never find the man of my life. But a girl with a healthy mind, with a healthy psychology, will know that the way she sees this situation makes all the difference. She could take another path: the break up hurts me, but it is not the end of the world. If he is the one for me, time will tell. If not, another good man will come, and so I will ask God to meet this man. And that's it."

"But there are situations that no matter how much you think about them and try to fix them, you will not feel good when they occur," Luis said.

"Sure, Luis, and here you give me the opportunity to explain. Think about this carefully: I'm not saying that life doesn't have real and clear problems. I am saying that the interpretation I make of them can help me grow or sink. Look at how the book I told you expresses it:"

"The first principle of cognitive therapy is that all your moods are created by your 'cognitions' or thoughts. Cognition refers to the way you look at things: your perceptions, mental attitudes, and beliefs."[36]

"This tells us that many of the negative emotions that we feel are a product of negative thinking. There is, in fact, a very good film that illustrates this, Luis. During World War II a group of women flee in a boat to Hawaii. Suddenly, they are intercepted by the

There are many people who live and decide according to their passions. In them, conscience and will do not play a fundamental role.

Japanese and taken to a concentration camp. In this camp, the film shows how one of the women lives hell, while another becomes a leader, living internally the freedom to think and decide how to approach each event of each day."

Luis started thinking about these new ideas that were stirring his mind; tickling his curiosity. He was processing subjects that were natural to him.

"Alejandro, this is very interesting. And I'm seeing that maybe at home, with my parents, there is some negativism. Maybe I'm not in the habit of thinking positively or turning what happens to me around. Things just happen to me, and I react."

"And it's okay that now you don't have the habit. But that's what we're talking about. You have to grow as a person. Do you remember to improve yourself? Well, now we are going from knowing ourselves to accepting ourselves and, later, to improving ourselves."

"It's about conceiving yourself as a project, as a task. You are a task for yourself in these fields of integration, of being more human. Just as it is your task to study what you study and then become a better professional. But let me tell you, these issues are much more important to me than the career, because they are the ones that save us from depression, family conflicts, abuse, divorces, and breakups—all these things that were never meant to happen."

"Yes, I guess that's why Sofia's parents are separated. There's a lot of dysfunction in their house too. I sometimes wonder if my parents will be together forever or not."

"Well, you have an incredible task there. Start with yourself. As part of personal growth, you need to have structure and discipline within."

Internal structure and discipline

"Let's see, where are you going now? What kind of structure and discipline?" Luis asked.

"Well, I would say that, in general, to begin with, our generation does not appreciate the term structure much. It sounds to us like rigidity, little freedom, intrusion into our lives. But in reality, the structure in ethics, in morals, in principles, in rules... we live it all the time. We do not realize it, but that's how it is."

"What would I say is structure and what is discipline? Structure seems to me like a scaffold. I also like the image of lockers in a post office. Many letters arrive—or situations and ideas—and the postman knows where to put them. There is structure. He knows that letters for a certain town go here, letters for a certain city go here, and discipline is the same, constant and persevering work of the postman. Socially, I see it this way."

"We walk through the streets with rules. The government gives us rules for living together. We don't bring guns to school because it's a law. We behave in certain way in our homes and society because the structures are a support for life. They are not there to

In life we encounter and produce many ideas and each one of us has the task of knowing where to store them. This is necessary in order to have discipline both mentally as in life.

restrict, but to drive. Perhaps we see the structure as something to be rejected, otherwise we are not authentic and free. But in reality, freedom is something more internal than external, and a soldier who is in a structure and follows rules is no less free. He exercises his freedom there in that structure, and it helps him."

"But a structure can make people rigid, right?" asked Luis.

"Of course it can. But that depends on the person. That's where being free inside comes in, enjoying the freedom that the structure gives you. When we think about external structures, if they are not accompanied by inner freedom, of course they become a burden. They are straitjackets that only enslave the person, and do not make them free."

"I give you an example that unfortunately happens every day. Two adult male friends get together for a beer. One says to the other: 'Hey, you have to go to dinner with your wife every Friday. Doesn't your wife let you go out with us?' To which he replies:

'That's not how it is, in the sense that is not as if I don't have a choice. I choose to be with her. Do I always feel like it? No, sometimes I might want to go out with my friends more than with her. But I have chosen to add discipline to the structure of my family and marriage life.'"

"That man, Luis, is freer than the one who goes to a cabaret with his friends and feels that he can do whatever he wants. The structure and disciplines he has chosen are the means that allow him to have true freedom. The freedom to say: I am faithful and firm with the decisions I made some time ago. No one imposes them on me but me. This is just because I am free. I am not a slave to my tastes and passions, or to what I crave."

"Would you say that is what many call maturity?" Luis asked.

"Yes. Maturity in a person is not about doing everything you want to do without being told. It consists in his integrating his freedom with what is convenient, and that usually requires a structure of values and principles that need discipline."

There was satisfaction in the air. They both felt that the foundations they had laid in previous conversations were now laying a firm surface to get down to business. After all, Luis was eager to live his life in a better way, to begin to integrate his life now that he was getting to know himself more. His greater knowledge of what his family was like, of the challenges they had in terms of training and education, now began to show him how to transform himself. He was beginning to see how he could not only know and accept the realities of his life and past, but also envision ways to improve.

"You know, Alejandro, I'm starting to feel a little bit of remorse."

Luis didn't speak for a few seconds. You could tell he wanted Alejandro to throw the question at him, and he did:

"Do you feel remorse, Luis? Let's see, why?"

"Because Sofia and I are always doing what we feel we should not do, we fail again and again. We often live as if we were a married couple. We have intercourse very often and then look at each other with a guilty face, only to do it again two days later. And we haven't had anyone to give us any advice."

"And, how do you think your relationship relates to what we're talking about?" Alejandro asked.

"Because of what you say, I see that we have neither structure nor discipline. On the one hand, we don't know—we only intuit—why that is not convenient. And even less do we have the discipline to avoid it. With the example of the guy you talked about before, when you said that he is free to do just what he sometimes does not want, you touched some sensibilities in me. Something tells me that it is so."

"I understand," Alejandro said. He wanted to leave a space for silence. He felt that Luis was processing something fundamental, and didn't want to interrupt the key moment. Some light was shining inside Luis.

"Alejandro, with your example of the lockers in a post office, let me get this straight. The lockers in people's lives, which correspond to the structure, are the clear ideas that make one think and live well, right? That is, knowing what things are more important than others, what to avoid, and what to do in life. How to live in a more dignified way. And, on the other hand, the act of putting the cards where they belong, that is the discipline we see in concrete behaviors."

Alejandro smiled at Luis with a smile of deep satisfaction. He was feeling the joy of seeing himself being an instrument to change a life, to accompany a friend who was clearly disoriented. If nothing changed, Alejandro knew that it would not be strange for Luis to fall into serious acts or depression. The light he saw in his eyes now was like a door opening.

Hierarchy of values and the meaning of life

"Another thing, Luis. In life you always have to have a hierarchy of values. What comes first? What is not so important and what can be this way or the other? What values are more fundamental than others? Not everything has the same importance. There are higher goods and more serious evils."

"Do you mean that there are acts that deviate and harm more than others?" Luis asked.

"Yes, later on, as I told you, we must talk about ethics. But for now, keep in mind the importance of a hierarchy of values needed in every person. Besides, all this gives meaning to life. Although usually this topic is the first thing to keep in mind—the meaning of life—I mention it now because it has come up in the conversation."

"A person who has no sense of life, is a person who will soon become depressed or suicidal. Passion is born from finding the substance of life. What am I passionate about? What mountain do I want to climb? What noble ideal does my nature call me to?"

"For now, the meaning of my life has been to finish my degree and be successful. Then see if Sofia and I are on the same page and get married or not."

"That's good," Alejandro replied. "Those two goals are part of the meaning of life. But I'm afraid you have to have something even bigger. Everyone discovers it. Just as a company is there to sell, and that's not wrong at all, but in its vision, mission, and goals, it goes beyond selling. Good companies, like good people, exist to transform lives. If you don't live to transform those around you, why live at all?"

"I would say that finishing the degree is a means for that, and the person with whom you want to live this adventure could be Sofia. Or perhaps you will make a decision on that in the future. But the goal of life is not to marry a particular person. Raise your mind and spirit and dedicate yourself to discovering what is the great dream that gives meaning to your whole life. Something that will fill you up completely and that humans cannot take away from you, and that no financial crisis can undo."

ANALYZING THE CONVERSATION

If we ask any person what the difference is between the human being and the rest of creation, he or she would tell us something similar to the fact that human beings have consciousness. Perhaps someone else would say that they have intelligence. Someone else out there would say that he or she is a being who makes reasonings on which he or she builds his or her knowledge.

They would all be right. The power of the mind has been emphasized by hundreds of authors. The power of the mind is enormous, to avoid saying infinite, because that does not correspond to the human being. We learn from each other, and together we are advancing towards increasingly sustainable development.

Much of what we achieve in life depends on how we train our minds. What we think, what we allow in, the attitudes we discipline ourselves to have. There is no doubt that there are individuals, families, and societies that have learned not to see the black dot on the white wall, people that know how to focus on that which does not diminish the person's energies to continue dreaming and aspiring to the highest that their being can conceive and conquer.

To achieve that you have to be rigorous. You have to follow the methods and principles that have worked. How wonderful it is that people who were not born with too high of an IQ have great achievements! A historical example, among thousands, is Demosthenes, considered one of the best orators of all time. The truth is that he was born with a terrible stutter.

If we manage to put a clear hierarchy of values in our life, if we can identify the activities that will be carriers of satisfaction and achievement in life, the repetition of them will achieve the prize. Let's not forget that drops of water constantly in action break the most solid stones..

Questions to think about:

1. Do you recognize the power of your mind and that it is responsible for what you have achieved or not achieved, both for better and for worse?

2. Let's talk about inner discipline: In which field are you strong, and in which do you have a lot to work on?

3. If you were to write down the five activities that are most important to you, would they coincide in that order with the amount of time you spend on them?

Chapter 12:
Healing your Whole Being

"Love heals. Healing is an integral part of human love. Where love is, healing is happening all the time".

Bob Schuchts

They both arrived at the same time in the pews. They were both very motivated by the topic they had agreed to discuss today. In Alejandro's case, he was moving forward and introducing his friend to what he wanted so badly for him: integration. Integration which, as we have seen, is the opposite of being alive, as if dragged in all directions. Integration is the strengthening of the trunk of one's "tree of life". Alejandro felt that in Luis' life, for various reasons, there were many loose cables, many aspects of his life that were not in harmony with each other. He felt that he could contribute a lot to Luis' life by talking to him about healing.

"What's up, Alejandro?" Luis asked.

"Hey, Luis, how's it going?" Alejandro said.

"All right," said Alejandro, settling into the usual part where he liked to approach the subjects.

"Yesterday you said you wanted to talk about the wounds that people carry on their backs, and from which no one is free."

"Well, Alejandro," Luis said, "that stuff about everyone being hurt, it doesn't ring a bell. I'm not. People are hurt, but a lot of

197

people aren't. I do consider myself among those who have some things unresolved, I suppose, but there are many people who are perfect or almost perfect."

Alejandro did not respond immediately. He knew he was now entering holy ground. The subject was immense and he could have begun in any of a thousand ways. He did it with a soft, slow and understanding tone, as if he only wanted to propose and make himself heard, without imposing:

"Luis, look. If there's one broad topic in life, it's this one of human wounds. It's like an ocean. You don't finish it. But we can't keep moving forward in our quest for fulfillment and happiness without this theme. And although we can't in any way exhaust every detail, since I myself have a thousand things to learn and I am still learning, we are going to launch ourselves."

"Luis, tell me, do you know anyone who has problems with their parents? Who would like to share more family time? Any girl who has given everything to her boyfriend and then cut the relationship off?

Someone who has suffered from bullying because of their physical appearance? Or even if we go deeper... do you know of any cases of an abused friend? We all have injuries, some more visible than others, we're afraid to talk about them, to tell about them, to admit to them... but they're there."

"The first thing I tell you is that survey after survey that comes out about suicides, depressions, and stress levels in the world, confirms that humanity is very wounded. The levels that are being experienced today are very high. In fact, you know that here at the university we've had two suicides in the last six months."

Luis was curious. "Ok, sure. The world is not having a good time is clear. But to what do they say these facts are attributed?"

"About the causes of suicides, there isn't one. There are many. There is almost no field of life that is not multi-causal. But I'm going to get a little philosophical, or I should say, theological. Well, a little of both. There's a line by Pope Benedict XVI that was put on the screen the other day that blew my mind, impressed me. He said this."

Healing, every man's way

'Understood at a sufficiently deep level, healing is an essential part of the whole Christian journey.'37

"Look carefully, Luis, at what he's saying. He is saying that the whole Christian way, the whole journey of man in this world, is a way of healing. If you're wondering where I get this, it's from an intensive course I took on a weekend in Florida. It's about healing. I took a lot of notes. My dad went to one of these courses, and recommended I go. But let's keep going."

"Look, everyone has a very deep longing to reach a state of wholeness that they believe is possible to achieve. It's a state of great peace, serenity, love and a sense that 'here I can't ask for anything more.' Many authors say that this is a longing for a return to fullness with God. That is a principle line."

"In the course at the beginning, the main speaker said that when God created man, everything was in harmony. Before the great fall of man, everything was in union with God and complete health. When man fell into sin, there was a great rupture, a great crack that was generated in existence. That's what we call, you know, original sin. You can read about it carefully in the book of Genesis, chapter three. Man, made in the image and likeness of God, voluntarily separated himself from his Creator and began a journey of pain and fatigue, even of ignorance."

"Alejandro, but again, we're getting into things of faith. Not everyone believes this."

"Yes, all right. I agree that it is part of God's revelation, but I tell you two things: let me go and explain it to you and you see if we can make sense of it. But more than that, look at your own human experience and see for yourself how you absorb it. I am convinced, as I told you before, that the Revelation of God to man comes and connects with human nature, since the same God who brought the people of Israel out of Egypt, that same God is the one who created the world. In other words, the God of the universe is the God of the Christians. The God of the Bible is the only one who exists. But then you'll tell me if this makes sense, just like when start putting together the pieces to a riddle."

"I was telling you that man was made by God to delight in the great dignity he received. Each one is precious and perfect for God. But when man decided to turn away from God, that's when the difficulty began. We are made for God, and when we turn away from Him, we begin to feel limited. I would say, we began to move away from our center, from the most intimate nucleus of each one of us."

"The harmony of creation was broken, and then in the heart of every man and woman a kind of storm began. An inner restlessness came over man. An inability to feel full and at peace with himself. Something was missing. Having been created for the love of the Heavenly Father, without that love man began to lose himself. Every difficulty, in the end, can be summed up in the absence of God in the person. Where the person is not full of God, in those aspects there will be difficulties. This seems too simplistic, but I am convinced that, if we possessed God fully, we would lack nothing. Saint Teresa of Jesus said in a poem: 'He who has God lacks nothing. God alone is enough.'

"Let's see, Alejandro, give me a more concrete example," Luis said.

"Well, let's see," Alejandro replied. "If in your imagination you don't have God, then surely what you are going to imagine in life is going to be imperfect. If in your will you don't have God, the things you will seek to do will not be those God calls you to. Where God is not found in man's intentions, history has shown that man generates other gods. We make idols of so many things to which we devote too much time. That is why atheist regimes, like communism, generate deep meaninglessness, absence of deep joy and social confusion."

"Do you think it's that rigid, that if you don't have God, you begin to do bad things automatically?" Luis asked.

"What I mean," said Alejandro, "is that when a man's heart, which is made for God, is not taken from God, he must look for other things to fill it for the time being. Those are the idols of this world. Let's see, Luis, tell me:

What are the most common attractions of every human being? What do you dream about and what do you do with your money?"

"Normally the obsessions of the world are sex, money, power and endless life. But I know people who don't abuse those things and live more moderately."

"We agree. These people have found in faith, through experience, that throwing themselves at creatures does not do them any good. They have a sense of what to do and what to avoid that comes from God."

Injured Travelers

They both took a pause. As they paused for a few seconds, they each took a drink and a snack to give themselves some time to think. Now it was time to continue building, to continue sharing their ideas and perceptions of this issue of wounds and human life.

"Look at an image that's served me well, Luis. When a boat is thrown into the water after it has been built in the yard, it is safer in the port. But the boat wasn't made for the port. It was made for the sea. There, when it leaves, it will inevitably start to suffer. The sea water, the winds, the waves, they will all tear at it. The same as with a car. No matter how perfect the road is."

"Even though we are going through a country like Switzerland, every car that takes to the road can't help but start to get dirty."

"Well, let's apply that to us. The wounds of life come to us, as we have said, from many sides. If you recall our conversation earlier, one source of injury is undoubtedly the family. We said there are families that nurture and others that don't."

"Yes, and I recognized that mine is one that nourishes little," Luis said.

Alejandro looked at him with affection, and did not say so in his commentary, because he wanted little by little to make Luis see that he had to be grateful for the great good that his parents surely gave him. He simply continued:

"In addition to the family, then we started to be independent. We didn't always make the best decisions. Maybe bad friends when we were innocent affected us somehow. Maybe there was an experience of physical or psychological abuse, an uncle or aunt who wanted to touch us inappropriately, maybe a combination of factors. Let's sum it up in family and experiences."

"The fact is, we have injuries and we're not entirely healthy. The greatest proof is that at least at various times in our week, in our life, we feel that 'something is not filling us.' There is a longing for something more. It is the eternal dissatisfaction that we feel here in life."

"Well, let's talk about those traumas. There's an author who also calls them "poorly processed memories." Let me explain. In life, we all live through a thousand things. For some reason, perhaps a great majority of those experiences don't cause us any trauma, don't cause us any injuries. But we can also recognize that there are some things we don't want to talk about. Others we don't even detect that they hurt us, but that's it: something is wrong. Others may notice and say: he or she is very painful. Or they say things like: "He has an explosive character. And you know what? There's nothing scientific about that description. What if with a thorough review, of the person, with spirituality and therapy, we could give a name to this wound?"

In life, we need to have someone to accompany us.

"What if we could identify that there was an experience or series of experiences in their growth that made them who they are today?"

"Wow! This really makes me think a lot," Luis said.

"So, what you're saying is that many strange attitudes in people which we think are part of their personality, can actually be overcome with help and a conscious process. That is to say, what can we show more precisely that makes those rare attitudes come out?"

"Of course, Luis. It is very common, for example, that some men marry their girlfriend and find something strange at the time of intimacy. They suddenly feel a rejection when they're most bringing their physical love—you know, making love—and they start thinking things that have nothing to do with it: Has she been unfaithful to me? Doesn't she like me? And you know, the fact is that the poor thing was raped by an uncle or an acquaintance fifteen years earlier. It's sad, but she never said anything to anyone."

Luis looked at Alejandro with eyes of impression for finding so much light in this.

"Another example, Luis, and a very common one, is that man who saw for a long time his father being patriarchal and dominant in his house. No one ever put a name to that attitude. He, during many years of adolescence and adulthood, only saw his father treat his mother that way. No one ever talked to him about doing a healthy analysis and putting a name to his dad's attitudes. Maybe his dad had a dad who was an obsessive, domineering man. And that's passed on from generation to generation. So, he marries his wife, and in the relationship after the honeymoon, he subconsciously repeats his dad's exact patterns. You know what I mean?"

"I mean, are we called upon to repeat our parents' ways, Alejandro?"

"No. Let's get this straight. We are NOT called to repeat, in the sense that no one calls us to that. But there is a certain proclivity, an inclination. If we do not detect in ourselves those wounds, those blind spots, it is certain that we will end up repeating the negative things of our parents. Moreover, we will repeat them and say: "That's me, and you have to respect me". Or there are couples who believe that perfecting oneself in life, fighting to be a better person, to grow in virtue and to heal the wounds and vices of life is to want to change the other person. And here we must always have counselors, because there are fields in life that must be accepted from the other, but the mediocrity of the other can never be accepted, because if you love someone, love demands, motivates and drives the other to be the best that he or she can be."

"Let me get this straight," Luis said. "We are not conditioned to repeat our parents' attitudes, right? But there is a kind of natural imitation by children of their parents that later must be revised maturely to remove what are family defects. They are those things that characterize us and that can be buried once and for all, if we know how to recognize the phrase that you told me from Pope Benedict: a whole life is about healing us of the errors and wounds that come, whether from the past or the present."

"Perfect, Luis. Just like that. I think I explained it to you well and you got it very well. Let me dig a little deeper. Have you noticed how people's eyes show you the health of the soul or not? People's eyes are usually like a window to the soul. And when you go to mental hospitals, when you go to a prison or to places where people are suffering, their gaze tells you everything. Similarly, and in the opposite sense, when we find men or women full of light, that is seen in their eyes, a clean, pure, bright gaze."

"A great family friend of mine who is a neurosurgeon and at the same time a mechanical engineer, and very Catholic, says a lot in his conversations that more than half of his patients' problems are of the soul. Wounds of the soul affect the body. As they say, problems become somaticized, that is, they manifest themselves in the body. Take a good look at your experience and you will see if this is true."

"Yes, now that you mention it, it sounds like it. My dad's brother just has serious health problems and his life has been a real mess since he cheated on my aunt and walked out on the family. It seems like body and soul are intimately connected."

"Exactly. When traumas are left unattended, they create holes in our souls that can eventually damage our bodies and spirits in significant ways. These wounds become part of our everyday language and reveal the effects of sin in our lives."

Knowing you are loved

"Alejandro, how should we go about healing those wounds and enjoying better health, both in body and soul?" Luis asked.

"Look, let's go to the depths of the human being. "What is the greatest need that exists in every man?"

"Ah, I know that answer. To love and be loved," Luis said.

"Good. Yeah, fair enough. We can't live without love. Especially if we think of life, not just as the present life, but the life within, which includes eternal life. We are not beings to live only on Earth. We have an immortal soul. We will live after death. Well, since we were created by love, with love, and for love, the essence of healing is to know that we are loved."

"How the external beauty of a girl or a man changes when they start dating the person they like! Insecurities become assurances. Their complexes disappear, the smile comes out, their walk is firmer and safer. When a person knows that he is in the heart of another person to whom he gives importance, everything changes. Everything!"

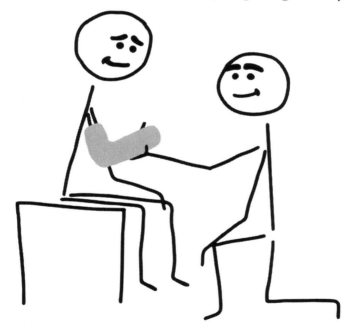

The life in a Christian entails being
attentive to one's own wounds.

"Yes, there's nothing like when the girl you like also shows you that she likes you."

"Yes, but let's go deeper, Luis. A girl will not last forever. We often like them before we get married. But even so, when you get married, one of two things happens: either one of us dies or that person is not enough. Why? Because no matter how much love there is, we are not meant to be completely satisfied with each other. Again, it is only the love of God, for whom we were created, that defines us."

"When we know that we are loved by the Father in Heaven, when we know that there is someone who cannot be fond of trivial or foolish things; when we know that someone who knows all the truth, including all my limits and sins still says to me, 'I am always with you'—that is the foundation of a person's health."

"Alejandro, but many people are healthy and don't believe in God.

That cannot be the foundation and reason for health," Luis said.

"Yes, all right. Many people are healthy. And that's possible, because in human love we can find traces of God's love. A person who does not believe in God can surely find someone who loves him, and that love will be his strength. I don't dispute that. What I'm saying is that, one day, that human love will be lost. That's for sure too. And what will he have left? He will have the love of the one who is life itself, the eternal one, the one who will always be with you. That is why, Luis, to be a Christian is an undeserved gift. For the one who loves best, the one who created love itself, the one who is the source of all kinds of love existing among men, that one tells you: 'You are my beloved son, in whom I rejoice to the death.'"

"There will not be, then, Luis, a safer and more healing love than God's love, which gives each of us the assurance that our worth does not depend on the humans who are there today and not tomorrow, humans who are faithful today and unfaithful tomorrow. God's love is stronger than death, as Pope Francis has said so clearly."

Luis and Alejandro kept quiet for a while. The intensity and the subject forced them to slow down. The cool morning wind and a few faint rays of sun caressed each one in a unique and particular way. The silence gave a new air to their conversion.

Unconditional love

"One last thought, Luis, is crucial. There are wounded areas in life that were never loved in an unconditional way. When a mother or father says to their son or daughter, 'I don't love you when you do this,' because they got bad grades, or because they got in trouble, what message do they send?"

"I guess the message that there are times when they're wanted and times when they're not," Luis replied.

"Right. That love is a conditioned love. It's not unconditional. If you do this, if you win my love, I will love you. But you have to win it. That is perhaps the greatest generator of emotional illness and dysfunction in life."

"Children, Luis, spend their whole lives deserving the love of their parents. They don't feel loved just for being, for existing. Their love will be based on achievement, on reaching a goal, on conquering some summit, many times they don't even want to. It's a daddy's peak. It's not theirs. Do you have a goal of your own or do you live with goals of your parents?"

Luis kept thinking and couldn't answer. His eyes filled with tears, and one of them ran down his cheek. Alejandro was sorry for having caused that emotional moment. In order not to cause more difficulty, he continued with his thoughts.

"Well, Luis, many of the family difficulties in every home are because those adults are actually injured children. They have learned only one way to live: I am worth what I conquer. I am worth what I achieve. I am worth what I prove I am worth. I am not loved just for living. I have to conquer that love."

"And if you look at it, a very common consequence is perfectionism and rigidity that breaks the harmony of homes. Why? Because the obsession of life, the aim of everything is to achieve my worth. We all have such a need to be loved that we will do anything to be loved, even if it means hurting or breaking up with others. For our greatest objective, which is really a distortion, is the external, that goal, that career or that business. Without that, the person is worthless, according to those criteria."

"One of Jesus' parables, that of the prodigal son, speaks of the cancer of the eldest son. The eldest son justifies himself before the Father. He says, "I have always done everything you ask of me. He was surely a wounded son, someone who felt he had to earn his father's love. And he was there believing that his worth depended on his accomplishments. It is a wound that is very difficult to uproot, because man gets used to working in everything to seek to be loved. He is not free. He is not autonomous. He has not achieved the integration of his being."

Alejandro left a silence before the emotional situation that Luis was discovering. Alejandro hoped that with this he was achieving an opening, a great discovery for his friend. He just asked him:

"Luis, does all this make sense to you?"

Luis did not respond immediately. He was moved.

"Yes. Not only does it look familiar, but it's the description of my house. All of us kids might be living in that kind of tension. The problems between my parents and the way they conceive life are like this: obsessive perfectionism. And that stresses and creates a lot of our fights."

"The key for you and me, Luis, because we can all feel this, is to know that we are loved by the Father. To know that there is a God who looks at us with an eternal gaze. And do not forget something that the Gospel says: 'God so loved the world that he sent his only Son, so that everyone who believes might not perish but have eternal life.'" (Jn 3:16)

"It's almost time to go. We can't see each other tomorrow, but let's get on with this wounding thing or close the subject on Thursday, shall we?"

Alejandro patted Luis on the shoulder.

Luis nodded. There was a growing bond between these two friends who in three weeks of conversations had already gone far in their exploration of life. A solid life. A life founded on rock.

There was the traditional farewell, this time with a big hug, and both went off to their class.

ANALYZING THE CONVERSATION

A few years ago, psychology had a bad reputation in the world. Going to a psychologist was something strange, something embarrassing that should be hidden. Maybe there's a good reason for that. The first modern psychologists like Jung, Spencer and Freud raised many doubts about their methods.

However, the Church itself has discovered the need for good psychology. Why has it discovered this? Because of a very solid principle that the Church has always upheld: grace (from God) presupposes (human) nature. In other words, when the

foundations of a house, when the basic nature of a man, are weak, it is of little use to ask for miracles. God ordinarily acts on a platform.

If a human being has great wounds in his spirit and soul, his work to live harmoniously with himself and with others will not come from praying alone. Of course, God is capable of everything in a soul, but ordinarily he uses what he has at his disposal. He respects the same laws of life, the real situations of the families and the hurtful experiences that each one has lived. And on that basis, working both in human nature and with the grace of God that comes into the life of the believer through prayer and the sacraments, then God can build on rock.

Every human being must be open to perfection. That perfection involves opening the chest and allowing the doctor to enter. But no one is a good doctor of himself. And that is where good psychology, together with the Christian faith, which is healing, can repair the damage.

The depressions and stresses of modern life that are increasingly plaguing our surroundings and families come by the great crash of life's waves to our boat. We sail without realizing it through more dangerous, harmful seas. Above all, pornography and social media have given a new shape to social life and human relations.

Pornography, on the other hand, has come to objectify and destroy something so essential to the complete health of the human being, as is the capacity to love and give oneself generously within marriage. Both men and women today have become objects of desire of the opposite sex (and, to an even greater detriment, of the same sex), and since they are not meant to be used, but to be loved, they eventually feel a huge void in the connection with others. Friendships have become less personal, and many of the good requirements of meeting in person, of expressing oneself by showing one's face, of courting women

being present, and many other effects, have been manufacturing a much more fragile human being. A human being that needs more attention. Hence, constant healing becomes necessary.

If we succeed in putting true love at the center of the society, we can resist the intrusion of pornography and social media. It is not a question of becoming obsessed or seeing grow in everyone and in all behavior, but it is a question of accepting that today we are much more exposed to the bombardment of a world that no longer carries Christian seeds in its winds. It is a neo-pagan world, with new ideas that are not in favor of man, but against him.

Healing, then, will have to be a subject to which one turns consciously, and then, when one has succeeded in polishing the effects of the present world, look ahead to living with strength, decision and perseverance the conquest of virtue. We will talk about this in the third part of the book.

Questions to think about:

1. Do you recognize that in you there are unprocessed memories, memories that do not allow you to advance on the path of peace and fulfillment? Can you call them wounds?

2. Could you spend about five minutes differentiating between the wounds you have acquired in your home and those you have acquired on your own?

3. Do you notice in your home that there was unconditional love, or have you had to fight to conquer the love of those who matter most in your life—your parents?

Chapter 13:
Our Blind Spots and Freedom

*"We come to know ourselves and our place in the love of others
in the human family, and ultimately in the love of God"*

Leanne Payne

On Thursday morning, with the same enthusiasm that brought them to their meeting place, Luis and Alejandro met.

Alejandro didn't want to let go of what he had noticed at the last sit-down together. He remembered how Luis had become emotional on Tuesday, just as he had brought up the subject of homes where unconditional love did not exist or existed in very limited ways. He felt and could tell that he had touched a sensitive key in his friend. And he didn't want to let it go this time. He wanted to find out how he could help Luis.

"How are you, Luis?" asked Alejandro.

"Alejandro, what about you? How are you doing?" Luis asked.

"Well, everything's going smoothly. Here we go now, getting closer to a partial exam, right? You, do you have any soon?"

"Yes, said Luis, "in fact, next week I have two and the week after that two more. But I feel that I'm more or less getting along."

Alejandro opened his bag of potato chips and began to eat a little. He hadn't eaten much breakfast and today was his day of junk food. Luis saw them and licked his lips, to which Alejandro responded by stretching out his bag of potato chips to share. Luis in turn got his tomato juice, the one he liked so much and they started the conversation.

"Luis, you've brought up something strange recently. You're worried about something. What's going on with you?"

"Yes, I think so," said Luis, giving a space to finish his chips. More than unconditional love, when you described homes where everyone is required to be perfect, to have no faults and a spirit of constant pressure and tension, for the first time it was as if I were being shown a stained picture of my home. I saw it clearly."

Stiffness and disorders in the home

"Luis, do you remember when we were talking about all this healing stuff yesterday? Well, I have a friend with whom I have resolved many doubts in this field. I couldn't get my hands on you the way I wanted to. And yesterday I told him that you and I talked a lot and that probably today we would enter more fully into these issues. The truth is that this guy is very wise. He told me that he loves to share his experience. I just told him the basics of our conversations and a little bit about you."

"Yeah, why not? I mean, you're saying that he could come right now and all three of us could talk?"

"Yes, of course. You can really trust my recommendation."

Luis thought for a moment, and then he said, "Go ahead. Sure. Tell him to come. Is he available now?"

"Yes. I'll text him." Alejandro took his cell phone and texted his friend. In three minutes he was there. When he arrived, Luis was surprised, but tried to hide his surprise.

"Father Andrew, how are you? Thanks for coming," said Alejandro. "Let me introduce Luis, who I told you I was having these conversations with."

"How do you do, Luis? I'm a friend of Alejandro's and a chaplain here at the university. I come here four or five days a week. I have my office in building C. So this is where all that philosophy comes out between you?"

Luis was still puzzled that Alejandro had brought a priest to this conversation. However he was attracted by his personality. Pretending to be normal, he reached out his hand:

"Hello, Father. Well, yes, we've been talking about subjects for a few weeks now that I haven't had anyone to talk to about for a long time. There are not many friends who care or even know about these subjects, and Alejandro has been very wise in my thousands of doubts."

"Father Andrew," Alejandro said, "I took the liberty of inviting you, because Luis and I have been discovering and talking about the subject of the wounds we carry in our lives, and how to heal ourselves from that so as not to go around depressed or tempted to commit suicide. Every time it happens, many of our colleagues and friends talk about it as something too close."

The priest looked at Alejandro with an affable smile, then he looked at Luis, and with a penetrating and soft look at the same time, he told him:

"Luis, I've been helping young and not-so-young people with their lives, their difficulties and weaknesses for nearly 20 years. Nothing should frighten us. We all have things. We are all fragile. I am happy to accompany you in these conversations, in the subjects that where I can enlighten you."

Luis responded quickly, prompted by a first impression of confidence given by Father Andrew: "Thank you, really, Father. Well, let's see, I'll tell you."

"My house is not a very functional place. In Alejandro's words, it's not a nurturing home. Among other things, my dad has an obsession with work, because he is a perfectionist, and when he comes home, that becomes his new area to pursue perfection at all costs. We all get stressed out, and everyone starts putting on their best face, not the one they have, but posing for my dad. My mom somehow gets into the same game, and my dad's compulsion makes the mood stiff."

"That makes peace reign as long as there is nothing out of place, no broken glass, no human error. Everything has to be almost perfect. It's my dad's eternal dissatisfaction, because now that I think about it, he didn't get that from my grandparents himself."

"Yes, Luis. I understand, and I am sorry," said Father Andrew. "I've seen that in some homes. I see that you describe something similar. I'll tell you some things. I can only accompany you, and at the same time thank God for putting you in my way. I know that kind of situation. Some people do, some people don't. But in every home there are things for improvement. Everywhere there are at least minor tensions."

"Yes, wow," said Luis. "The truth is, now this is starting to give me clues to things I have. I realize that I'm always like a kid who feels he needs to jump higher to meet my dad's expectations. And that makes me insecure and I think it's affecting me with Sofia, who's my girlfriend. I treat her according to these insecurities. I'm pushing her to be perfect. She can't be wrong about anything, I get angry, and then we fight. I keep telling her about my dad."

Alejandro intervened, "Well, shall I tell you something? I'm so glad we're talking about this now. Do you realize how healthy it is now that we're still young and you can see those blind spots, seek help, and not bring those things to the table of your future marriage? The problem is when someone realizes that already in the marriage and they are to proud to change. If you're already in a marriage and you have some humility, there's a solution. But right now you can take this as something you can make better, check, and also you can see if this girl has what you are looking for and and are willing to endure with patience."

There was a pause in the conversation. On Alejandro's side, there was great satisfaction. He said to himself internally, "Well, this is paying off!" And Luis, on his side, felt like his own friend was really a doorway to the light. The priest observed the good synergy between the friends.

Blind spots

"Several times Alejandro," said Luis looking at Father Andrew, "has mentioned the subject that we can all have blind spots. What do you know about blind spots? Tell me more about it."

"Yes, well, blind spots are, I would say, things that we do not see about ourselves, and others have to tell us that we act in such and such a way, because we do not see them. And we come to see that no one is the best judge of his own cause, no one is a good doctor

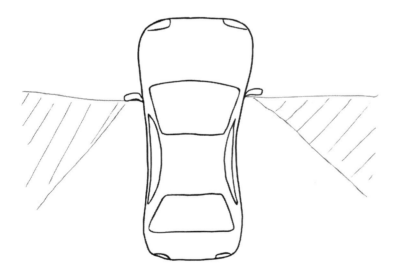

As in a car there are blind spots, in each person as well. They are "blind" precisely because the one who does not see them is the person himself.

of himself. We need other doctors. In a sense, a blind spot is something I discover through another person who points it out to me."

"Many times we go through life believing in an image of ourselves that is not real. Everyone sees us one way, and we another. And God has to wait, our beloved people have to wait years until something breaks that mold. There is some light. And many times that light doesn't come except with pain. The human being—he doesn't usually learn much from the good times. He learns much more when it suffers."

"Give me examples of common blind spots, or if you, Alejandro, notice something in me, show it to me," said Luis to both of them.

"So," father said, "these are the examples you were saying about your house. Your father's pressures make you dissatisfied with everything, and it sticks to you. And when you demand things of your girlfriend, you probably do it believing that you are asking for fair things. But for her maybe—and I invite you to have this conversation with her—these are silly things or things that aren't worth discussing, because they're of little relevance. Those points are blind to you, because when you react you probably do so thinking that you are being objective, that what you are claiming is legitimate. But you see, it gives you problems."

"Another example is often when we project things onto others that we do. Perhaps sometimes a blind spot can be that we are offended by everything. We are so sensitive that someone says something to us that they don't mean to, or they say it spontaneously, and we are already doubting our whole personality: 'Could it be that I am a failure, could it be that I always cause these reactions in others?' And so, we go through a sea of doubts and thoughts."

"Okay," said Luis. "I was thinking about all this. And how do you remove those blind spots? What do you have to do to not have them?"

"Well, taking them off completely may be impossible," said Father Andrw. "But they can be drastically reduced. If a person starts by picking up his weakness, his fragility—and you know, Luis, that is impossible without a dose of humility—then he is on the right track. Starting with language is very helpful. I'll give you examples."

"If I start talking and arguing by putting in phrases like 'in my humble opinion', 'it seems to me', 'I don't know if I'll think differently later, but at least now what I think is...' or even 'I could be wrong, but I understand that...' The problem is the phrases that, we don't even discuss them, because they no longer leave room for objection. They generate fear in us. There are people with such arrogance that they pontificate, they are categorical and their ways of seeing seem to be the only ones. So, start with the way they speak."

"Yes, I think if the listener hears that there's moderation, that always encourages openness. What else can you think of?"

"Another important element is to live by checking yourself. Whoever checks himself and makes examinations of conscience and attitudes, that person will constantly see how he or she could have improved and gets used to the fact that just as he or she finds faults in himself, others see them too, and perhaps even bigger ones. So, making examinations of conscience, taking moments of silence to check oneself."

"Do you do that?" Luis asked Alejandro.

"Yes," said Alejandro, "the truth is that every day, before going to sleep, I spend five to ten minutes to review a little bit how I have lived. That's something Father Andrew recommended to me. I turn it into prayer, talking to God about it. But there are people who benefit only from reviewing themselves in the light of their own conscience. You choose the way. I recommend that that might be one way you fly, and you're going to get closer to God. It's very effective."

"And then, as I told you in a previous conversation, you can also remove blind spots with people who love you if you open the door of your soul to be told when you see things that only they see, and you don't. A friend, or a good spiritual director or psychologist, are instruments that do this. They have attended to so many people that they can see how what one does is similar to other cases they have treated and perhaps they have already seen how to solve the issue. Father Andrew serves many young people and sometimes adults. His presence has been key for me."

"I don't know," said Luis. "Father, it seems to me that we can do a lot of this, but at the same time I feel a little bit of I don't know what, like rejection. Sometimes it seems to me that it's a woman's thing. Walking around all day being vulnerable and telling people your faults and insecurities. I think that's debilitating. Don't you?"

"I understand the feeling, said father. "Yes, you can pray like that. But let's be clear. There is an author, John Eldredge, who has a book called Wild at Heart. It is a book that speaks of the needs of every man's heart. And he has this sentence, 'It is no shame that you need healing; it is no shame to look to another for strength.'"[38].

Looking for Help

"If we are sincere, we will see that it is braver and more humane to recognize that if we do not seek help, in our weakness we will not admit to destroying our relationships. And relationships are the most important things in life, more than business, careers, or human successes. For what makes people happiest in the hour of truth are people. It is in our relationships that we find much of our joy and fulfillment."

"Yes, but how do you know who to tell and what to tell?"

"Well, there's no perfect answer, Luis. I agree that you have to choose a few people who are extremely trustworthy and who really love you to tell them a little about you and to focus your vision. And the same goes for counselors, whether they are priests, guides or psychologists. The important thing is that you feel comfortable and see that they know how to guide you."

"But I insist on something important: many of our ancestors, many of our grandparents, with the excuse that all the problems had to be kept inside, that men do not cry, that man cannot show vulnerability, did a lot of damage. Some women did the same. Crying was looked down upon. For many years there was a style of education more of fear and discipline than of conviction. In many films, those that reflect the ways of acting of times before the eighties and nineties, we do see some elements that today we know do not fly. We must have at least some people who can serve us (and us them) as an escape. It is necessary for men to remove tensions and difficulties outside their system."

"I see, Father, but I guess you're not saying that people in the past didn't know how to live well. I mean, for example, Alejandro says that many of the values of yesterday have been lost in our generation," said Luis.

"No, no, of course it's not all black and white. I am the number one fan of many of our ancestors' values. Notice I'm simply mentioning some aspects here. Those aspects are what I think is good that have evolved. I'm talking about a discretion that was misunderstood. They were dying of stress or pain for something, and they felt that 'a man never cries,' or that 'nobody should know what Grandpa or Grandma is going through.' These tensions make people sick, cause heart attacks, cause discomfort, etc. Love between people can manifest itself in a healthy and attentive listening."

"What I want to emphasize, Luis, is that we must seek healing and be open to it. All our lives we have to admit that we are

broken by original sin and its consequences. As we said, it is almost impossible for us not to be affected, even a little in the rolling of life. And that is why every person should make a self-revision."

Everyone was silent for a few moments. These silences were necessary from time to time for ideas to take hold. Each one ate from his snack a little, taking also some time to think about the conversation.

Effects of Not Seeking Help: Internal Lying and Strengths

"Father. If you don't seek help, that is, if there is a lot of pride in a person or no one points out that they need to seek healing, what are the consequences? In other words, what happens if you go through life without addressing the issue?"

"Many things happen. The most obvious ones are that tensions start between everyone in the house. We start to create environments in the house where what reigns is not peace. There is very little harmony. Arriving at your home is not what recharges your batteries. Rather, you have to find others to recharge your batteries."

Luis looked at the horizon, as if hypnotized, and from time to time he looked at either the priest or Alejandro. He couldn't talk much. He was overwhelmed in his thoughts.

The priest continued, "And so spending time in the house ceases to be nice. You have to find a place to go to avoid those closest to you."

"That's what I've felt many times in my house, you know? And now it saddens me to connect the dots—now that I hear it—in the way that you are doing. Now I'm putting a name to the feelings I've had in the past. I've been looking forward to being out of the house constantly."

"Yes, Luis. Well, I feel bad for hearing that, but believe me: I am sure that those bad environments in other cases have been modified by one person. It's enough that someone from the family establish a different pattern. For one person alone, there can be new air in a house. Now, let me tell you something very interesting."

"There are two other effects of these unhealthy, unbalanced and dysfunctional environments. The first, Luis, is that all these things generate in us **'internal lies'.'** Let me explain: harmful environments make us compensate for lack of balance. They hurt us.

And we begin to generate in our minds an internal conversation in which we fall into defeatist internal lies. Not everyone does that. But it lends itself to that temptation. One's self-image must be healthy, neither inflated nor insufficient."

"If you'll allow me an example, it's like when someone in a sport is walking or running badly. The athlete starts compensating for that bad footfall or pain, and ends up hurting other parts. In other words, he ends by hurting himself even more."

"Yes, it sounds logical to me," said Luis. "I mean, I guess he means that when the environment is unhealthy, it doesn't just affect you in the obvious, but it can also affect you in ways you don't even realize."

"Absolutely. Yes, and the experience of psychologists, counselors, and me as a priest is that by the time they realize it, it's all a tangle. It's not easy to untangle the issue. So many things have been mixed up already that it's not easy to identify what came first and what came after. That is why there are times of hard purification in many cases."

"I mean, can you think of an example of an internal lie that a person might develop?" asked Luis.

"An example of an internal lie is this: in a home where people have never been allowed to express what they feel, what they perceive, what they take in from the environment, but where mom or dad tells them that 'they can't think that about their dad' or 'they can't say that about their mom', when that's really what they're seeing, they can say to themselves: I distort reality. I don't get things right."

"Another example, Luis, happens a lot. When in a house there is little affirmation and affection, or when there is a spirit of rigid perfectionism and tension, what can happen is that the person says to himself clearly and deeply: 'I am not enough.' That is why many girls, when they do not even feel the look of their father who considers them to be princesses, these princesses go and seek love in the arms of the first boy who gives them that attention."

"Wow! Well, that totally makes sense. I wonder if I have internal lies that affect me on a daily basis."

Alejandro wanted to intervene, but father stepped forward without looking at him, as he was on the bench to his left and not in his line of sight.

"Well, it's a good thing that everyone, not just you, can constantly do a self-review. It's not something you just check once. It's something that needs to be done. Hence the Pope's phrase that 'the whole spiritual life, understood in a sufficiently profound way, is healing. We are all in the same boat. St. Paul is an author who is not afraid to manifest without shame that he himself carries a thorn in the flesh. And he says that when he is weak, then he is strong.'"

Luis looked at Alejandro with a smile. It was clear that he had learned that phrase of Benedict XVI from Father Andrew, since both were using it. Luis said:

"Yes, Alejandro had told me that phrase which is extremely enlightening, or at least it has been for me. This is very interesting. I've never read St Paul. Do you recommend it?"

"Of course. It's not easy to read, but once you understand it, it sheds a lot of light."

"Father, and what is the second effect of not seeking healing or grasping these things?" asked Luis.

"The second effect is that we build up fortresses. When I say fortress, I mean like in the Middle Ages, like a castle. I'll explain. A fortress is a belief under which we operate automatically, but which hurts us. When we have fortresses in our souls, we have made a promise or oath to ourselves that we will defend them at all costs. But in trying, we don't realize that we are hurting ourselves. I'll give you an example."

"Someone might say: I don't trust anyone anymore. To trust someone is to expose yourself to being hurt. That strength was created by someone who was hurt by someone else, disrespected by someone else, let down by trust."

"And what about these fortresses, I mean, how do they affect you?" asked Luis.

"Well, those strengths create barriers in the mind and heart. Bob, who teaches the course in Texas, which I think Alejandro told you about, says that fortresses are effects of traumatic wounds, of poorly processed memories. Strengths are often formed by the internal lies we have just seen. It's those lies sown there by the devil, or by our weak minds that have been fooled."

"Possessing these strengths means that God's love, the love that heals every heart and is its greatest need and desire, cannot come. Many times strength is the inability to forgive someone for an offense. Where there has been a moment, a season of frustration, of hatred, of anger, of dissatisfaction, there is a possibility that a strength has been formed. And you know what? A fortress is just the place where the devil has a door open to do more harm. That's why it's called a fortress. In fact, St. Paul, in the letter to the Ephesians, tells us to '...give the devil no place.'" (Eph 4:27)

Healing by Grace

They came to a pause and left a moment to reflect. Alejandro wondered if Luis would object to the fact that the priest had mentioned the devil, but Luis said nothing. He didn't mind that he had mentioned something religious. Luis took a drink and a bite into the sandwich. This led Father Andrew to say what he felt was essential to close the subject:

"Luis, as you realize, this topic of healing is not easy, but at the same time, when it's actually done, it becomes precious and exciting. You have to be open with the means I told you earlier. But there are other means without which it is impossible to leave. I am referring to something that some may not like to hear, however, the gospels are full of this. I mean the power of Christ. That power that is found in the sacraments, prayer, fasting and grace in general."

Alejandro was surprised at Luis' openness at this moment, and stared at father, who continued.

"Throughout the Bible we see how what the whole world is— but the envoy, the Messiah, is coming to cure all kinds of diseases. That was Jesus' task. The book of Isaiah says so:

'The Spirit of the Lord God is upon me, because the Lord has anointed me to bring good tidings to the afflicted; he has sent me to bind up the brokenhearted, to proclaim liberty to the captives, and the opening of the prison to those who are bound; to proclaim the year of the Lord's favor, and the day of vengeance of our God; to comfort all who mourn; to grant to those who mourn in Zion—to give them a garland instead of ashes, the oil of gladness instead of mourning, the mantle of praise instead of a faint spirit; that they may be called oaks of righteousness, the planting of the Lord, that he may be glorified.' (Isaiah 61:1-3 RSVCE)

"Through the life of grace, Luis, that which comes from Jesus, in a privileged way God wants to insert his grace into our souls to heal us of all the things that are attached to us."

"One of the things I value very much about the Catholic faith is the meaning we give to suffering. Many religions do not know how to give it the high and redemptive, saving meaning that we can give it. The cross of Christ is what makes all pain meaningful. We do not have to suffer without meaning."

"St. Paul, in fact, invites us to suffer something in our lives in order to follow the same path as Christ: '...I fulfill in my flesh what is lacking in Christ's afflictions...' (Col 2:24). He realized the good he could do for his spirit if he learned to bear his daily crosses and difficulties with patience and a supernatural sense. Do you understand me, Luis?"

"Yes," answered Luis, "although it's been a long time since I've practiced, I do remember that one day someone told me about offering our acts to God. I hadn't heard it for a long time, until now from you, Do you live with that? Do you sometimes make sacrifices?"

"Less than I would like, said father, "but yes. I try to do it a little, especially during Lent. But not alone. This is always good. One way to sacrifice is through fasting. When we don't eat something we like or eat something we don't like, we turn to something that Jesus himself did two-thousand years ago before he began his task of announcing the good news. He went into the desert and went hungry voluntarily. He knew that this kind of sacrifice, fasting, would make him very strong for a task that was not easy."

"Many years ago there were two human groups during the Roman Empire that did this for pure human strength. The Stoics and the Epicureans were groups that fasted just because of the willpower involved. They deprived themselves of many things in order to be strong for life. However, this is not the Christian way. We do it to follow the example of Jesus who offered it for his Father, but also because he knew the good effect on him."

"Something that complements sacrifices very well, Luis, is prayer. Every human being enjoys having a relationship with God. And the best way to do this, to meet Jesus, is through prayer. Today it is fashionable to do meditation everywhere. But many times meditation is an encounter with oneself. That is not Christian prayer. Christian prayer is meeting the great You of life, the person who loves us, who came to save us and heal us, and who looks at each other with loving eyes. God is love. That love he gives to me. And that's what I go to prayer for."

Smiling a little, Luis replied to father, "I am a little afraid of these co-workers. Sometimes they seem a little bit fanatical to me. I don't understand how that could please God or how it benefits God if you don't eat something or make sacrifices."

"We received an ancient Jewish tradition, Luis, from a people chosen by God and very religious, and at the same time very decomposed in its early stages. They also knew how to fast as something that pleased God. And as I told you, Jesus himself did it. If imitating Jesus is the main task of the Christian, then doing so will do him good. And history does not let us lie."

"All this that we are talking about, Luis, is situated in the context of God's grace. Whoever is baptized lives with the qualifying grace of God. It is the life of God in his soul. It is sad that we do not talk much about this nowadays, but it is one of the greatest miracles that can exist: that God lives in the soul of the human being. Of course, this is as long as the human being cultivates it and does not live in opposition to God. If not, God leaves. Because of mortal sin, God does not dwell in the soul. But that is what the beautiful and undeserved gift of the sacrament of forgiveness is for. We go to a priest, who in reality only takes the place of God, and we meet the witnesses of the mercy of God who always forgives. I myself, who am a priest, go with another priest and he gives me forgiveness. I cannot forgive myself." Father Andrew made the gesture with his hand to turn it to himself and give himself the blessing that forgives sins. He did it with a comical gesture, as if he were making fun of what he was saying.

Luis thought a little. Inside, he felt a movement in his heart, like a light that suddenly opened him up to the things of God. In all this time of conversation with his friend, he always felt a rejection of faith. On this occasion, before Father Andrew, he began to feel a certain openness, a kind of docility to the things of faith. Not feeling rejection, he asked:

"Are you saying that this life in grace is the best path to healing? In other words, are these tools, prayer, sacrifices, fasting and the life of grace... the means God gives us to solve these difficulties?"

"I would say, Luis, that they are both. God always works on two levels: the natural and the supernatural. The life of grace, in itself, does not ordinarily solve all the problems of nature. It could be that it does, for God does what he wants and heals when he wants. But if man is able to take care of himself and go to a good psychologist in some cases that already deserve it, he must do so. And then, the popular saying 'help yourself, I will help you' is fulfilled. Saint Augustine expressed it differently. He said that God spoke to him saying: 'Give me what you ask for, and ask for what you want.' It is as if God said: 'You put everything on your side, and then you ask me to help you with my grace to do so.'"

"What I can tell you is this: the total and final healing of the person will never come without the grace of God. It is not in man's hands to be completely healed. Only in Christ can one be completely happy and only in life in Christ can one be completely healthy."

"Christ comes to heal, then, Luis. He not only forgives all our sins, but also cures all our illnesses, as the psalmist says (Ps 103:3). Bob Schuchts puts it this way: 'Healing is a process that will be completely fulfilled in heaven. But the process must begin now in each of our lives, as we face our various physical ailments, psychological difficulties, and spiritual afflictions.'39

"As you see, therefore, both realities are needed: the natural and the supernatural."

Luis felt a deep satisfaction at the pleasure of human wisdom, to have this friend, and now with this surprise of talking to a priest. The feeling that he was beginning to accept without so much suspicion and rejection many of the things that his friend was living and saying filled him with an assurance that he was going the right way. In addition, he could now ask more questions about religion, things which had always been on his mind.

Suddenly he felt a pain in his stomach. The question of whether Sofia would accept these things came to him like a flash. Luis' resolution to start living better as these conversations with his friend inspired him was unsettling, for he asked himself, "I want to start transforming my life. But what about Sofia? Will she get on my boat?"

They had already talked a lot and it was getting close to the end. Given everyone's strong desire to continue, they agreed to meet again on Friday. Father wasn't sure he would be able to be there, but he said that if he took off a commitment, he would be there. e It was necessary to continue to learn, now with more tools, how to make all these things fit the person. The part of self-improvement that Alejandro had been mentioning as part of the pedagogy of improving who one is, that was the part that was coming right away. It's good to know and accept yourself, but action was now necessary. And father's contribution on the spiritual theme now gave another meaning to everything.

"Well, I want to tell you something: the truth is that until now I have not been grateful enough for all that these conversations are serving me,' said Luis. "I feel a new light on my path to help me with my problems, which include my family and Sofia. I don't know how much I can change them, but I can begin to change myself."

"Yes, Luis, the key is this, said Alejandro, "control what you can control. You cannot change them. But you can do much to change yourself. That is why there is that very wise and ancient prayer that says:

'Lord, give me the serenity to accept the things I cannot change, the courage to change the things I can, and the wisdom to know the difference.'"

"Let's continue tomorrow, Luis. But I recommend something. As you have come to know yourself and know more about human beings and their wounds, you are getting more light. Now, as we go further, we're getting to the point of self-improvement. And I would say that the key to everything is integration. Please, Luis, do not forget this word. If you have to forget many things that we have been talking about in these weeks, I only ask you not to forget this one: in integration there is happiness, peace and integral health. And if you want, we can start there tomorrow."

Father Andrew looked at Alejandro with pride, since he did not have many acquaintances among the university students who had that passion for attending to their friends' concerns in this way.

God grant me the serenity to accept the things I cannot change, courage to change the things I can, and wisdom to know the difference.

"Luis, Alejandro: I sincerely congratulate you. It is a pleasure and pride for me to be able to come to your conversations and help in any poor way I can. Whenever I have the time, I will accompany you. Tomorrow I do not guarantee to be there, but I will do my best."

Father headed to his office, and Luis punched Alejandro in the shoulder.

"Why didn't you tell me your friend was a priest?"

"Because I know what you're like. I thought you'd say no."

"I was actually surprised by the way he explained, and especially by the fact that he presented it to you and let you decide. I didn't feel the typical imposition of the Church."

"It's just that you're kind of stubborn. You talk about the Church as if you knew all the Christians and all the priests, and you have already proved that it is as you say. But you don't realize that you live by what others say," said Alejandro.

They shook hands, Luis looked at his watch and realized he had four minutes to get to his room, which was on the other side of the building. "Let's run!"

ANALYZING THE CONVERSATION

It's amazing what happens in our world today. Although we know it, we forget that the smiling faces, the supposedly happy and full lives, the great fortune that many seem to have in life, judging by social networks (Snapchat, Instagram, Facebook, etc.) are a mask, a lie. Day by day, every human being, whether they know it or not, wonders whether it is worth getting out of bed. Every day we all search for the meaning of the next twelve hours we will be awake. And many times we have people very close to us who do not dare to say: "Help me, I can't stand it anymore".

Maybe that person is ourselves, or has been in the past. Either way, we're not alive to be dragged through life. We are called to live fully, even if that includes the beauty of imperfection and human difficulties. That's what Jesus meant when he said, "Whoever wants to come after me and follow me, let him deny himself..." (Mt 16:24)

In life there are some people who have discovered the good that can be done to walk lightly through life. Walk lightly because they are pruning the excesses of the soul, those elements that have been introduced by the home in which we were born or by the decisions and experiences we have had. Sometimes we are not to blame, many other times we are. But the important thing is not to look back. What is important, as in every human endeavor, is to analyze, recognize and solve. Where am I now? Where do I dream of going? What does it take to get there?

When Jesus said that we must be vigilant and pray, he did so because his human experience and divine wisdom told him that one does not go through life without suffering, without bewilderment, but suddenly finds that I do not understand myself. What happened to me? How did I get here? Believe me, as a priest I have seen many bitter tears shed in retreat after retreat, error after error. Weeds appears in our lives even if we set ourselves the goal that will never happen. One couple after another suddenly finds themselves feeling the other is no longer the same. He is full of blind spots, and I can't tell him anything, because he doesn't believe me. He takes it all personally, there's no way to breach his walls. I am not the person who has the key to open his heart.

That is why this conversation between the two friends and with the help of Father Andrew is key in your life. You must not resist in life to be checked by others. We must give the opportunity to believe that some things have interfered with us. Wounds, lies, fortresses, foolishness, blind spots... The name of the elements is not relevant. What is relevant is that we observe, we are open and we overcome. The key we have given here is to know, accept and overcome ourselves.

It is important, then, that we also know that every change that lasts and that takes us like a boat to the next life—my own—understand that, without God's grace, the changes will be only a varnish, something that lasts today, and tomorrow will not appear. There is no possibility of survival without the strength that emanates from the redeeming power of Jesus Christ, King of the Universe and Lord of life. Humanity's long history makes this clear to us. Just like Alcoholics Anonymous, we know that without God there is no salvation. There are no human methods sufficiently capable of healing the whole person. The human soul is incomplete without grace. And that grace comes to us through prayer, the sacraments, and the union of our being with the sufferings of that King who looked at us tenderly and breathed his last, from a cross.

Questions to think about:

1. Can you think of people who clearly have blind spots? Have you ever thought about your own blind spots, things you don't notice about yourself but that affect your relationships?

2. In your family, what kind of relationships do you have? Healthy ones? Or does the environment have certain toxic elements?

3. Can you identify inner lies or strengths (in the sense of this chapter) that you have built that are hurting you?

Chapter 14:
Integrating the Whole Person

"The task of every human being: the serene integration of emotional forces under the dominion of faith, reason, will and love"

David Abad

It was a Friday and Alejandro arrived at the university early. He felt a great satisfaction for what had happened the day before. It was risky to have invited Father Andrew, but it was worth the risk. The weeks of conversations had made Luis almost completely confident in Alejandro, although by nature he was a guide and would remain inquisitive. And there is nothing wrong with that. Where there are questions, there is potential wisdom.

In the distance he saw Luis. He was entertaining himself by greeting Monica Mendez, a mutual friend. Meanwhile, Alejandro took advantage of the brief delay to send a couple of WhatsApp messages and review Instagram.

"How are you, Alejandro?" said Luis as he arrived at the bank.

"Well, what about you, Luis? I'm not sure."

"I'm not complaining. Hey, that was a good conversation yesterday with Father Andrew, wasn't it?"

"Yes," said Alejandro. "The truth is that it is very useful for me to have a priest friend, and especially someone who won't leave you with a thirst for life's questions. There are too many people who have faith and do not know how to explain the most important things, the questions of life. And thanks to the fact that my parents have always been more or less educated in these more existential and faith-based issues, I have faith today. Well, I've realized that faith and reason, as we talked about a few weeks ago, never clash."

They both stopped for a moment to talk and each took out his mug of coffee and food. It was a little cold.

"Alejandro," said Luis. "all this time you've been explaining things to me in simple ways. We have talked about many things and it has become clear to me that, in life, knowing your identity and achieving your integration is key. I would say that without this, as you have told me, we will not get rid of it. We will not live a life of peace and harmony. The subject of grace that Father Andrew spoke about is something I have to start analyzing. Even so, I can't get it all straight in my mind."

Alejandro saw the opportunity to offer a little more clarity according to the scheme he had previously talked about.

"Luis, yes. Don't worry about not having it all figured out. Let's take time today to talk about something that's not new, but to integrate it all."

"You remember the three phases we talked about, right? We spent quite a bit of time getting to know each other, then accepting each other, and now we're getting there."

"Yes, yes. You haven't stopped talking about them, as if they were mantras."

"Well, you will find," said Alejandro, "that they are like a world in which we operate. He who does not know himself forgets himself. He can never be a good human being. He will go around crushing others."

"Then, to be accepted—we went into that in depth as well."

Luis stopped Alejandro in his tracks, a little frustrated:

"Alejandro, but you've mentioned getting to know each other, accepting each other, and improving each other several times, and I can't see the line where one starts and the other stops."

"Luis. You take it easy. This isn't exact engineering and math, man. This is the human soul, existential issues, psychology and spirit issues. All your life you walk through knowing, accepting and overcoming yourself. When you accept yourself, you overcome yourself. When you overcome yourself, you can accept yourself a little better. And all the time you are getting to know yourself more and more, at different ages. And I'm sure we'll never stop being surprised. But now again, and trying to help you close the 'getting over yourself' part a little, I want to touch on one more subject."

Luis looked at Alejandro, intrigued. He couldn't help but appreciate the amount of knowledge and ways of living and thinking that his friend brought to him. No doubt his maturity was admirable and came from his ability to reflect and from his home.

Living with Big Dreams

—Algo que a mí me ha funcionado mucho, Luis, es algo que sie"Something that has worked for me a lot, Luis, is something that I always saw in my father's attitudes, and he preached it to me a lot when I was something like thirteen or fourteen years old. In order to have the gas, the enthusiasm, the passion in life to become someone great—in other words, to be able to surpass myself—I had to be great. Huge dreams, I would say. And I always loved stories and movies about heroes or ordinary men and women, but with high goals. Characters like William Wallace, Michael Jordan, Frodo, Roger Federer, stories of tenacity and perseverance."

"In fact, I don't know if you've ever heard the saying that 'many people die at twenty-five, but are buried at seventy-five.'"

"I don't understand," said Luis.

"Yes, think about it. There are many people who don't have big dreams. There are people who do not have it in their souls to do great things in life. In a recent survey by Barna Group, three out of ten young people in the United States do not consider themselves or want to be leaders. And that's in the United States, a place where leadership and achievement seem to be everything. And yet, God gave us all talents to be leaders, even on a small level. We all have a calling for greatness."

"I should see that statistic, because they do all kinds of surveys and you don't know what to believe anymore. But what's the problem with not wanting to be a leader?"

"Well, I'm sure that a person who brings works on himself in the sense we've been talking about becomes an attractive leader. I'm convinced of that. And in many, many motivational leadership conferences I've been to, I've met people who say that no one gave anything to them when it all started."

"What do you mean, nobody gave anything to them?"

"Yes, that there was a time in their lives when they were nobody. They didn't always have the virtues or qualities they have today. But they started out with a very big desire, and now people admire them. People who don't even have legs or arms, or people who have serious disabilities, they give us a master class in self-improvement, passion, desire and dreaming. People who have been through very hard things, and now they can talk about them with authority, for they have endured many pains and doors slammed in their faces."

"Luis, in short: 'If you don't live with passion, better not to live at all.' God didn't bring us into the world to be average."

"There is a seminarian legionary of Christ, Luis, who died recently and suddenly. He was close to being ordained a priest, but God had other plans. He had a phrase: Your life is too big to play small."

They both left a pause before going on. They both wanted a moment of reflection.

If you don't live
with passion,
better not to
live whatsoever.

"So, Alejandro, how do you make big dreams come true?"

"I feel like I have it in me. But maybe not. From very early on in life, my parents sowed the seed of excellence for me. Les Brown, a world communication professional, used to say that in every child a 'yes' or 'no' is sown in the first five years. I feel that I was sown a 'yes.'"

"I wouldn't know what to call it. I think I have both 'no' and 'yes' in me, according to this guy you're talking about."

"I think, Luis, there's probably more of a 'yes' in you. But they are seeds that have to be watered and then, by taking that responsibility away from our parents and making us carry ourselves, one has to polish them. That is, the seed can also be planted later in life. Thousands of cases show this."

"I mean, Alejandro, if I'm not that passionate about something, can I be?"

"Of course. Ask yourself: What do I love? What would I do with excellence in life?

Luis kept thinking. Then he answered:

"I think the truth is that one thing I'd love to do well is stand out as an architect. To make designs and houses that will earn me money. Or if they didn't win prizes, at least that people liked them a lot and asked me for more."

"Well, there it is. And I'm sure if you're looking for more, you could score two or three more passions. And don't forget that being a good dad, a husband and a Christian should be on the list, and it's all connected."

Luis looked at Alejandro smiling, now charged with motivation:

"You're cheering me up, man! I think I do find it easy to have our motivations always in front of us. To be attracted to big things. And I guess when you have big dreams, things get easier."

"Mmmh! Not exactly," said Alejandro. "I mean, yes, but not so fast. It is important to live with big dreams both for oneself and for the things one will do. In that sense you do have more of an advantage if you dream big than if you don't. But already at the execution, it doesn't necessarily make things easier for you. Anyway, there will be obstacles all your life."

The Obstacle is the Road

"How so? So what's the point of having big dreams if they'll only bring you trouble?"

"No, that's not what I said. What I said was that, even if you have big dreams, to achieve them you will have to go through a lot of difficulties. That's for sure. And that's logical. Otherwise, life would be too easy."

"Now that we are talking about the third phase of overcoming, much will have to do with the combination of great ideals and a willingness to be tough."

"One of the best books I've read about this, Luis, and which gave me too much, is called "The Obstacle is the way". It's really good."

"What's it about?"

"The book deals with the mentality attributed to Marcus Aurelius, the great Roman emperor. He was one of the so-called 'five good emperors.' The point is that he had a mettle and courage that made him conquer what he set out to do because of his ability to see the negative not as an obstacle, but as a tool to be used in his favor.

"Luis said. "Tell me some of the things the book says."

Alejandro looked at him with the satisfaction of one who expected him to ask. The book had impacted him decisively.

"I love it when he talks about how in battles and historical moments where there was no way out, this or that character saw an

The will is the inner strength that cannot be affected by the ourside world.

opportunity. And for that, he talks about the will in a person. He says that 'the will is an inner force that cannot be affected by the outside world.'

"In fact, Luis, I have a lot of phrases on my cell phone that I saved when I read the book, because the truth is that sometimes when I need energy or fly low, I read them."

"You, flying low? I can't imagine you flying low," said Luis.

"What do you mean? It's not like I'm Superman. Many times I feel as bad as anyone, or sometimes I'm tempted to throw in the towel on a lot of things."

"Let's see. You were going to read me some ideas about obstacles."

"Yes, yes. Calm down. Look."

Alejandro took out his cell phone and did a search of the book quotations.

"Look," said Alejandro. "The book says that 'the hindrance to progress, advances the work. What gets in the way, that is the way itself. It's cool, isn't it? I thought it was very clever. It's given me a kick in the pants."

"Wait. I don't understand. What's the big news?"

"Well, look here, Luis. How many times do we start careers, jobs or relationships and leave them because there are obstacles? We don't realize that when we enter something, the obstacles are special. That's why it's called 'The Obstacle is the way.' We can't stand setbacks. If it's not exciting anymore, we quit. Whatever it is."

"That's where he has some great chapters on tenacity and perseverance. Notice this sentence: 'The obstacle in the way becomes the way. Never forget: within each obstacle there is an opportunity to improve your condition."40 Then look at this one. It is Benjamin Franklin's phrase: 'Those things that hurt, instruct.'

Within each
obstacle lies an
opportunity to
improve your
condition

"That's good, man," said Luis, visibly moved and motivated.

"The book is a shot of adrenaline, because it tells you stories and it gives you great quotes, just like these," Alejandro concluded.

"And of course I got a lot out of it," Alejandro continued. "The whole attitude thing. Remember?"

"Yes, I remember. Convictions, attitudes and... and..."

"Behaviors, Luis! Behaviors! It's easy to remember if you think from the inside out. My convictions help me to have attitudes and from there the behaviors manifest themselves externally."

"Ah, yes. You've told me this before. It's coming back to me."

There was a necessary pause. They took a bite of their rolls and a sip of their drink. Alejandro continued:

"And I'll give you one more sentence about obstacles and will, look at this one: 'What matters most is not what these obstacles are, but how they appear to be, how we react to them and whether we always keep our composure.'"

Alejandro saw in Luis a hungry look, a gleam in his eye that was beginning to be far from the Luis who started this series of conversations. Something was going on in Luis, and the only regret was that his discoveries were not shared by Sofia and her family. They were on two different channels.

"If you look, Luis, in everything we are talking about we are assuming in the person an intelligence that is using reason for the good of itself. It is by using reason properly that one can discern in life what is most convenient, what is best."

"I'm really excited about this part," said Luis. He wondered a little internally where to start. But he had already started a long time ago. Without realizing it, his life was changing for the better.

"Wow, but there seems to be a lot of homework, Alejandro! There's too many things to consider."

"Not so much, Luis. It's not about being perfect anymore. I would say that in fact it's not about being perfect ever in this life. It is about moving forward little by little, working—as Father Andrew said—every day a little more and better. Taking one lesson into account, then another, and then asking the Holy Spirit, who is the coach of our sanctification, for light."

As he said that phrase, Alejandro looked down to see if Luis didn't mind getting into the subject of faith. To his surprise, Luis nodded silently.

The Power of Imagination

"And one more faculty that comes to help us integrate well all our life, Luis, is imagination. With imagination we can go very far. Man has received from God the power to plan a great future, with great projects and great deeds. To put it first in the intention and then, with planning and perseverance, to arrive at the execution."

"I have always heard," interrupted Luis, "that imagination is something more appropriate for magicians, for those who use their imagination to invent something that is imaginary. Imaginary, imagination. They look alike, don't they?"

"Yes, that definition is also valid. But it's not the most complete. Imagination is the ability to visualize something you want to conquer. That step is required. An animal does not imagine anything. It just follows its instinct and does it. We are builders together with God. Imagination, says one author, 'is concerned with giving substance to passions and making plans to satisfy them.' When we speak of passions, Luis, we obviously speak in the technical sense, and not in the sense of something negative. The passions in the sense as spoken of by St. Thomas, are faculties of man which must be mastered and oriented towards the good.

Luis didn't respond much to let the idea settle.

Then he asked:

"So is imagination something we should all strengthen?"

"Yes, obviously. It's good to do it. It will make us much more constructive of a beautiful, good and true world, Luis."

We are called to--with help of others or on our own, integrate all the pieces of ourself until harmony is acquired.

Integration

"Alejandro, I'm not very good at this, but I do want to take this opportunity to thank you for these conversations. They've really started to do me a lot of good. Actually, thank you."

Luis fixed his eyes on Alejandro, and then a sense of grief and excitement at the same time made him look down at the floor. His head nodded with a sense of satisfaction that he felt for the sake of it.

"Luis, I rather thank you because you continue to give me the opportunity to learn how to apply and explain so many things that I cannot talk about with others. Thank you, indeed."

The integrated man or woman is a harmonious man or woman

"Now, before we run out of time, I would like to seal one thing up well, because if I do not make it clear, we may lose sight of the essentials."

"We've talked about identity for a long time. We have also made it clear that it is essential that all parts of the human being are properly integrated. This phrase serves as a motivation for me: "The integrated man or woman is a harmonious man or woman.""

"The man and woman that everyone wishes to have in their lives, Luis, whether as a father, mother, brother, husband or wife, will be the one or the one that reflects harmony. A person within. I always admire the balance in people. When they are neither tense nor passive. When the joy is genuine, not false, not forced or superficial. When it knows how to harmonize softness with firmness. Conviction with flexibility. These people are an empire of harmony. They can also be defined as equable people. That comes from Latin, and means 'soul in balance.'"

Silence reigned between the two. Luis put on a face that said this challenge was too difficult and questioned:

"Alejandro, but I'm afraid of such a big challenge! We've talked about so much and there's so much to consider. Where do I start?"

"My experience, Luis, is that they look like a lot of things. In reality, life has a few fundamental principles, and the others are things to be taken into account. Good conversations, good books, and good friends will slowly bring everything into place. It should not be a distressing process. When I have been distressed, and I feel your same doubt, I have been reassured by Father Andrew saying: 'Every day has its own anxiety.'"

"Does every day have its zeal?"

"Yes, it's a phrase of Jesus. The idea is that I don't have to worry about tomorrow. I do today what is right for today. Every day has its worries. And here, Luis, let me add something I want to close this conversation with."

"This work for the Christian is very comforting. For the Christian is in an intimate relationship with Jesus Christ, his Master. He is the one who stopped calling him a servant, and now calls him a friend. And this friend does not demand without being present, does not blame for the falls, but accompanies. This friend is a companion in life, in the journey, in life. He himself was a man in everything but sin. He knows that there will be frustration, anger, crying, and discouragement. He knows that in the end we will feel very lonely, with the desire not to get up and stick our faces to the ground. And just when we do, he will say to us, "Come to me, all you who are tired and weary, and I will give you rest. For my yoke is easy and my burden is light."

"Wow, the mystic," said Luis to Alejandro.

Alejandro did not hesitate, visibly moved and transmitting his own experience:

"Try it, Luis. Between our efforts that use the intellect, the will and the whole heart to build the person, and the help from God, His Holy Spirit, everything is possible: 'What is impossible with men is possible with God.'" (Lk 18:27 RSVCE)

"It's this integration of all our powers, thoughts, feelings, fears, sadness, illusions, through human effort. All of this, together with God's grace and his help within us and with his constant guidance, gives each one of us all that our soul longs for. Both in this life and in the eternal one."

"Let's go, we're not there yet."

ANALYZING THE CONVERSATION

We have reached the end of the second part. In the first part, it was important to lay a firm and solid foundation on the capacity of the human being. It was also necessary to understand what man is, from his roots. What is the truth, if there is one? Thus, we arrive at his identity. Knowing what identity I have and why we were created, how we make use of our humanity and what hurts us. That is the foundation of everything.

Then it was all about integration. The cart that has been driven through life has not been able to avoid getting dirty, defying itself. It is normal in life. That's why a life begins where you and I have to be those musical instrument tuners. We have to be able to readjust what our decisions and the influence of family may have thrown off course.

That's where three key concepts have come in. The ability to dream, the power of imagination, and the transformation of obstacles into fuel for life. We can never stop having an end in mind. And that end, that goal must be possible, but it must also be hard to reach. With trained imagination and constant demand, we will have the ability to visualize things that will bring much good to people. Dreams must never fall short. "If we can dream it, we can do it," as Walt Disney said.

And the third key is to sharpen your eyes. Setbacks hit, disorientate, and create bewilderment. But whoever has made a habit of seeing in them a golden opportunity to grow and become stronger, that person becomes almost invincible.

And this is where the hand of God comes in. We cannot want all this for ourselves and for ourselves alone. The greatest transcendence is achieved with God. And God is Love itself. Man can never live happily if he does not live to love, to give himself, and to give himself to others in a way that leaves every last drop of blood and sweat.

Therefore, the desire of reaching that longed-for integration is made with God. He makes the dream possible. He gives strength for the task. He rewards when there is a fall. Now, in the third part, it is time to look at what is most inscribed in the human heart: happiness.

Questions to think about:

1. Do you have a habit of dreaming big?

2. How much have you filled your mind with desire so that it projects and imagines great plans for you and yours?

3. How do you react to defeats and obstacles? Do they make you want to throw in the towel or do they encourage you to look for another option?

PART III: HAPPINESS

What am I called to?
Where do I find my happiness?

253

Chapter 15:
Man's Deepest Longing

"I have committed the worst sin one can commit. I have not been happy".

Jorge Luis Borges.

The weekend had been one of family time and relative calm for both of them. Luis spent time with his girlfriend at a nearby ranch where they usually did many things: horseback riding, walking through the forest full of pine trees and wide spaces, having a drink with the family around the huge rustic table of the house, lighting the fire, going for a run...

Alejandro, for his part, had not left the city. On Friday he had had a quiet evening with friends at Ruben's house, a friend from years ago. About five couples got together and each did what they liked: some played Catan, chatted or watched the league football match.

Alejandro felt a special moment was coming in the conversations. They had spent a lot of time solidly building two great concepts essential to each person: identity and integration. Now, he felt that it was time to let Luis speak, but to take him towards something that he was passionate about and was the reason for having laid these two foundations: what is the deepest thing that man longs for? However, he felt uncomfortable, unprepared to address these issues with the same wisdom as he had done with the previous ones. He therefore arranged in advance with Father Andrew to be attentive to his call. He needed his help again.

When he arrived at the site, he thought for a moment that Luis would not arrive. Then he immediately saw him in the distance, and waited. When he arrived, Luis gave him the usual hug, asking about the weekend:

"What´s up, Alejandro. How are we doing?"

"Luis, everything's in order. I thought for a moment that maybe you'd cancelled today and I'd forgotten."

"No, no. I'm not that casual. I would have told you in time." They both took their usual seats.

"How did the weekend go?" asked Alejandro.

"Really nice. I went with my girlfriend and her family to the mountain house. A little bit of everything. There I keep winning over the in-laws, although I don't know what for. You can see the difficulties Sofia and I have at every moment."

"And this time, there were no fights or misunderstandings?"

"There's always something," said Luis, "but why get into it? Hey, Alejandro, Friday you ended up with something that attracted me. We've seen the whole issue of integrating everyone, of how everything has to be aligned and oriented in the same direction. I just... I don't know exactly where to start. And, besides, I always ask myself one question. What is it that a man must do? I mean, I want to know, what inspires you? How do you get happy?"

Alejandro felt that this was just the hook to go where he wanted. And he dove in:

"Let's see. You, what do you think each person should do?"

"I have a notion, but I'm asking you the question."

"Yes, and of course I'll share my point of view with you. But go ahead, you tell me first. How is the best way to spend your time?"

Luis, somewhat reluctantly, looked at the horizon to think a little. He took a deep breath and said:

"Since you insist, for me, I think everyone has to do what makes them happy. What you find in your heart, what you want, do that. In other words, everyone must throw themselves into it without restriction because of what they want, in their heart."

"That is to say, said Alejandro, "that what each of us wants, what we have in our desires, will make us happy. Did I express it well?"

"I think so, don't you?"

"Luis, this is an exciting topic. But now I must add that, although I have heard it well, I have not mastered it. I am afraid I cannot give you the best explanation on this particular question that every human being asks himself: what to do? How to be happy? Do you think we should call Father Andrew to see if he is free to come over for a while?"

Luis nodded, and Alejandro pretended he hadn't arranged things. He took his cell phone and called the priest: "Father, how are you? How are things?"

Alejandro and father greeted each other and then he asked him if he would join them for a while. Father came down in three minutes from his office to be with them.

He arrived with the same smile as always, they hugged and greeted each other, and Alejandro brought him a chair from the side table.

"How are you, young people? Luis, how have you been?"

"Good, Father. Everything's going well. Alejandro and I have continued to philosophize here and we've done quite well. That doesn't mean the situation with my girlfriend or at home is any better, but I do recognize that I've become much more human with all this."

Father nodded in satisfaction at what he heard, and turned to look at Alejandro.

"Alejandro, so, what's the topic now?"

"Father, do you remember the sessions on human freedom you gave us last year? I thought they were great and Luis and I have been talking, actually getting to that point. But, although everything sounded good to me and I agreed with everything when you talked to us, I don't want to mess up. You do better."

"But put me in context," said father. "How did you get to this point?"

Alejandro took the floor.

"Of course, of course. Sorry. It's true. Well, Luis and I have already talked a lot about the foundation of everything, which is the personal identity of each one. And we said that without it, it's impossible to become someone, because you don't even know who you are."

"Then, in the last two weeks the conversation was about integrating everything we are to build a great person."

"I mean, the higher and lower powers, the feelings, the personal wounds, the motivation and meaning of life, all that?"

asked father.

"Yes, right. It seems to me that since I'm new to this, it seemed like a lot of stuff. But I think it was clear to me," said Luis.

"Okay," said father.

"Then," continued Alejandro, "now we have reached the outer limits. That is, we have questions about happiness and the actions that lead to it. Luis and I would like you to tell us about this question: what things make one happy? How do you achieve happiness?"

"Luis said something that everyone around me responds to, but you explained that it's not that simple. He said, in short, that you have to do what you want. That is, what each one wants to do, let him do it, and then he will be happy. I guess a lot of today's culture says more or less: Do what you love."

"I understand," said Father Andrew.

He was thinking for a moment, like he was trying to find the best place to start.

Freedom and Happiness

"This topic is exciting. But I need to give some historical context."

"In Jesus' time, Christianity basically knew that living and imitating Jesus was the best thing you could do. This is because Jesus said: 'I have come that they may have life, and have it abundantly' Jn 10:10. For centuries, more than thirteen centuries, human beings—at least in the West—lived with an ideal that came from Jesus and his Word, which is the Bible. The Christian culture of the West that created the universities, that prepared the ground for the great Renaissance, that discovered America, that translated the texts of the great Greek sages, like Aristotle, lived clearly from a thinking that took into account where man comes from and where he is going. And no one was arguing about God's role in this. God created man and man is heading towards an encounter with God."

"Suddenly, there was a great philosophical cataclysm. Pretend you've been told all your life that football is played with your feet and between two teams of eleven players. And now you're told that football is played with your hand, and it's six against six."

"In the fourteenth century, there was a big change. A certain William of Ockham—you can Google him—decided that God has an absolute will to do whatever he wants, even if it goes against his own laws. That is, if there is a square, He can make it round. That was called 'God's absolute will,' according to Ockham."

Father slowed down. He felt he was going down a high road. He asked, "Are you following me, or is this too much trouble?"

They nodded. As long as he didn't get too high, there was a lot of interest in the subject.

"Okay. Well, although I studied this both in Spain and in Italy, it is what a good course in universal ethics and philosophy should make you see. What this man did was to create a great division between the supernatural and the natural world. I will try to be simpler. Only two centuries after this man came Rene Descartes, who rode on Ockham's theories, generated a Copernican revolution of immeasurable effect, which is still going on today. He turned things upside down, or at least said things that others after him would use to turn many realities upside down. In essence, man became the central point of interpretation of everything, and not God. He opened the door for man to be 'the measure of all things.' There was a great division where the transcendental, the spiritual, no longer counted so much. It was a private matter for people, but it was not objective and real. The only objective thing was what science could measure, what matter showed to the human senses."

"Obviously there were many other contributors to this, but just keep in mind that the unitary vision that St. Thomas Aquinas had left us and that today is still a reference in Christian circles, was lost. And Thomas Aquinas took as a basis for his thinking Aristotle, who is possibly the most brilliant mind that existed before the coming of Jesus."

"Then, some of the results were that soul and body, supernatural and natural, theology and philosophy, morality and obligation, all those concepts, now became two separate islands, untouchable from each other."

"I'm coming down from my mountain now, young men. The consequence of that was that the objective truth of things was lost. Now it's not that there are acts that are always and everywhere good, but that everyone decides what they want to do. But without reference to a truth. A metaphysical vision of life where God sets the rules of good and evil was lost."

At that moment Alejandro, moved, interrupted abruptly:

"Luis, do you remember when we talked about this a few weeks ago, talking about whether there was truth?"

Luis nodded in agreement that father should continue. He was trying to understand.

"What? You, Alejandro, talked to him about metaphysics?"

"Of course, Father. I did it when we talked about ways to find out whether or not there can be an objective truth, clear to everyone."

"Wow! "Excellent, guys. Well, that which you converted and which applies to the material and measurable world, that also works the same for man's actions, his behaviors, good and evil. In a word, for ethics and morals."

"These ethics and morals are based on something called 'natural law.'"

"Yes, yes, Luis spoke of it this time. Alejandro spoke of it too. How do you understand that again? What is it?"

Father was happy to be able to discuss this with these two young friends. He felt sad for the superficiality and lack of interest of most of the young people he had to work with.

They only know what works here and now. They have little capacity for wisdom.

"Sure, Luis. The natural law is a law that we find inscribed in the heart of every human being and which must be known by reason. In the human heart there is already a 'chip', Luis, which tells us: 'badly done' or 'well done.' But it must be cultivated. If we go astray and live like animals, that law is no longer so clear."

Alejandro interrupted:

"That's why there's the famous phrase that says, 'If you don't live like you think, you'll end up thinking like a live.'"

261

If you don´t live according to how you think, you will end up thinking according to how you live.

"That's right," said Father Andrew. "Trying to get where he wanted to go, a new and erroneous ethics emerged. But here I must slow down a little and explain something simple, or at least I will try to put it in an easy way."

Freedom for Excellence

"The concept of freedom has taken a huge hit, young people. Many today consider that freedom is 'to do what I want', 'that nobody tells me anything', 'that there are no restrictions on my actions.' If you say to someone, 'Hey, you must do this or that,' what do they say?"

Luis immediately said: "Nobody can say that, because everyone thinks differently. No one can, forgive me, father, think that they have a higher truth than the other."

There was a silence. The father looked at him very kindly, and then he looked at Alejandro, who was beginning to get restless. Then Luis followed up:

"Wow! I think, although I don't understand why, but you said something to me, Alejandro, about this being called a relationship."

"Relativism, Luis. Both of you laughed at his new word." Father took advantage:

"And in this case, Luis, it's moral relativism. That is, that in reality there are more truths—if you will let me speak so—than others. That's exactly why Alejandro was telling you about metaphysics."

"Let's see, Father. Explain to me well then why one can tell another what to do without being wrong."

"Sure, Luis. I'll explain it with a sport or an art. Do you play a sport? What do you like?"

"I like football. And as for art, I don't play, but I admire violinists a lot. We went to a concert at the Vienna Philharmonic Orchestra's main theater, and I'm very passionate about it."

"Perfect. Let's talk about football. If someone asks you if you play well, how do you measure it?"

"In my case, for goals. I'm a forward. If I score goals or at least assists, I'm a good player."

"I agree. So, football tells you there's a way to have good football, and there's a way to have bad football."

"Sure. There's not only bad, but pathetic football."

"All right," said Father Andrew, enthusiastically. "And like every sport, there are rules and a tradition, which, if you follow them, you play well. No one would ever think of answering the question of whether you play good football by saying: 'Well, I don't leave the field,' or 'I'm good because I don't touch the ball with my hand.' There are rules. And it's not about being mediocre and making up our own rules. There's a way to play good and a way to play bad."

The two young men looked on attentively and satisfied with the father's clarity.

"Let's go to the violinist now. If a child wants to play the violin he goes to a teacher, and the teacher starts to teach him and says, 'Look, take it like this, take the strings with your other hand, then turn like this...' and if he turns like this he says, 'Who are you to tell me how to play the violin?'"

"Well, the master would look at him with horror."

"In every sport, in every art, in every discipline, there are rules, there is a nature, there is a way. And to follow the way, or to have someone who guides you to do it with mastery, is not to impose anything on anyone. It is simply to show the way to do it well.

"What difference does this make to life and our actions? Very little. If someone tells another person, a friend, a boyfriend or girlfriend: 'this was wrong,' or something like that, it is only teaching the other how to be free, but free for the excellence that that art requires. That's the key: the classics, the people of the first fifteen centuries after the beginning of Christianity, knew that there was freedom to do something excellently and according to rules, or to do it badly. And they knew that, by natural law, it is not up to man to decide whether he likes it or not. It is simply so."

Luis and Alejandro looked at each other. Their eyes were shining on each other for different reasons. In one, Alejandro, because he was hearing this again. In Luis, because he had no objection to father's logical explanation.

"So this is what we called it and it became known as freedom for excellence. Human beings are not free to determine where there is good and evil. We are not free to reinvent football or how to play the violin. If you play it wrong or if I play it wrong, that is wrong. It is not simply 'my way of playing.'"

"It makes perfect sense," Luis said.

"And this, Luis, is crucial. You know why?"

"Why," he asked.

"For what happened and is happening in modern times, when there is no longer the transcendent, when there is no God, when therefore there is no natural law, is that each man sets his law, his rule, his justice. This is called positive law. The word 'positive' is a neutral word. It simply means law 'that is set or established' on the part of men. Today it is set by the ruler, even if he is a rogue or an immoral one."

"In the present, for many, one must have freedom to do anything. No perennial rules, no natural law, no transcendence, no voice of God in any of this. The important thing is not to play football according to the rules, but to play as 'I feel like it.' That's the new freedom of the world. You know what we call that freedom?"

Freedom from indifference

"What?"

265

"Freedom of indifference. That is, it is indifferent to do it like this or like that. It doesn't matter, because as there is no truth, there is no better or worse. It doesn't matter. The important thing, I repeat, is that you do what you want. Have you heard the 'Do what you love?' Or also, 'Be free'? It's the promotion of this kind of indifference."

"That being the case, there is no truth about human acts that applies to everyone and always. It's up to the government to make the laws. Unfortunately, violations of all kinds of fundamental rights occur every day. The clearest example of all is the terrible crime of killing babies when they are not yet born. We call it abortion."

Father left time to process. Whenever there was a silence, everyone would look into the distance, trying to reflect upon the many words heard or spoken with their mind.

"The happiest player on the field and the artist who best performs his discipline according to the rules that are proper to his field, that is the happiest one. That is why it is called freedom of excellence. Because excellence is as much on a human level as it is on a transcendental, supernatural level."

"Unbelievable!" said Luis. "I don't understand why it isn't easy to access these subjects as we are doing. To me It sounds exciting, but why don't they teach it to you in college? Why don't my parents have any idea about this? It should be mandatory for everyone to know about this, right father?"

"Luis, I couldn't agree with you more. In fact, all this so-called 'classical humanism' has been lost on us enormously. But there is light: some universities in Europe and the United States have begun to recover that part of their curricula."

"William Dix, a writer in Forbes magazine, clearly says that amputating the classical sciences in universities has been enacted by policies to get rid of students who teach more and ask them complex questions that are not always about productivity and economic systems.[42]

266

"If we look closely, humanism will win us all over. Whether we have faith or not, humanism puts man at the center of human decisions. At the center, but without neglecting the presence of a Creator who has set rules for how to play in this life. Take a good look:

"Materialists, since there is no longer any initial or final cause-because these are philosophical terms—since the transcendent no longer exists, answer only the two questions of 'what' and 'how.' Humanists, on the other hand, have a much broader vision. They give answers to 'why', 'what for', 'how' and 'what'. This is exactly what two great philosophers who have influenced the West made clear: Thomas Aquinas and Augustine of Hippo.

"True happiness always has to be linked to truth. And the freedom of the human being is limited, just as the freedom of a child is limited. The father has to guide him, take care of him, because he does not always know what is good for him."

Maturity

"Father, how does one acquire this wisdom both at the level of understanding and at the level of action? That is to say, first I have to know these things and then live these things. Are we agreed?" asked Alejandro this time.

"Well said, Alejandro. Everything has a logic. First we form our conscience, our mind, so that it is bright and true. Then we form our habits, which reside in the will."

"Yes, yes, said Luis, "he spoke to me clearly a few weeks ago about those superior powers of man."

"Potencies, potencies, Luis! Not powers." and he laughed again, seeing the confusion of words in Luis.

"That's right, "potencies."

"Well, yes," said Father Andrew, "the way to mature every human being is to know right from wrong, and then to do right from wrong."

"Maturity, young people, is not something that comes with the years. There are immature people at all ages. Maturity is knowing the truth—not making it up—and then living it. But I'm not getting into that, because I understand that you've talked about this before."

Father Andrew looked at his watch, and then everyone looked at theirs. Time had flown by and the break between classes was over.

"Look, we're running out of time. But let me just finish with something. The other day I read about a lady who was asked by the doctors to stay at home so as not to infect someone with a virus. And she didn't want to, and she just said:

"Everyone makes choices. Some of us make some, some of us make others. There are some who choose their life over their freedom, and others our freedom over their life."

"You don't know how much it fired me up to read that. Well, it's in those words that we find moral relativism. We find the freedom of indifference. Why? Well, for her, clearly, whether she knows it or not, the important thing is to do what you want, not what you ought. If you have a virus and you can infect people or die, it's not just a choice, it's a good choice. And that 'right' is denied by many. They say, 'It's up to each person to decide what's right for him or her. The self-determination of the human being is limited, because he is limited.'"

"Father, since we have entered into ethics and morals, will you come again tomorrow to talk about some more details that I don't handle well?" asked Alejandro.

"Tomorrow, Tuesday?" Father took out his diary and saw that he was free.

"Yes, would that be 9:00?"

Both young people nodded, eager to finish off the ethical issue with father.

They shook hands, said goodbye, and each went on to their next activity.

ANALYZING THE CONVERSATION

The individualism we are witnessing in today's world has many motives, much history, and sometimes it is not so obvious where it began.

As Luis and Alejandro discussed with Father Andrew, the decline of the spiritual vocation of the man who had begun in the fifteenth century generated a domino effect that reaches us today. Intellectual and moral relativism is not new. It simply takes on new and diverse forms today. The ideology of gender, where the human being tramples on biology by deciding what he is with his mind, is an example. Abortion, euthanasia, the relativization of sex, the right to religion, are many of the ways in which we find this current today.

Instead of human beings receiving from their creator, through humanism and philosophy, how to become happy, new paths are invented each time, dangerous and slippery routes that do nothing but prolong the agony. This is no exaggeration. We see it in the increase in suicides and stress levels and illnesses of the souls, minds and hearts of so many. All of this is having a huge impact on children, homes, marriages and social life. And it ends up being paid for by the whole of civil society, and the economies of the world. For someone has to pay the price for the lack of humanism, of understanding why and what we live for. Simon Sinek says it very well in his book and Ted conference: Start with why. But he didn't invent that term. That comes from the great classics.

It is essential that today's generations know well the difference between freedom of indifference and freedom of excellence. Man cannot play God. They have to mature, and maturity is impossible without humility. For the humble person who asks, listens, consults, knows that he does not know much. The attempts that have been made by man trying to be God have been catastrophic: the tower of Babel, the rebellions of the Israelite people, the Marxist and Communist thinking that presupposes that God does not exist, the current of death that we are living today. Two world wars and millions of abortions a year are witnesses to this. This cannot go on.

Questions to think about:

1. Do you understand well the difference between freedom of excellence and freedom of indifference? Have you ever acted with freedom of indifference?

2. What was the cause of the loss of a sense of transcendence in the modern world?

3. How can you work on maturity for your life?

Chapter 16:
Doing Good, Feeling Good

"Never has man had such a keen sense of his freedom, and meanwhile new forms of social and psychological slavery are emerging"

Gaudium et Spes #4

It was already 9 a.m., and everyone was right on time for the appointment. Father Andrew arrived from the sides of the Humanities area, where his office was, and with his characteristic smile. Luis and Alejandro arrived together, since they had parked their cars very close to each other.

"Young people, how's it going?"

"Good, Father. You?" They answered almost in unison.

They each took their place where they had been yesterday. There was a bit of homework, a bit of exams coming up. Luis was acquiring a new clarity, and he felt that his inner self was burning with light and truth.

"Where did we stop yesterday?" asked father.

Luis took the floor, restless and eager to find answers to his concerns.

"Yesterday you spoke to us," said Luis, looking intently at father, "of maturity, which does not come only through the passing of the years. And you said that part of that maturity consists of being able to know what is right and what is wrong. We're talking about ethics, obviously, aren't we?"

Alejandro nodded, and added: "Yes, Father. When you told me about this in the group sessions you first mentioned how human ethics and religious morality are actually linked, but I don't remember how or why. I didn't know, in other words, how to reconstruct the philosophy of ethics."

What is the Purpose of Ethics in Man?

Of course, of course, replied father. "Look, we're taking steps. The first thing is that we must ask ourselves: What is the purpose of ethics in life?"

"Well, the purpose of ethics is to protect man from all technological and scientific abuse. It intends to guide man to be full and happy, orienting his life towards the end for which he was created."

"But something that in classical times was known to all without question, and has now been lost, is that the acts of man here on Earth and the consequence of them have an impact on the afterlife as well. That is, his earthly life prepares for his eternal life. So, that revolution or turning point that the world underwent in modern times—what we talked about last time that had begun with William of Ockham—is lost. And it is obvious. If the transcendent, the supernatural no longer exists or is irrelevant, man's acts have no reference to any law of God, which we can simply call the natural law."

"I cannot go on without quoting a very important document of John Paul II, called 'Splendor of Truth,' which says:

'Jesus Christ gives the decisive answer to every question of man, in particular to his religious and moral questions.'"

"You know that I love Holy Scripture and that it enlightens man a lot. In the first letter of St. Peter, we read: 'They sanctify themselves 'by obeying the truth.'" (1 Pt 1:22)

Luis interrupted, saying, "Yes, Alejandro and I talked a lot about the truth a few weeks ago and how it's getting lost. But still, let me ask you, Father, the question we all ask ourselves:

How can I know the moral truth?"

Moral Conscience

"Excellent, Luis. Look: in every man's heart God put a chip. Don't take it literally. But it is an ability to detect good and evil, at least in broad strokes and in the simplest and most fundamental situations. Those, in broad terms, are found in the Ten Commandments that Moses gave to the people of Israel and that everyone lives, whether they know it or not. That chip, that capacity in every man and woman, makes us sound an alarm and turns on a red light, when we do wrong. When we do good, we feel a mysterious, mystical satisfaction. Something like an inner peace that says: 'You have done well, my beloved.' It is the soft voice of God that embraces us."

"I'm sorry, Father, but I have to play devil's advocate.

Thousands of people disagree on what is right and wrong."

Alejandro was now a spectator, amused between Luis' questions and father's answers.

"I must say you're right. That's why there are so many wars, fights and misunderstandings in the world. But that's only part of the truth, not all of it."

"Basically, every human being agrees. I'll give you examples: if a cannibal—and I'm going to extremes—eats someone, it could be that he doesn't know he's wrong because he's hungry, as well as because he has an extremely poorly formed conscience. But now, what would that cannibal feel and think if another cannibal ate his mother or his wife? Do you think it would give him joy? I'm sure it wouldn't."

Both stayed silent.

273

"Or, for example, young people, in what world civilization does a soldier who deserted in the middle of a war receive a medal of honor? Why are there certain films that make every human being fall in love, that touch every human fiber, such as 'Braveheart', 'The Shawshank Redemption' or 'Gladiator?' There is a common feeling in every human being about what is right and wrong. That's why we know today that that chip, called conscience, is in everyone's possession. Even St. Paul, in his letter to the Romans, says that even the pagans have this knowledge, even if they are not religious."

"The difference that causes wars and misunderstandings is that there are badly formed consciences and well-formed consciences. The perfect conscience is called a right conscience. And the malformed conscience has an infinite number of names: domesticated conscience, lax conscience, deformed consciousness, asleep conscience, erroneous conscience... but we will not get too involved. It is enough to know that there are upright consciences and wrong consciences."

"And what causes someone to have a bad conscience?" asked Alejandro.

"Many factors. You can't name just one. In many cases it happens that people do not have anyone around them to offer them this ethical or moral formation. They have not had an environment, a family, or friends to light their way."

"That's my case," said Luis, with a tone of regret. Father continued:

"I'll give you an example. I know a very polite and loyal boy who realized that his friend enjoyed liking girls, and he kept inviting them everywhere, feeding the illusion that he really cared about them. And he had nothing but the intention to have fun. So this young man went to his friend and told him that it was not right for him to be like that with girls, and that the moment he went out with one, and realized that she did not seem like a suitable companion and girlfriend, he should stop inviting her."

river

Some go around with a dormant or erroneous moral conscience. They act objectively wrong, even without being aware subjectively.

Both young men turned to look at each other with a smile, for Luis had told Alejandro long ago that he was like that. He dated one after another, until his relationship with Sofia began.

"Then," continued father, "if a person had no one to teach him, and there was no one to accompany him on the path of life or a class to open his eyes, he would probably have a wrong conscience, that is, a conscience which does not detect good and evil. He sees something, and he does not know whether it is a reprehensible act or a right one."

Alejandro took the floor: "Father, and what is the way to have a correct conscience, or straight, as you said?"

"The right way, Alejandro, is by having several elements: we already talk about friends and family, then having frequent soul-searches to ask God for light on one's actions. There is also reading books or listening to podcasts from people with right consciences in order to learn about good and evil. Moreover, one has to practice virtue in one's life, and that is just what it is good to do at each moment in life."

Universal Ethical Principles

The three of them left a moment for the ideas to settle down. Always in these pauses some or all of them took advantage of the opportunity to nibble at their food. On this occasion, each of the young people offered father a piece of their sandwich, and he took a piece of the croissant offered by Luis, who was right next to him.

Then Luis asked:

"Father, if we have an internal chip that is the same in all, what things or principles are we all capable of detecting, no matter what opportunities you just mentioned?

"Great question, Luis. The first principle that is sealed in the human soul is that we must do good and avoid evil. That is to say: just as the name says, the human being is called to seek to do good, to distribute goodness and truth to everyone who approaches him. Even, for the Christian, one must go to seek him out if he does not approach him, and do him good. For love of neighbor is at the center of the whole message of Jesus."

"Included in this is avoiding bad actions. Those things that that chip and the formation that later is obtained say that they are objectively bad. We must seek to know, with all our strength, what things violate the natural law, which is the will of God. It is His plan, His will and His design for each of us."

Alejandro added, "Yes, and there is another one too, isn't there? I remember something about the end and the means."

"Ah, right, right. It is known that, in a human action, the end does not justifies the means. I mean, I can want something good, but use bad methods to get it. For example, I can't steal food from a store to feed the poor. Or I can't pass a test by having stolen the questions from it the day before. For a good deed to be good, all its parts must be good."

"All its parts?" asked Luis.

"Yes, let's say the person's intention, his final act, the acts in between, everything! We even have to look for all the possible consequences to be good, although, to tell the truth, sometimes this is not achieved, because we could not calculate any undesired effect."

Luis and Alejandro looked at each other, nodding their heads in agreement as to how all this made a lot of sense to them. Some things were already known by Alejandro, very few by Luis. But they both felt—as we all do—the joy of seeing everything take shape. Then Alejandro asked:

"Father, and how is it that someone with a guilty conscience does a bad act, but is not guilty, since he did not know that what he was doing was bad?"

"Very good question, Alejandro. It's complex and we'd have to go much deeper into ethics. I highly recommend that you yourselves, with that same hunger, don't just stay with these conversations. Take your training into your own hands."

"But we can comment on something simple. A person could at some time, because he had no opportunities or people who instruct him, not be completely guilty of a bad act. For example, someone could avoid a pregnancy in many artificial ways, and not know that it is not right."

"What happens in those cases is that the person objectively acts wrongly, but subjectively not. That is, the fact is wrong, but since his conscience does not detect it, for moral purposes, it is not an act that can be imputed to him. What we should all try to do is to investigate what the truth is and to form our own conscience."

"In ordinary life, sometimes you don't get away with it. A person can commit a crime, and that doesn't mean the law won't punish him. I already know the saying: ignorance of the law does not exempt you from guilt."

"Ugh! But that's already confusing me. There seems to be justice there. How can someone who does evil without knowing is not punished, and the one who does evil while knowing it, is? Well then, is it better to be ignorant of the truth?" asked Luis.

"I argued exactly the same as you, Luis," said Father Andrew. "I made exactly the same logical observation in my moral theology class at the seminary. And little by little I observed in the following classes that there is so much to learn, for ethics is about human acts. And, these are an infinity! But obviously the thing to do is to know the good and to know the law. If you know what is good, God knows how much you know and how much you don't, and he judges you accordingly. As for the law, there you are not exempt from almost anything you should know and do not know."

"Well, I do like the subject. I would like you to recommend a book to us to go deeper into this. But I do understand that now we cannot have a complete course in ethics," said Alejandro.

Virtues and habits

Luis didn't forget the subject that Father Andrew had mentioned before. "Father, you mentioned virtue earlier. What can you tell us about virtue?"

"Yes, well, look. Do you know where the root of the word virtue comes from? They both looked at each other, and shook their heads, without pronouncing a word.

"It comes from 'vir', which is Latin for 'man'. A virile act is a male act, an act done by a man. With time, like so many things, it brought us the word virtue. It is to act decisively, and there one does not need to be a man at all. Woman is also called to virtue."

"Well, we must know that man, without discipline, without repeated, constant, persevering and orderly acts, besides being directed towards a good goal, cannot be virtuous. We are called to follow three steps: we must act with good acts. These good acts must be repeated until good habits are formed. And these good habits must be converted into virtues."

"Virtuous men and women are happy people. Aristotle, besides the Stoic and Epicurean currents, spoke of having virtue. What Christianity came to do was to direct it with the virtue of love. Good deeds, done with great love, make saints. So it is not only a matter of doing good only, but of doing it with great love, because love is what makes the world go. It is the engine of the world."

Luis' eyes lit up. Now, after so many weeks of nurturing his spirit with good conversation, things were coming more easily. It didn't mean that he always understood everything at first, but he was already beginning to put together the puzzle of a life well-lived, a life of virtue, a life of happiness. Once again, he spoke up:

"So, Father, is the Christian's life, in short, about doing things to attain virtue?"

"I can't say it better myself, Luis. Christian ethics is nothing other than the ethics of virtue, as Martin Rhonheimer, a well-known philosopher who teaches the virtue ethics in Rome, said.

Driven by the Holy Spirit

"Exactly where does religion come into this, Father?" Alejandro asked.

"I wanted to ask one of you," said Father Andrew, visibly moved. "I must tell you that this is my field, my passion, and my whole life is a testimony to this dream, this horizon."

"Listen well, for this is deep in my heart. In the Gospel there is a beautiful story. A young man came to see Jesus. This young man is known to be rich, for the text says so. And he confidently asks the Master a question. He says: 'Good Master, what must I do to gain eternal life?' To which Jesus, with an exquisite and intense love, replied: 'If you wish to enter into (eternal) life, keep the commandments. The young man said, 'Which ones?' To which Jesus replied: 'You shall not kill, you shall not commit adultery, you shall not steal...'" (Mt 19:16-19 RSVCE)

He who advances under the impulse of the Holy Spirit makes light years more progress than with his own effort.

"Young people, do you see what's going on here?"

The two young men sensed that the question went beyond what they were able to see, and for fear of not failing on such a sensitive issue, they said: "What?"

"What happens is that the one speaking with Jesus senses that there is a connection between the moral good and the full fulfillment of one's destiny. The young man realizes that there is an umbilical cord between his good acts and eternal life, the happy life. Do you get it?"

The two young people were now also moved to see the radiant, red face that looked at them intently. With laughter and an expectant look they nodded, not letting their words ruin the rhythm and cadence of father's speech. They let him go on.

"How sad that this has been lost! How sad that the young man of today does not have many ways of bringing reality together, instead of separating it! For many, daily life, their daily actions, how they study or how they go out with a girl, have no relation with their religion. But this rich young man is sensing that it has everything to do with it. What I want you to see is the intimate connection between life and faith, between Christian religion and human ethics, between natural life and supernatural life. They have a continuity. Modern people want to divide and fragment knowledge. But, in the end, things are bound together and they are understood together."

"The art of being alive today is to discover that some philosophies and ways of thinking have wanted to divide knowledge. They have wanted to take God out of the daily life of each one of us," said father passionately, so much so that a tear came to his eye.

"And where exactly, Father, is that connection between this life and the life of grace in us? In other words, how do we make our actions valuable on Earth as well as in heaven?" Alejandro asked.

"It happens when we understand one thing: that without God we can do nothing. And who is God? Well, there are three people, Father, Son and Holy Spirit. They're one heck of a team of three. And when Jesus left, he said, 'It is to you advantage that I go away' (Jn 16:7 RSVCE), for what he was about to do was to send the Holy Spirit. And the Holy Spirit dwells in every baptized heart. The Holy Spirit is the sanctifier and our partner. He is the one who helps us to be best we can be."

"Young people! Do you realize the treasure we've been given? When we learn, with the help of a spiritual director, to live attentive to the work that the Holy Spirit wants to do in us, we succeed in working, not only in an ethical way, but in a holy way. We even manage to open wide the doors of Heaven. For in Heaven, those who have arrived before us are there cheering us on so that we may do well. And that is much more than just an ethical way."

At this point, Father Andrew took out of his backpack a book that you could see he had been reading, and told them:

"Look, listen to this, which I was just reading yesterday:

'The meditation of the dialogue between Jesus and the rich young man has allowed us to gather the essential contents of the revelation of the Old and the New Testament on moral behavior. They are: the subordination of man and his work to God, who alone is 'Good'; the relationship, clearly indicated in the divine commandments, between the moral good of human acts and eternal life; the following of Christ, which opens to man the perspective of perfect love; and finally, the gift of the Holy Spirit, source and strength of the moral life of the 'new creature.'" (cf. 2 Cor 5:17)[44]

"This text that I have just read to you is from a writing by John Paul. Do you notice how he connects one thing with the other? How does the work of man then refer to the action of his soul working with the Holy Spirit?"

The two young men were absorbed, overwhelmed by father's explanation. They felt something burning in their hearts that now continued to make sense. Time had literally flown away. The young people, the priest, the atmosphere, exuded joy, happiness, satisfaction of being together to build a strong building full of wisdom. But it was time to leave. They could not be late for their respective classes. However, Luis asked for one more favor.

"Father, thank you very much for all this. I'm sorry. And you too, Alejandro. This is all changing my life. But, I want to ask you for a favor. I feel like I'm close to having to make a decision with Sofia. We think very differently and the issue of premature relationships has us confused, and I've felt that we should stop, but I don't know why and of course she does less. If I bring her in on Thursday—because I can't tomorrow—can we talk to her about it?"

Father shook his head, for he said he would be out that day giving a lecture. But he said to Luis:

"Luis, it's important that you make time for that. I can't be here on Thursday. But I think if there's one young man who can speak with intelligence and conviction about it, it's Alejandro. I trust that you, Alejandro," he said looking at him proudly, "can throw yourself into this conversation."

Alejandro smiled humbly, and said, "I will ask the Holy Spirit for light," to which the three of them nodded with smiles. And they went off to their class.

ANALYZING THE CONVERSATION

Men of all times have asked themselves: How should I act? And the answers have varied and been of all kinds. But in the intimate conscience of each one there is a compass. There is a compass; only this compass needs to be adjusted accordingly.

When human beings have been able to identify the claims of their nature and their moral sense, they have reached levels of virtue worthy of a poem or a painting. The sense of responsibility and justice of man has created legislation and moral rules that, without being perfect, have given rise to the multiform presence of peoples. In many moments of history, man has known how to live together and how to reach agreements for social coexistence.

At the same time we see that man has been seriously wounded by sin. That crack in his nature has been the cause of many disputes, wars and conflicts. It has led to great personal, family, and social dissatisfaction. Therefore, the great examples of life, those whom we can call the champions of life on Earth, are the saints. For the saints were not a Mandela, or a Gandhi or a Napoleon. The saints do not fight only for an earthly cause. They knew how to take into their hands the intellectual material and the firm faith in the proposal that has come to the human being from somewhere else, from the beyond.

When Nelson Mandela died, one author wrote about him saying, 'A hero dies, but not a saint.' He said this because while there is much to admire in him, there are also elements in every human being who has walked the Earth that have not counted on God's grace to rescue and uplift man.

God's grace, the work of the Holy Spirit, comes to heal and even to impel each human being to act beyond his or her nature, so that they can repeat with St. Paul: "It is no longer I who live, but Christ who lives in me" (Gal 2:20).

Questions to think about:

1. What knowledge of ethics did you have prior to reading this book? Did you have any idea or did you not even know about the subject?

2. How is your conscience formed? Right or wrong?

3. In your work, have you ever asked the Holy Spirit for light to work as God asks?

Chapter 17:
Sex Before Marriage, is it ok?

"Love between man and woman can only be built on sacrifice and self-denial."

John Paul II

It was 9 o'clock and Luis sent a message from WhatsApp to Alejandro. He told him he was a few minutes late. Sofia didn't know where they were meeting, so he had to pick her up at her car. From there he took her by the hand and they went to the traditional meeting place. Alejandro was sending some messages and as soon as he saw them, he got up to greet them.

"Hello, Sofia."

"Hello, Alejandro, how are you?"

"I'm fine, thank you for asking. Hey Luis, I see that you can't spend too much time without your girl, right?"

"Ha-ha yeah, Sofia is the one who always forces me to be with her." And he looked at her with a smile. She didn't approve much of his comment, but she didn't say anything.

"I am very excited to be with you; even though Luis is not so happy that I am here. I want to know what you talk about so much, he sometimes talks to me about it with such passion!" Sofia said.

The three sat down, and each, as usual, took out what they had brought for a snack while the conversation lasted. Then Alejandro began the conversation:

Sexual relations, yes or no?

"Sofia, I'll tell you what Luis and I have been talking about. That thing you say you're excited about."

Sofia was intrigued by the conversations. She thought maybe several friends and partners were making a plan to travel together, or maybe it was something related to a new business. Alejandro continued.

"In short, we have been answering the question: How to live life? And that question is so broad that it has many pre-concepts and answers. We are already talking about whether there is a truth or not, whether everyone has their own, whether God exists or not. We have talked about the human person, his wounds, his dreams and aspirations."

"What good topics, but how complicated, right? Very philosophical. What have you been left with after all these conversations?"

"They're philosophical, yes, but basic philosophy. You know that philosophy is love of wisdom, and we have talked about that for lack of thinking about these things and being alone in your area or your little hobby, this world is a disappointment for many. I don't know if you knew, Sofia, that last year was the year with the most suicides in the United States in the last fifty years."

"How hard it is, Alejandro, I had no idea so many people felt empty or lonely that they would kill themselves! What do you think takes them to that extreme in their lives? I know why they like to come and talk. I feel like this conversation is going to get good."

"Yes, because it's partly because of so much wounding and deception in the world. One of the subjects where there is most confusion is the subject of love. That word is manipulated too much.

286

We use it for everything. And since it is so central to the heart of every man and woman, it is not something that is done automatically. You need to have people and good influences, as well as books, to learn to love. The human being, automatically, does not know how to love. He has to spend time on it. You see how the subject of sex is today.--everyone with everyone, and on the first night, and it doesn't matter if it's with someone of the same sex or the other."

Alejandro had a passion for this subject, because shortly before he had finished a course on theology of the body that Father Andrew had organized with several other experts. He read constantly about the subject, and in his backpack he carried the course booklet with phrases that enlightened him enormously.

"Look, Sofia. This I have to quote literally to you. On this subject, John Paul II said:

"Love is never something you have initially, something simply 'given' to man and woman, it is always at the same time a 'task' assigned to them. Love must be seen as something that in one sense never 'is', but is always only 'a being converted', and what is converted depends on the contribution of both persons and the depth of their commitment.[45]"

"Oh, Alejandro, well, yes, it's a complex subject, this love thing. But I think there are also many ways of looking at love that depend on your state of life, if you have a boyfriend or girlfriend, if you're already married or if you're just looking for a little bit of acceptance or pleasure. And Alejandro, the truth is that this topic of love today is demonstrated in many ways and I think that most of them, as bad as someone may see it, are considered love," Sofia said.

Luis looked at Sofia with attention and concern, because now it was his turn to enter the scene, however uncomfortable it was. This subject had generated enough fights already.

"Sofia, part of the reason I wanted us to talk about this is because you and I haven't stopped having sex, and very often. But we've both said several times that we're not sure if this is the best thing or not, as much as we like it. And I haven't found as good answers to my questions as I did with Alejandro and Father Andrew. We hadn't talked about this subject, but I want to touch on it now, because it has worried us both. Well, no, more so for me, really."

Sofia was surprised by Luis' words, as she did not know that the purpose of the meeting was mainly that.

Sofia replied. "Luis, we both know that our relationship has not been forced and I wouldn't want either of us to make it conditional. The truth is that I don't have the answers you're looking for, but like you, I have many doubts about the subject. And Alejandro, since you're here, how are you living it with Natalia? It would help us if you would share with us, more than recommend books or the typical things that adults give as solutions."

Luis turned to Alejandro and said, before he could answer, "Hey, it's true. You never talk about your girlfriend. How come?"

"Well, you didn't ask me, but now Sofia has, so I'll tell you."

"We've never had sex. We talked about it on the second date before we officially started, and that's how we've managed the relationship.

"Haha. Stop pretending Alejandro, what do you mean you don't have relationships? Then how do you show her love? Or does she show you love? The truth is that for me, intercourse in a relationship is the ultimate test. When it is performed, you can be sure that he or she loves you."

"It would be good if, just as they talked about not having sex during the courtship, they would talk about it again and rethink it."

Alejandro drank from his coffee, looked out over the gardens, and knew right there that it would take all the patience, tact and kindness he could muster to explain this. Furthermore, he asked the Holy Spirit for light to know what to say. He already knew of Sophia's experience, and she probably meant no harm, but she had no one to offer her another viewpoint on the subject. Luis, meanwhile, remained silent, expectant.

"Sofia, surely sexual intercourse is important in a relationship. Very important, I would say. I don't deny it. I tell you beforehand that it's not that we don't want it. Sometimes we have been very close to having, but it is something we talked about and committed ourselves to. Look:

"One day I met a girl who met a guy who she was enchanted by. In fact, all the girls swooned over him at that event. It was a retreat, actually. And they were all after him. And she was very impressed with his personality, and she said, 'That whole time, I never saw him as an available man. And then I found out that he had a girlfriend. And I knew he wasn't having sex with her either.'

The deepest and most sincere love of a man towards a woman, the strongest sentiment is to promote one another. It is called oblative love.

Where am I going with this, Sofia?"

"Imagine if a man came up to you and said this: 'Sofia, you are so beautiful, so beautiful and so important to me, that even though what I want to do the most, is to sleep with you, I'm not going to do it. I want to put it off until we're totally together in marriage. Where there's no way out. Where we have God's blessing forever, and also to make a family. What would you feel?"

Sofia didn't answer anything, thoughtful.

"What that man would be telling you is that you are so special, that he wants to raise his love for you to a more spiritual level, precisely by waiting. Because if he will simply let go of his instincts towards you—which you know in men are strong—what guarantee would there be that you are everything to him?"

Look what the Pope says again about desire:

"If desire is predominant, it can distort the love between a man and a woman and rob them both."[46].

The Tests of Love

"I would think that he doubts his feelings for me, and I really wouldn't want him to be thinking about having relations with me. If he loves me, he gives his all for me and, as you say, that's all in the relationship. Why wait? He can give himself totally without the sacrament. I think that's what they say, right? That doesn't give you special powers. In the end, you see that there are couples married by the Church and who end up getting divorced and there are couples in free unions who are perfectly stable," said Sofia.

"Well, I have a different point of view. What you are telling me is in line with what other people are saying too, with what the world in general thinks. And if someone is going to model sex life for me, I think the argument falls apart. Never has there been so much single motherhood; never has there been so much abortion, so much sadness in woman; it makes me sad how women today allow themselves to be treated as objects of men's desire; the number of children who have to live without a father or mother is due to thinking that the greatest manifestation of love is found in sexual intercourse. What do a man and woman do when he goes off to war for six months? What does a man do when his wife is in post-partum depression? Can't he manifest his love for her at those times?"

"My experience, and validated by many couples and books on the subject, is that there is a place and time for sexual intercourse.

When two people who are dating look at each other lustfully and not seeing the whole reality and the project that each one is called to, relationships become blind

And that is when there is already a marriage, because there it is guaranteed that everyone feels safe and protected: he, she and the children to come. On the other hand, if in the most basic passions that we have, and which alone do not guarantee true love, we put the maximum expression, there are no guarantees. The physical has to be united with the spiritual, the psychological, and the biological and has to enjoy an atmosphere of total union. In courtships that does not exist, because there are so many that begin and end."

Sexual Compatibility

"But, Alejandro, if you don't experience that sexual relationship with your boyfriend or girlfriend, how do you know if it's true love, how do you know if it's the right one?" Sofia asked.

"Good question, Sofia. Well, it's not the first time some woman has asked me. You know, Sofia, we're back to the enormous dignity of every woman, and every man too. We test products, not people. It's not true that you have to be 'compatible' in the sexual relationship, 'because if you don't, it doesn't work.' The relationship between two people is much more than sexual union, without taking away the importance of it. Perhaps on the honeymoon or the first three times they will not understand each other as much as those who have done everything, but in a short time they will understand each other in this field as in others. Believe me, rarely are sexual issues the reason a couple goes to a therapist, psychologist or priest. Always the difficulties are due to moral or spiritual problems. If not, look around you."

Blind Sex

Sofia pondered these ideas in her mind and heart. She was quiet. Luis spoke.

"Sofia, one thing that does make a lot of sense to me from what Alejandro is saying is that I'm uncomfortable with this: a lot of times when you and I have a fight, we don't resolve it, because we just resort to having sex. And that doesn't address the problem, it hides it, it's a false solution. In marriage that doesn't happen, because you live with the person and you are obliged to solve it. I think that sex blinds us a lot."

"Again, look at John Paul II's words—perhaps a little bit complicated—about falling into lust alone:

"The person, especially a woman, can be disappointed by the fact that in time a man's affection turns out to be, so to speak, a cover for desire or even an explicit will to use."[47]

"What the author means is that the man can easily, but also the woman, no doubt, can use the other for her own benefit, for her own pleasure.".

How far can/must you go?

Luis and Sofia looked at each other with uneasy eyes, and Luis felt an acute frustration with this difference of views.

"Well, if, according to you, the best thing for dating is to wait until marriage to have sex, then what can you do in a dating relationship? Or is it always bad to feel pleasure with your boyfriend?" Sofia asked.

Alejandro intervened gently, without haste, so as not to cause her intimidation or fear of questioning:

"Of course in dating you can experience pleasure. And there are so many ways to do it. You know something, Sofia? Have you noticed that in the scene in the Garden of Eden, God tells Adam and Eve that all the trees in the garden are for them. He tells them to use everything. That everything is theirs. Only one of them, no. And the fools, they chose the one that the Creator is telling them of all things that they shouldn't use."

"So, to answer you. The first question to be asked is not so much whether you can have pleasure, but how much can you really love each other. And love, as we said, has to be well explained and understood. Love is donation, surrender, tenderness, concern and sacrifice for the other. That, Sofia, is what Jesus told us. That is the way."

"Oh, Alejandro, stop it, I still have the same question, what can we do in our relationship?" Sofia said.

"I understand the question. And I'm going to answer it. But there is no doubt that these are questions typical of a very pragmatic and unspiritual world. What can be done is a lot, but in the field of warmth, what can be done is to be very attentive to manifesting physical love—that is, kissing and caressing—in such a way that we do not start on the path of sexual intercourse, which we have already seen is not for those who are dating."

"If I have in my hands gunpowder or an arsenal of rifles, I am not always saying: how far can I use them without killing someone? You have to use each thing at its right time and with the right person. Natalia and I have a thousand ways of telling each other that we love each other, and the truth is that there is no shortage of them! It's a question of educating the heart to lov love well. And to love well is according to God's plan."

God's Plan for Human Love

"Let's see, Alejandro, I'm not very religious or spiritual like you, so how do I know this love as God sees it? Or according to his plan?" Sofia asked.

"Well, Sofia: How I would love it if you could take a course on theology of the body! You would love it!"

"Theology of the body? What's that? It sounds complex," Sophie said.

"Sure. The theology of the body is a doctrine that John Paul II expounded over many years. He loved to talk young people about love and sexuality. He developed the whole doctrine on this and there are many courses that offer it. And it answers the question you asked: what is God's plan for human love?"

"Above all, he makes an explanation based on the Sacred Scripture and his long experience working with couples. The first three chapters of the book of Genesis contain many texts that give the answer."

"God's plan is that man and woman aspire to become a gift to each other."

Luis, asked: "Let's see, Alejandro, so you're telling us that a pope uncovered this theory of the body, and it's through this that God reveals to us how to love our spouse? How's that? He's not married and probably didn't even have any girlfriends."

Alejandro had heard such objections several times, both in his course and after it, and each time he tried to share about what he was now passionate about.

"Yes. The Pope has given us this teaching in which man and woman become a gift to each other. He did so with the experience and the great wisdom he has in this matter. And as for what you say about whether or not he's married, that's an old question. If married people knew more about love, I don't understand why they cheat on each other. And it's clear that in the world today there are couples who treat each other like trash, and 'they're married.' One thing doesn't lead to the other."

Luis stayed silent, reflecting on Alejandro's words, while Sofia spoke.

"Alejandro, I don't quite understand, but this subject has already left me intrigued. I want to understand how all this about God's plan, about love and that, has to do with happiness. Because I have heard that God wants us humans to be happy, and what does all this have to do with happiness?"

"It's a paradox, I know," Alejandro said. "There is something I learned from a Spanish author who says: 'Happiness is only achieved when it is not pursued.' In men and women, when they try to seek happiness directly, it slips through their fingers. So, returning to the subject of love, when two couples really seek the good of each other, what they do is seek to think about the absolute good of the other person. They advise each other, they read, they learn, they talk, and in that way they come to know which is the path that will make them better lovers. And better lovers, Sofia and Luis, is not the same as best in bed. If better lovers were the best in bed, the Hollywood couples who have slept with hundreds, those would be the happiest and longest lasting. But we see that, unfortunately, almost all of them get divorced."

"The most luminous love of all is achieved most by promoting the person, by taking into account his past, present and future, and all the wisdom accumulated throughout history about what love really is and what, on the other hand, using is."

"So, Alejandro, you're telling me that sex, even between married people, doesn't satisfy us completely, doesn't make us happy?" asked Sofia.

Alejandro's eyes lit up, for this is just one concept that had intrigued and enlightened him greatly.

"Excellent question, Sofia. No, not quite. In fact, according to John Paul II, sexual intercourse is fills, but not completely. How do we know? Because a couple has an intimate relationship and the next day they are not completely satisfied. In fact, they always have to go back 'to the source' to try to satisfy their soul, and again they go away empty. Do you know why?"

"No. For what reason?" asked Sofia.

"Because the heart of man and woman is not made to be satisfied by another creature. The heart of man is made only to be filled by God. Remember the famous phrase of St. Augustine: "'You made us, Lord, for yourself, and our heart remains restless until it rests in you.'"

"If you allow me, Sofia, and you too, Luis, that yearning for intimacy and sexuality that is in the man and woman, and that time and time again remains unresolved, not satisfied, is, says the Pope, the unmistakable sign of their yearning for something more transcendent. We aspire to eternity. We are men and women, but with an eternal vocation. The earthly will never fill human aspirations."

The three of them were very quiet. Each looked down at the floor. There was a feeling in the couple both of illusion and of shame. How is it that no one had ever spoken to them so beautifully?

How is it that the world again did not promote this anywhere? How is it possible that this kind of love was not witnessed to even by their own parents? What a mystery! The silence lasted longer than usual. No one knew how to break it. What to say now?

Suddenly, there was a surprise for Luis and Alejandro. After a few seconds that seemed like minutes, Sofia started crying inconsolably. Something of what had been said on this Thursday had pierced her soul. Something had reached the most intimate fiber, where a woman actually wishes she had led another life. She wished to have had a close mother, a protective sister or some more feminine friends.

Luis just put his hand on her shoulder, and hugged her. He felt a little sorry for having caused this. It wasn't really his fault, though. It was clear that this was the hand of God through him, which now made Sophia and Luis think about their relationship. There was hardly any future in it. And if anything, they both had to start on a path of return, of healing.

Luis intervened: "I think we're already late, Alejandro. This has been a really good talk between the three of us. You have left us with a lot to think about and decisions to make."

"Luis, I am sorry to have caused this, but I am glad to have shared it with you, and I want you to know that we are all walking on this path that we want so much. I'll leave you alone and run to my class. See you soon, Luis!"

"Sure, Alejandro. I'll write to you."

Luis stayed with Sofia and, at the same time, thought about the next steps in his relationship with her.

ANALYZING THE CONVERSATION

There is no place in the world where the young person is not intrigued by the question: What about sex? What can you do? What can't you do? Why can't you do that? How should I show him all my love if I can't do it with my body? These and many other questions haunt the circles of young people who have an intuition, the intuition that sex is something that goes beyond the cravings and desires of the moment. Some will deny it because they are passionate about it, or because they have not known how to restrain themselves after having introduced a harem of women or men into their memory. But deep down they know that there is something else.

If you read the Old Testament of the Bible, you will see that it expounds extensively on a great many mistakes made in that area. And always, since the beginning of history, where there were former sexual excesses, there was decline, there was depravity, there was sadness, trauma and rupture. Many great films in history show the great drama of sex mishandled, misunderstood. Why does this happen with this facet of the human being?

One day we'll understand better. But one thing is clear: the Creator wanted to put in the procreative capacity and the union of man and woman a code, a series of stipulations, of rules, that if not taken into account, lead to intense suffering, infidelity and loss of control of oneself.

On the other hand, and seeing God's plan for human love, if each human being looks beyond the immediate, erotic pleasure, if he understands that he or she was made to love and be loved—far from using each other with the strong pleasure that the sexual act produces—then they achieve harmony with their partner and with themself, with their own soul. If they grasp it, they see that it enables them to fill their deepest longing: love.

Let us not forget what these young people have discussed with the priest. Every human being carries within himself a personal vocation of eternity. His body is a gift called to be a gift for others. To discover the code that God has placed in him or her to give himself or herself entirely when the circumstance offers a safe environment, that is in the vocation of man. To know that in the intimate union between husband and wife man finds a sanctifying realization that imitates the immense love of the Trinity.

For some people, these rules are binding and exaggerated, the product of a world of the past that wants to restrict, wants to limit. They are products of past traumas. However, one only has to look at our world to ask it: "What advice do you give me to live human sexuality?" And this world responds with tears, with crying, with disappointment and rupture. It does not have words of freedom, but of libertinism. The statistics don't let you lie. Those who remain faithful to chastity before marriage have a higher rate of perseverance in marriage than others. We must refer to the facts and results, if we do not want the discussion to become pure theory. Against the facts, there is no argument.

And in case something is missing: let us not forget that the Jewish-Christian culture has been receiving commandments and traditions for 3,200 years. In it, the correct use of human sexuality has oriented us towards true wisdom. Conversely, the misuse of it has led to the fall of entire civilizations and cultures.

Questions to think about:

1. What concept of sexuality do you have? What can and cannot be done?

2. Have you ever noticed that using sex to solve difficulties in a couple does not go to the root of the problems, but hides them? Does it leave them for another time?

3. What do you think about sexual compatibility? Do you have to test first to find out if you are sexually compatible? Why do you? Why not?

4. What did you know about the conversation about God's plan for human love?

Chapter 18:
How Can We Achieve Happiness?

"When you seek happiness, it is Jesus you seek."

John Paul II

After having a somewhat tense Thursday because of Sofia's reaction, Alejandro and Luis met again. The scene that they had repeated so much, however, was today surrounded by a certain sadness, not without a deep joy.

It happened to be Friday. It was the last day of official classes before entering final exams. This meant that, because of the intensity of the time, this would be the last conversation until a new semester. And to this we must add the sorrow that Alejandro felt with Luis about the scene the day before. Sofia had unloaded what she had perhaps been storing for a long time, what she had long denied in her own heart.

They met for this new and last time. The day was beautiful. The sun was radiating, but not generating heat. Everyone was wearing jeans and a light shirt. The two already had a mutual appreciation for each other. Let's say even a mutual admiration, albeit for different reasons.

"Luis, too bad about yesterday, man! How's Sofia doing? How do you see things?"

"You have nothing to worry about," said Luis to Alejandro.

"The problem is us. But perhaps this has already come to an end. I am still reflecting, but I sincerely believe that our future is numbered. It's not that we don't deserve it. I simply believe that there are times when couples need to give themselves time to resolve, on their own, the most fundamental questions and concerns in their lives."

Alejandro put his hand on Luis' shoulder for a moment. He wanted to comfort him a little, for he did look a little more sad. At the same time, the Luis in front of him was another being. This man had grown up like few others in a matter of a few months of constant conversations. He had been able to contribute to Luis' solitary ideas in such a fluid world.

Luis took the floor:

"Alejandro, we're not having these conversations anymore. But in case I forget, I want to thank you infinitely for existing. You have awakened me to so many realities. The past subject, yes, has hit us, but I feel it was necessary."

"I want to ask you something: What is, then, the vocation of every man? How can I, now that I have seen the changes I have to make in my thinking and my living, walk the path to happiness?"

Again, as several times in the past, Alejandro felt a warmth in being able to end these talks with a theme that was at the center of his passion, his faith and his convictions.

"Luis, I want to repeat what Father Andrew has been telling us about this in our philosophy sessions. This is a topic for which I even keep on my iPhone important quotes that keep me focused a lot as a person."

Each Man's Vocation

"The vocation of every man and woman is something that escapes words. God has been very great to us. He had already said earlier that there is a psalm that says, 'He made him a little lower than the angels.'" (Psalm 8)

"Something that I have learned little by little through some readings and conversations with father, is that God, Jesus, wanted to leave us an institution that is a Mother and a Teacher: I am referring to the Church."

Luis frowned, but said nothing.

"I know, I know. Everyone makes that face when they know little or only by hearsay. But listen to me: the Church is expert in humanity, and for two-thousand years it has done nothing but watch over man's knowledge of how to get to Heaven. She has pointed out the way. Look at this sentence I have here:

"The joys and hopes, the sorrows and anxieties of the men and women of our time, especially of the poor and those who suffer, are at once the joys and hopes, the sorrows and anxieties of the disciples of Christ."[48]

"That phrase tells us that she, the Church, has received from God a mission to guide the hopes of the human heart. There is nothing truly human that does not find an echo in her heart.[49] And within what she has told us, there is a phrase that impacts me too much. She says: 'Really, the mystery of man is only clarified in the mystery of the Word Incarnate.'[50] This phrase says only one thing in simple words, Luis. That man will only know himself well when the Son of God, Christ, reveals it to him."

"I don't understand. What does Christ have to do with me knowing myself? That is, how can man know himself only if Christ reveals him?"

"Since we started talking you and I," said Alejandro, "how much do you feel you've known more about yourself?"

"Ugh, so much."

"So?"

"So what?" asked Luis, confused.

"All that we have been talking about is nothing but doctrine, the wisdom that I too have learned and continue to learn. And guess

303

where it comes from? Well, it is the doctrine of Christ through his bride, the Church. It is the message of the Church. It is the good news, the Gospel."

"Everything we have talked about, the whole central theme of identity, integration and now happiness, who do you think is the first speaker on all this?"

"The Church?" asked Luis.

"Sure. And within that message is the central message of all Christianity, and without exaggeration, the greatest truth in the history of humanity."

"And what's that truth?"

Alejandro took a sip of his chocolate milk, and resumed, with slow and emphatic words:

"Christ died for all (Rom 8:32), and the supreme vocation of man is in fact one, that is, the divine vocation. That the love of God was so great for man that he sent his son to be born, live, and die with us, for our salvation. And all this, out of pure love."

Luis kept thinking. It crossed his mind that this language now sounded true to him. Only a few months ago he would never have accepted this language or these ideas. But something was working inside him. Something bigger than himself. He wondered if it might not be the same Holy Spirit that Alejandro had spoken of only three days ago.

Happiness is Found in Giving, in Love

"If then, Luis, all this was done by God out of love, only with love can we be happy. Because love is paid for with love. And that is man's vocation. There we are coming to your question: How can I be happy? Well, there it is, Luis! Alone in love. Only in giving oneself to others and to God does man find meaning. In everything else, he will find emptiness and hollowness."

304

"And why does the world of today always think that happiness is in total freedom and everything?" asked Luis.

"For all that we have said," said Alejandro passionately, "I fight. Because man has never had such a keen sense of his freedom, and meanwhile new forms of social and psychological slavery are emerging[51]. Because we have confused the fact that man is fulfilled in love, not in rebellion or debauchery. Man, Luis, cannot turn away from God for too long without at the same time turning away from himself. Without God, existence has no meaning."

"St. Paul says it like this: 'Aim for the higher charisms! And I will show you a more excellent way' (1 Cor 2:31). And right after that, he gave a beautiful description of love. Look for it later, Luis."

Luis was now really moved. He was a little embarrassed to tell his friend. But after all the gratitude he felt, he thought it was the least he could do:

"I really thank God for you, Alejandro. I admire you very much for what you know and have let your parents form in you, and as far as I can see, Father Andrew too."

Alejandro was embarrassed by his friend's words of praise. He accepted them with gratitude, but still wanted to finish the subject.

"Alejandro, what are the concrete ways to live this love, given that you were telling Sofia and me yesterday that love is very devalued?"

"Yes, Luis. That's right. I'd say love can be broken down into selfless giving to others. That is, when we do good to others, but not to receive applause, thans or have the favor returned. But to do it only for God."

"For God's sake? How's that?" asked Luis.

"Yes, Luis. In the Our Father, which is the most important prayer, we find that we are brothers. And that we have, as brothers, a common Father. And what more could a father want than to see his children love each other? So, when we do something small and full of detail and love for someone: a poor girl, a beggar, your brother, a stranger, your classmate... God is in them. And it's not my invention, Luis. Jesus himself said this: 'Truly, I say to you, as you did it to one of the least of these my brethren, you did it to me.'" (Mt 25:40 RSVCE).

"And another way to do it, Luis, is through effort, will and virtue. What we talked about on Tuesday. God allows man to learn about his supernatural end, his place of destiny, but the decision to walk towards that end, the choice, I mean, is in the freedom of each man. God does not redeem or save man against his own will."

"I imagine that correct application of the freedom to do good is part of what you called the freedom for excellence the other day."

"High five," said Alejandro, raising his hand so that Luis could give him a high five. "Excellent, Luis!" said Alejandro, "I'm swimming."

"And now I will give you three laws of happiness that Father Andrew once dictated to us. Wait, I have them here.

First: happiness is only achieved when it is not pursued.

Second, the doors of happiness always open outwards.

And thirdly, happiness is always in direct relation to virtue."

"Let's see, Alejandro. I don't think I quite understood the first two. The third one, that one's clear."

Alejandro bit into his sandwich, took a few seconds to drink from his chocolate milk, and responded:

"They simply mean this: that happiness is not something to be sought directly. It is something that comes to the heart and feelings as a result of a good deed. Do you understand?"

Luis nodded.

"And the second one is just a summary of what I have already said about love: the doors that bring me happiness are those that I have oriented to others, to give myself and to be a gift for others."

Luis was left thinking, "Alejandro is a gift to me, but I can't tell him that. It would sound too effeminate."

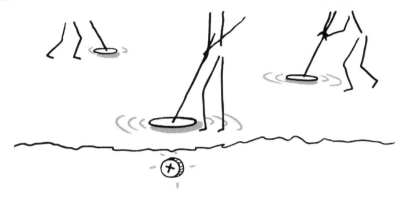

Que quest for the great treasure of our lives should end when we find it.

No one Outside of Christ can Give you True Happiness

Alejandro looked at his watch. There were only 10 minutes left to have to close this conversation and go to his class.

"Luis, tell me something. What do you plan to do, then, with the Sofia thing?"

Luis thought a little and hesitated to respond.

"Actually, we'll almost certainly have to end things. I'll have to do it this weekend, because I don't want to be suffering during exam time."

There was a silence. Then Luis added:

"I hope this breaking up with someone, after so much time doesn't lead to me losing some of my happiness."

Alejandro spoke. "Now that we're finishing up, I'll share with you the most profound thing I have, Luis. In my experience, no one outside of Christ can give you true happiness. No one, Luis."

Nothing asside from Christ can give you true happiness

"I loved a line I heard from a fellow at a conference once. He said, 'When you've seen the sun, all the other lights go dim' When you have had an experience of Christ, Luis, then you understand that no one can fill the human heart like He does. Look for him."

"Billions of people every day are looking for it, wherever they are: sex, money, power, alcohol, drugs... and look: they can't find it. How wise: when you've seen the sun, all the other lights become opaque."

"How I wish I could experience Christ the way you do, Alejandro."

"Luis, listen to you! Of course you can! I know that through all these conversations, the first person to enter your life has been Him. I am sure that He has been working on you so that you would realize that you need the break with Sophie so that you can work on you."

"But I don't know where to start. I've never prayed, I've never been taught that."

"It doesn't matter, said Alejandro, "it's a question of throwing yourself into it. God is looking for you. Start talking to Him, little by little, every day, for a while. And nothing else. He will know how to guide you. I will be here for you. And it's not about running. God has his times."

"Some specific advice?"

"Yes. What I told you. Pray a little bit every day, asking Jesus to reveal Himself to you more. To show you who He is, and how good He is. Take the psalms from the Bible or the gospels, read a little, and start talking. Later on, I will invite you to a good retreat, one that I know you will like."

"And, uh, anything I can read or anyone I can talk to?"

"Yes, I think you can talk to Father Andrew, since you already know him.

Why don't you make an appointment to talk? And about reading, I highly recommend a book called 'Solid Ideas for a Fluid World." It's very good."

"Luis, I have to go now. But if, of all that we have talked about in these times, of all that we have shared and of all that you have heard, you were to ask me to tell you what to keep, I would say only one sentence. John Paul II said it to two million young people gathered in Rome in the year 2000. It goes like this:

"When you seek happiness, it's Jesus you're looking for."

They both stood up, gave each other a hug, and each took his backpack and left, lost in the horizon.

ANALYZING THE CONVERSATION

Man's vocation—that's what his soul screams—is one of eternity. He knows in his heart that it is repugnant to his mind that this is all. He constantly asks himself about the legacy he wants to leave. But why leave a legacy, if you'll leave life and become nothing? And then, later, the one or those to whom you left your legacy, will also return to nothingness.

The songs, the poems, the words of the lovers, the last words of the dying, the speeches of funerals, everything points to a reunion. It doesn't all end here. Pio de Pieltrecina already said it: "O death, I do not know who can fear you, since because of you, life opens up for us".

God has put a seed of eternity in every man and woman. We are not made for death, but for life. Again, what the Master of Nazareth said resounds in our heart: "I have come that they may have life, and have it to the full" (Jn 10:10). Every pore of the body, every dream that one has while awake, every intense feeling that one has for a person, all of this I ask that this not end. Could God place in man that desire for eternity in the depths of the soul without such a destiny existing?

Mankind is very lucky. Perhaps to call it luck is trivial. Perhaps it should be said that we have been very much loved, and for that

When you seek happiness, it is Jesus whom you seek.

we are fortunate. For there was a Man, if you can call him a man, who came to tell us what is behind the curtain. He was very clear and reassured us: "I am going to prepare a place for you" (Jn 14:2). His triumph is our triumph. His entrance into the New City is a guarantee of our entrance into it. His Resurrection is the proof and seal that our destiny does not end in this theater. For we are indeed beings of eternity! It is His gift, and we only have to want it and act upon it.

St. Paul, when he wanted to describe the experience of Heaven that he had in a totally singular event in life, having seen paradise, clumsily described the indescribable: "what neither eye saw, nor ear heard, nor the heart of man came to know, what God prepared for those who love him." (1 Cor 2:9).

Millions of people have raised this prayer to the Queen of Heaven billions of times: "Pray for us, now and in the hour of our death, Amen." They do this because they know that the happiness they have longed for is on the other side of death. And so death is not something to fear, but something to embrace.

As we come to the end of this book, one last idea remains: happiness is what everyone wants. It is a possibility and a gift that God has wanted to offer us. It's a participation in His own divine life. And the way to this is one: Jesus Christ. One and a thousand times we have to ask God to clearly understand: "No one outside of Christ can give you true happiness."

Questions to think about:

1. At what age did you know that man has a vocation for eternity? Or have you never heard that?

2. Have you ever had a moment when by giving yourself to others you have realized the reality that happiness here on Earth is found by giving yourself?

3. Are you willing to prove in your flesh that no one but Christ can give you true happiness? Do you dare?

REFERENCES

1. Santo Tomás de Aquino, Quaestiones Disputatae de veritate, De veritate, q. 2 a. 3 arg. 19.

2. Robert Barron, To Light a Fire on Earth, New York. Image Books, 2017.

3. Catecismo de la Iglesia Católica #38,

4. Fides et Ratio #1, encíclica de Juan Pablo II, 14 septiembre 1998, Roma.

5. Evangelio según San Juan 8,32.

6. Benedicto XVI, Luz del Mundo, Herder, 2010.

7. Collins, The Language of God, p. 6.

8. Robert Jastrow, God and the Astronomers (W. W. Norton, 1992), pp.107,14.

9. Polkinghorne, One World, p.57.

10. C. S. Lewis, Mero Cristianismo, (Fount, 1952), p.39. (traducción del autor)

11. Sarah, Robert Cardinal. El Poder del Silencio: contra la dictadura del ruido (p. 4). Ignatius Press. Kindle Edition.

12. C. S. Lewis, Mero Cristianismo, (Fount, 1952) (traducción del autor)

13. Agustín, Confesiones, versión Kindle. Libro 1, Cap. 1

14. Juan Pablo II, homilía del Santo Padre en Toronto, 2002. http://w2.vatican.va/content/john-paul-ii/es/homilies/2002/documents/hf_jp-ii_hom_20020728_xvii-wyd.html

15. Kant Immanuel, Fundamentación de la Metafísica de las Costumbres, 429, Traducción de Manuel García Morente.

16. Gaudium et Spes, Constitución Dogmática sobre la Iglesia en el mundo actual, #24.

17. Carta de los Derechos Universales del hombre, https://www.un.org/es/universal-declaration-human-rights/. Asamblea General de las Naciones Unidas, 10 de diciembre 1948.

18. Schuchts, Bob. Be Healed. Ave Maria Press, 2014, p. 64

19. Schuchts, Bob. Be Healed. Ave Maria Press, 2014, p. 55.

20. Juan Pablo II, homilía del Santo Padre en Toronto, 2002. http://w2.vatican.va/content/john-paul-ii/es/homilies/2002/documents/hf_jp-ii_hom_20020728_xvii-wyd.html

21. https://www.ted.com/talks/simon_sinek_how_great_leaders_inspire_action?language=en

22. Papa Francisco, Audiencia General del Papa, miércoles 29 de agosto, 2018.

23. Eldridge, John, Wild at heart, Nashville, Tennessee, Thomas Nelson, 2010, P. 68

24.

25. Eldredge, John, Wild at heart, Nashville, Tennessee, Thomas Nelson, 2010, P. 182

26. Siegel, Daniel, Mindsight, Bantam Books, 2010. P. 64

27. Siegel, Daniel, Mindsight, Bantam Books, 2010, p. 10.

28. Ratio de los legionarios de Cristo, #212.

29. Ratio Institutionis de la Legión de Cristo, #18

30. Palmer, Arnold, A Life well played, St. Martin's press, 2016, p. 147.

31. Discurso del 26 de abril, 2013. https://www.catholicworldreport. com/2013/04/26/pres-obama-praises-planned-parenthood-slams-pro-lifers/

32. Suma Teológica, Aquino, Tomás. Parte I-II q.9 a.5 ad 3

33. Discurso Papa Francisco a los consagrados, Roma, Italia, 28 de enero 2017.

34. Rotella, Bob. Golf is not a game of perfect, Simon & Shuster, New York, p. 35.

35. Tal Ben Shahar. Choose the life you want. The Experiment, New York, p. 61.

36. Tal Ben Shahar...p. 2.

37. Burns, David. Feeling Good. Harper, p. 26.

38. Schuchts, Bob. Be Healed. Ave María Press. 2014. P. 77

39. Eldredge, John. Wild at Heart. Thomas Nelson. Nashville, Tenn. P. 125.

40. Schuchts, Bob. Be Healed. Ave María Press. 2014. P. 10

41. Holiday, Ryan. The Obstacle is the Way. Penguin Group. New York. 2014. P. 7.

42. Holiday, Ryan. The Obstacle is the Way. Penguin Group. New York. 2014. P. 16.

43. https://www.forbes.com/sites/willarddix/2018/03/28/eliminating-the-human-ities-decimates-every-students-education/#5ea9bcf55803

44. http://www.vatican.va/content/john-paul-ii/es/encyclicals/documents/hf_jp-ii_enc_06081993_veritatis-splendor.html

45. http://www.vatican.va/content/john-paul-ii/es/encyclicals/documents/hf_jp-ii_enc_06081993_veritatis-splendor.html. VS#28

46. Juan Pablo II, Amor y Responsabilidad, P. 139, Caparrós Editores. Madrid, 2008.

47. Juan Pablo II, Amor y Responsabilidad, P. 82, Caparrós Editores. Madrid, 2008.

48. Juan Pablo II, Amor y Responsabilidad, P. 124, Caparrós Editores. Madrid, 2008.

49. Gaudium et Spes, Constitución Dogmática del Concilio Vaticano II, #1

50. Ibid..., #1

51. Ibid..., #22

52. Ibid, #4.

53. Juan Pablo II, Amor y Responsabilidad. P. 83

JORGE OBREGON GONZALES

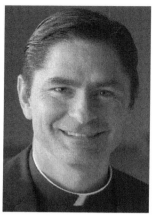

Sporty, restless, fond of culture, photography, golf, soccer, and squash. He went from being a young businessman to a servant of God and man, a priest since 2009. He loves to work with young adults and is committed to the values that endure.

Jorge Obregón was born in Monterrey. After living in Houston, Texas, during his childhood, his family settled in Guadalajara. He studied Business Administration at the Tec in Monterrey. After working at Flextronics International, as a 'Program Manager" for Motorola, he felt a deep desire to dedicate his life to forming young people and families, to give his life to God. At the age of 26, this voice said to him with clarity: "Jorge, I want you for me."

Fr. Jorge began his journey in Medellin, Colombia, after having finished his degree. A year later, he went to Salamanca, Spain, to study classical humanities. His formation path has taken him to Germany, Spain, and Italy to prepare for the priesthood. After finishing his bachelor's degree in philosophy, Jorge began his youth ministry in Colombia to sow values and make young people dream about being authentic leaders who transcend.

In 2013 he went to Caracas, Venezuela, to serve as a youth director within Regnum Christi. During that time and in addition to his ministry, he traveled to several cities in four countries to expand Search, a constantly expanding youth retreat. This retreat is now in twenty cities and nine countries, including the United States. He is also the founder of New Fire, a Catholic content platform for young people. He then spent six months in Mexico City doing youth ministry.

He has just completed a Master's Degree in Biblical Theology at John Paul the Great Catholic University in San Diego, CA.

He currently gives talks, organizes spiritual retreats, and personally guides many young people in their human and integral growth. In New York, he is the international director of Search and dedicates himself to forming young people in their human and spiritual leadership.

Made in the USA
Middletown, DE
30 November 2020